# iPod® & iTunes®

## PORTABLE GENIUS

# iPod® & iTunes®

## PORTABLE GENIUS

Jesse David Hollington

WILEY

Wiley Publishing, Inc.

iPod® & iTunes® Portable Genius

Published by
Wiley Publishing, Inc.
10475 Crosspoint Blvd.
Indianapolis, IN 46256
www.wiley.com

ISBN: 978-0-470-38259-2

Manufactured in the United States of America

10 9 8 7 6 5 4 3 2 1

For general information on our other products and services or to obtain technical support, please contact our Customer Care Department within the U.S. at (800) 762-2974, outside the U.S. at (317) 572-3993 or fax (317) 572-4002.

Wiley also publishes its books in a variety of electronic formats. Some content that appears in print may not be available in electronic books.

Library of Congress Control Number: 2009921473

WILEY

# About the Author

Jesse David Hollington is a Contributing Editor for iLounge.com, a site about all things iPod, iPhone, and iTunes, where he writes a number of technical articles and tutorials as well as penning their weekly Ask iLounge column. Outside of the world of iPods, Jesse is also self-employed as an IT Consultant working in the networking and collaborative services space and, in his spare time, is also an officer in the Canadian Forces Reserve working with Air Cadets.

# Credits

**Senior Acquistions Editor**
Jody Lefevere

**Senior Project Editor**
Cricket Krengel

**Technical Editor**
Brian Joseph

**Copy Editor**
Marylouise Wiack

**Editorial Manager**
Robyn B. Siesky

**Vice President and Group Executive Publisher**
Richard Swadley

**Vice President and Executive Publisher**
Barry Pruett

**Business Manager**
Amy Knies

**Senior Marketing Manager**
Sandy Smith

**Project Coordinator**
Kristie Rees

**Graphics and Production Specialists**
Jennifer Henry
Andrea Hornberger
Melissa K. Smith

**Quality Control Technician**
Caitie Copple

**Proofreading**
Melissa D. Buddendeck

**Indexing**
Potomac Indexing, LLC

*To my beautiful and devoted wife, Nina, for her ongoing support, dedication, and continuously adding much-needed perspective to my life.*

# Acknowledgments

I would like to express my thanks to a number of people who have made invaluable contributions to both my general iPod and iTunes experiences as well as this book specifically. Firstly, I would like to thank Jeremy Horwitz and Dennis Lloyd and the rest of the staff at iLounge.com for their guidance, support and assistance; Rob Stewart for his assistance in testing and serving as a sounding board; Andreas and Lianne Bach for their ongoing encouragement and support; and Thomas Rogan for his understanding and willingness to accommodate the time commitment that goes into a project of this magnitude, even while other projects were demanding our attention. Finally, I would be remiss if I did not thank my editors, specifically Jody Lefevere and Cricket Krengel for their support and patience as I undertook this first major writing project amidst a very busy schedule and several moving targets.

# Contents

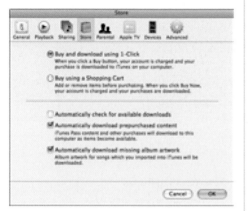

## chapter 8

How Do I Get the Most Out
of My iPod? 168

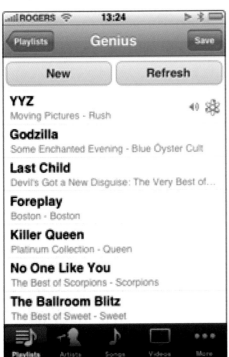

## chapter 9

How Do I Get My Own Movies
onto My iPod? 194

## chapter 12

How Do I Manage Content
on an Apple TV?                          254

## chapter 13

How Do I Manage a Large
iTunes Library?                          282

# Introduction

**Seven years ago,** Apple Computer announced that they would be taking their first steps into the world of digital media with a new portable media player that they chose to simply name the iPod. Although Apple was not the first company to introduce a portable digital media player, they took the unique approach of providing more than just a stand-alone device. Instead, they provided many of the other pieces necessary to make the user experience work, ultimately building an entire ecosystem around this device, with a desktop media management application and later an online digital media store, providing the average user with all of the pieces they needed to enjoy their music at a time when most other digital media players were simply too technical for the average consumer.

The result of this accessibility was that the iPod, which started as a little-known media player for Mac users because a huge success, adding support for Windows users, expanding the reach of the iTunes Store, and adding support for video content and games. Not content to stop there, Apple moved into the living room with the Apple TV and expanded their reach even further with the iPhone, a game-changing cellular phone unlike anything else the world had seen up to that point.

Today, Apple enjoys continued success in the market, with sales of over 174 million iPods, almost 10 million iPhones, and over two billion tracks sold on the iTunes Store. Although some may dismiss the iPod as little more than a fad, the overwhelming success shows that there's something there which speaks to the average user: Put simply, the iPod is a device that for the most part just works and allows you to spend more time enjoying your media content and less time managing it.

Out of the box, the iPod and iTunes are pretty straightforward; this is after all the primary strength of the iPod brand. However, one would be mistaken in assuming that iTunes is little more than a conduit to manage content on an iPod. While Apple has done an excellent job of making iTunes simple for the average user, there is a lot of hidden power under the hood of the iTunes application, making it one of the best media management applications available, even for users who don't own an iPod or any other Apple device.

This book assumes that you understand the basics of media management and how to use iTunes itself and takes you deeper — into the aspects of iTunes and the iPod that are hidden beneath the surface and explore the real power of iTunes and how it interacts with your iPod, iPhone and Apple TV devices. By exploring the power of iTunes, you will discover how to better manage and get more enjoyment from your media collection.

# What Do I Really Need to Know about iTunes?

Managing a library of music and other media content can be a challenging task, and iTunes is a powerful tool for this, even if you're not planning to use an iPod right away. A good understanding of how iTunes manages your digital media collection helps you to get the most out of your digital media experience and allows you to spend more time enjoying your media collection rather than managing it.

# Understanding iTunes

iTunes is pretty much the only game in town to get the most out of all of the features on your iPod, but even for non-iPod users, it can be a great tool for managing an ever-increasing library of digital content. For those who have experience with other media-management applications, however, it's important to understand that iTunes takes a slightly different philosophy to how it manages your content, and it's important to get a good understanding of these differences so that you can get the most benefit out of it.

## Types of audio content supported by iTunes

There is a popular misconception among non-iPod owners that all of the content that you put into iTunes must come from the iTunes Store. Nothing could be further from the truth. Not only does iTunes support any standard audio CD that you give it, but it also supports the MP3 format — the most popular digital audio format available on the Internet today.

In addition to the MP3 format, iTunes provides support for the Advanced Audio Coding (AAC) format. Contrary to another common misconception, this is not an Apple proprietary format, but is actually an MPEG standard audio format originally designed to replace the MP3 format. It is also the standard audio format used by other devices such as the Sony PlayStation 3 and the Nintendo Wii, and many other modern portable music players and cellular phones have also added support for this format.

Content that you do purchase from the iTunes Store comes in AAC format, and iTunes imports your CDs in this format by default, but you can import any standard MP3 file directly into iTunes without needing to convert it first, and you can play these same files on your iPod, iPhone, or Apple TV without having to worry about converting them to another format. Changing your default import format is discussed later in this chapter.

**Note**

Windows users may be familiar with the Windows Media Audio (WMA) format, which is the default format used by the Microsoft Windows Media Player application and many Windows-compatible portable media players. Although iTunes does not support the WMA format directly, the Windows version of iTunes offers to automatically convert any *unprotected* WMA files to your preferred format as you import them, as discussed later in this chapter. Note that this option is not available to Mac users, as Mac OS X does not include the necessary WMA components.

iTunes also provides support for several other less-commonly used formats, including Apple Lossless format, Waveform audio format (WAV), and Audio Interchange File Format (AIFF). These are lossless formats in that they preserve the full original sound quality of the source, but they also consume a lot of storage space as a result.

## Understanding lossless and lossy

Digital music formats fit into two broad categories: *lossless* and *lossy*.

Lossless, as the name implies, refers to those formats that preserve the full sound quality of the original recording. Common lossless formats include WAV, AIFF, and Apple Lossless. The WAV and AIFF formats are essentially a direct copy of the audio from an original CD, while the Apple Lossless format performs lossless compression on the audio file to reduce the size slightly, although still without losing any of the original audio fidelity. This is the same way in which a ZIP file on your computer works — when you ZIP up a document or other file, the size is reduced, but you don't lose any of the actual information.

The problem is that even with compression, lossless files are generally still very large — between 6MB and 10MB per minute of audio. To solve this problem, a number of *lossy* compression methods were developed.

The idea here is, because most people's ears cannot hear the full fidelity of most audio recordings, a simple analysis can be performed to throw out those sounds that are of a frequency above or below normal hearing range. By selectively discarding information that the average listener can't hear anyway, the remaining music can be stored in a much smaller file.

The most common lossy formats are MP3, AAC, and WMA. Each of these formats can be set to different bit-rates, with the simple rule of thumb being that the lower the bit-rate, the smaller the file but the lower the sound quality. Bit-rates are expressed in kbps (short for *kilobits per second*), and although many audio enthusiasts prefer much higher bit-rates, most users consider 128 kbps to be the lowest acceptable quality for a digital audio file.

## Changing your default audio format

If you're importing existing media files that are directly supported by iTunes, such as MP3 or AAC files, these are simply left in their original format and cataloged into your iTunes library. No conversion ever takes place with an existing supported media file format during import.

However, when importing CDs or WMA files, it's necessary for iTunes to convert the audio into a supported digital media file format. Rather than pestering you each time, iTunes uses a default format that you set under your iTunes preferences. To set your import preferences, follow these steps:

1. **Open your iTunes preferences, click the General tab, and then click the Import Settings button.** A screen similar to the one shown in figure 1.1 appears.

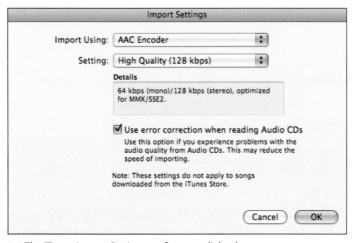

1.1 The iTunes Import Settings preferences dialog box

2. **Select the format you want iTunes to use for imports from the Import Using drop-down menu.** The format chosen here is used as the default for all conversion operations — importing from CD, converting WMA files automatically, or even converting tracks manually. The choices are

- **AAC Encoder.** The default encoder used by iTunes. This is a lossy format that provides reasonable quality at lower file sizes. This is the best-quality lossy encoder in iTunes, but the AAC file format is not as widely supported as MP3.

- **AIFF Encoder.** An uncompressed, lossless format that is just a direct copy of the audio from a CD.

- **Apple Lossless Encoder.** A lossless compression format. Files encoded using the Apple Lossless Encoder are the same quality as the original CD, but they are compressed to about 50 to 80 percent of their original size using lossless compression.

## Calculating Audio File Sizes

You can easily compute the size of an MP3 or AAC file based on the bit-rate you've chosen. The bit-rate is actually just the number of bits of data stored for each second of audio. So for a 128 kbps audio file, each second of audio requires 128,000 bits of data. Because there are 8 bits in a byte, with a given bit-rate and length of a song, you can figure out almost exactly how much space each track takes up if you want to do the math.

For example, for a 5-minute track encoded at 128 kbps

5 minutes = 300 seconds

128 kbps × 300 seconds = 38,400 kilobits of data

38,400 kilobits / 8 = **4,800K**

For a quick approximate calculation, however, you can just multiply the bit-rate by 7.5 and this tells you approximately how many kilobytes each minute of a song takes up.

Another good rule of thumb is to remember that a 192 kbps track is 50 percent larger than a 128 kbps track, and a 256 kbps track is twice the size of a 128 kbps track.

- **MP3 Encoder.** The standard digital audio file format used by most content and digital audio software and hardware. This provides the widest range of compatibility with other software and hardware; however, the MP3 encoder in iTunes generally requires a slightly higher bit-rate to be used than AAC to produce the same audio quality.

- **WAV Encoder.** An uncompressed, lossless format that is just a direct copy of the audio from a CD.

3. **Select a quality setting from the Setting drop-down menu.** For the MP3 and AAC lossy formats, select one of the predefined quality settings. Each quality setting corresponds to a specific bit-rate for that format. If you would like to set your own specific bit-rate, select Custom and an additional dialog box opens to allow you to select a more specific bit-rate. Note that this does not apply to AIFF, Apple Lossless, or WAV formats, as these formats provide the same quality as the original audio.

**Note**

Once you have actually imported your music into iTunes you can view the size of your files by enabling the Size column in the View ⇨ Options menu in iTunes.

# Types of video content supported by iTunes

iTunes also supports organizing and viewing your video content. Although the world of digital audio formats is much more well-defined, with MP3 being the dominant standard, the world of online digital video content is a great deal murkier, with a wide variety of different formats out there and no clear standard.

iTunes uses QuickTime as its underlying video engine, and you can therefore use any video format supported by QuickTime in iTunes. In a default configuration, this includes the QuickTime MOV format, as well as the H.264 and MPEG-4 video formats. A number of plug-ins are available for QuickTime, however, that extend this video playback to include numerous other popular formats such as WMV and DivX.

Keep in mind, however, that although iTunes supports any video format compatible with QuickTime, this is not the case with Apple media hardware. These devices are limited to the H.264 and MPEG-4 formats, and have certain additional limitations on maximum resolutions and bitrates that are discussed in Chapter 9. This becomes important if you plan to watch your video content on any device other than your computer.

# How iTunes organizes and stores media

iTunes takes a considerably different approach from many other media-management applications in terms of how media content is organized on your computer. Basically, iTunes expects that you are performing all of your music and other media management using the iTunes application as the front-end, and it takes care of all of the little details like file and folder management for you in the background..

Ironically, it's often the most experienced digital media users that have the hardest time coming to grips with how iTunes works. If you've been collecting digital media for a long time, even with another media-management application, you may have become used to managing your media collection through a file and folder structure. You've probably become quite comfortable with this organization and grown to expect that things are only ever where you put them and nowhere else.

However, the problem with a file and folder structure is that it's limiting by its very nature. Say you choose to organize your music into a folder structure by Artist and Album, with each song file named after the track. Now, how do you find all the music of a particular genre? How do you deal with songs from albums with various artists such as movie soundtracks? For a few tracks, this may not be much of a challenge, but it can quickly become unwieldy as your library grows to thousands of songs — which it will.

Most digital audio formats already include room for tags stored within the files themselves to contain information such as the artist, album, song title, and genre. In most cases this information is already at least partially filled in for your existing media files — it merely needs to be read in and put to good use, which is essentially what iTunes does as you import your media files into your iTunes library. The information from the tags is stored in a database for quick access, and so iTunes can generally find a given track for you much faster than you could otherwise.

**Genius**

If you want to actually see a specific file, simply select the track in iTunes and choose File ➪ Show in Finder (Mac) or Show in Windows Explorer (Windows); iTunes opens the appropriate window to that location, with the selected file highlighted.

So what about the files themselves? Well, the point is that you don't really need to care where those files are. There's no longer a need to deal with the original files — you can locate, play, copy, organize, and retag your media from within iTunes, and it takes care of all of the other trivial details like file storage for you automatically under the hood.

**Genius**

Need to copy a set of tracks? Try highlighting a single track or set of tracks in iTunes and then drag-and-drop them directly onto a Finder or Windows Explorer window. iTunes copies those files to that location.

# Configuring Your Library Storage Settings

Armed with a basic understanding of the types of media that you can use in iTunes and how it's all stored, the next step is to actually get that content into iTunes. Of course, there's always a temptation to jump right in, but this is one of these situations where just a little bit of initial understanding and planning can help you avoid a whole bunch of headaches later.

## Selecting a location for your iTunes media

By default, iTunes stores its library folder under your *Music/iTunes/iTunes Music* folder on a Mac or your *My Music\Music\iTunes Music* folder in Windows. Both of these folders are normally located on your system drive, and if you're importing a large library, this may not be the ideal place for it. Even if you choose to leave your existing media files where they are, the iTunes Music Folder path is still used for tracks that you import from audio CDs, as well as any content purchased from the iTunes Store, including podcasts.

Although iTunes stores its library database on the system drive by default, you can specify any location you like for the storage of your media content, and it does not need to be stored with the actual database. You seldom need to be concerned with changing the database location — it doesn't grow particularly large. Your media content, however, can quickly take over your entire hard drive if you're not careful.

Note that it is possible to move your media content to another location in the future, and I discuss that in Chapter 13. However, moving the media content can still be a time-consuming process, and it's better to plan ahead and place it in a location where you want to keep it for the long run now.

To change the location of your iTunes music folder, follow these steps:

1. **Open your iTunes preferences and click the Advanced tab, as shown in figure 1.2.**

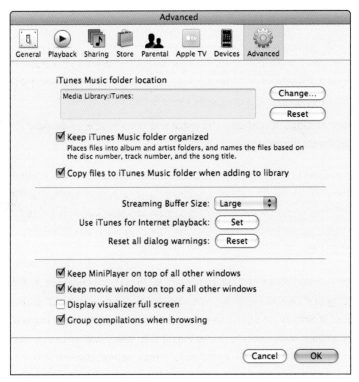

1.2 The Advanced tab of the iTunes preferences dialog box

2. **Click Change.**

3. **From the file browser dialog box that appears, specify a new folder location and click OK; this is the folder that contains your media content.** The actual library database remains in your Music or My Music folder.

4. **Back in the Advanced tab, click the check boxes to select the other options you want to apply with regard to your folder location.** There are two to choose from:

   - **Keep iTunes Music folder organized.** This option determines whether iTunes reorganizes content in your iTunes Music folder as you change the tags and other information. For example, if you change the Artist field for a track, iTunes moves that track into a new folder according to the new artist name. This only affects tracks that are located in the iTunes Music folder.

   - **Copy files to iTunes Music folder when adding to library.** When this option is enabled, any existing files that you import into your iTunes library are copied to the iTunes Music folder. iTunes uses the copy for its library, but the original file is also left in its original location. If this option is not selected, iTunes simply references each file from its original location. It does not rename or move the file in any way, even if you later update the track information. Further, iTunes stores the full path to each file, and so if you rename or move the file later, iTunes will lose track of it, resulting in a broken link to the file. Note that content imported from CDs or downloaded from the iTunes Store (including podcast subscriptions) is always placed in the iTunes Music folder, regardless of this setting. Further, if you import a track that is already in the iTunes Music folder, it is moved or renamed if this option is enabled because it's already in the iTunes Music folder.

5. **Click OK so that the new settings take effect.** The remaining options on the Advanced tab do not apply to your iTunes library storage.

The basic point that you should keep in mind here is that iTunes considers your iTunes Music folder to be its home folder. Anything in this folder can be reorganized and managed (subject to the options mentioned in the previous steps). Files outside of this folder location are never managed or reorganized by iTunes. In fact, if you remove a track from your iTunes library, iTunes doesn't even offer to delete the file if it's not already located in your iTunes Music folder.

Keep in mind that if you're concerned about maintaining your own file system organization and choose not to copy files into your iTunes Music folder when importing them, you should ensure that your file and folder layout is already set up the way you want it, as it is not easy to move or rename these files once they've been imported into iTunes. Personally, unless you have a very specific reason to maintain your own file and folder organization, I strongly recommend letting iTunes manage your file organization for you. You save a lot of time and hassle in the long term, particularly if you ever need to move your library to another drive or another computer, and after all, aren't computers supposed to make our lives easier?

**Note** If you have selected the option to do so, iTunes *copies* files into your iTunes Music folder during import, and so if you're importing a large number of media files, you need to make sure that you have enough disk space for this. Alternatively, you can move all of the files into the iTunes Music folder manually before adding them to your iTunes library. If they're already in your Music folder, then iTunes just imports them in-place and reorganizes them as necessary.

## Adjusting your CD import settings

Importing an audio CD into iTunes is normally as simple as putting it into your computer's CD drive. With default import settings, iTunes simply asks you if you want to import the CD, and then does this for you. If you want to be a bit more selective about what you import from CD, however, you can either adjust your import settings to not automatically prompt you, or simply select No when asked to import your newly inserted CD.

If you choose No, iTunes displays the CD in your Source list on the left-hand side and a list of the tracks it contains, as shown in figure 1.3.

1.3 The iTunes CD track listing

From here, you can choose specific tracks that you want to import simply by placing a check mark beside them, and unchecking the tracks that you do not want to import — a useful feature if you only want to grab a single track or two from a CD, rather than importing the entire disc.

**Genius**

Many audio enthusiasts consider the quality of the iTunes built-in MP3 encoder to be less than acceptable. If you're concerned about audio quality and want to use the MP3 format for your imported music, you might want to consider ripping your CDs using a third-party tool such as Exact Audio Copy (EAC) from www.exactaudiocopy.de and then converting them to MP3 using the popular L.A.M.E. conversion tool, which can be downloaded from lame.sourceforge.net. The result is a standard MP3 file that you can just import directly into iTunes.

# Changing CD track information

When you insert a CD, iTunes tries to look up the correct track information for it using the Gracenote CD Database (or CDDB). You can turn this behavior off by unchecking the Automatically retrieve CD track names from the Internet option in your Importing preferences.

**Note**

If you're not connected to the Internet when you insert your CD, or iTunes doesn't retrieve the track information for some other reason, you can force it to try again by choosing Advanced ➪ Get CD Track Names.

For most commercial CDs, it does a pretty reasonable job, but keep in mind that the information that goes into CDDB is based on user submissions, and it's only as accurate as the information provided by end users like you. If you notice an error, you can easily correct it before importing your CD simply by editing the information in the CD track listing as you would for any other file in iTunes:

1. **Select a CD track.**

2. **Choose File ➪ Get Info from the iTunes menu.** You should see a dialog box similar to the one shown in figure 1.4.

3. **Fill in the correct information for that track.**

4. **Click OK.**

If you want to change an entry for several tracks at once, such as for an incorrectly spelled album name, you can simply select all of the tracks you want to change and follow the previous steps to edit the common properties for all of them.

1.4 The iTunes CD track properties window

**Genius**

When editing the properties for an individual track, you'll notice a pair of Previous and Next buttons at the bottom-left corner of the window. If you're changing information on multiple tracks, you can use these buttons to quickly navigate through the entire set of tracks. You can even use the keyboard shortcuts ⌘+P and ⌘+N, respectively, on a Mac, or Ctrl+P and Ctrl+N in Windows.

If you've corrected some obvious error in the track information from CDDB, why not share your experience with the rest of the world? Follow these steps to submit your own information to CDDB:

1.  **With the CD still inserted in your computer, select Advanced ⇨ Submit CD Track Names to submit your changes to the CDDB database.** You should see a dialog box similar to the one shown in figure 1.5. Note that as long as the CD is still inserted, you can also display this dialog box at any time by right-clicking the CD in the iTunes Source list and choosing Get Info. Once you eject the CD, the option is grayed out.

2. **Fill in the requested information in the dialog box in figure 1.5 for the CD.** At a minimum, you should include the artist, album, and genre information.

**CD Info**

Artist

Band of the Royal Regiment of Canada

Composer

Album                         Disc Number

Footsteps in Time        1   of  1

Genre                           Year

Classical                     1998

☐ Compilation CD     ☐ Gapless Album

Cancel       OK

1.5 The CD Info dialog box

3. **If the album has more than one artist, type** Various Artists **in the Artist field, and click the Compilation CD check box.** Note that the Compilation CD check box is only for albums with multiple artists, not albums that are merely special collections of a single artist's work.

4. **If the CD is designed to be played back with no breaks of silence in between tracks, click the Gapless Album check box.** More on gapless playback is discussed in Chapter 4.

Keep in mind that your submission won't show up immediately, as there's a review process for user-submitted changes, but it can certainly help the CDDB team to keep its information accurate.

# Importing your existing media files

If you already have a collection of media files lying around on your computer, you can import them directly into iTunes. iTunes does not offer any means of converting from another media-management application such as Windows Media Player, but if your files are correctly tagged, most of the information you need is already contained within the actual files.

The easiest and most obvious way to get the tracks into iTunes is simply by dragging-and-dropping a track onto the iTunes window. You can also do this with complete folders.

**Caution** iTunes can be strangely unhelpful when you try to import unsupported file formats, particularly where video files are concerned. If a file format is incompatible and cannot be imported into iTunes, you often get no feedback — it just doesn't appear in your library.

If you're importing a lot of content, and drag-and-drop doesn't work for you, then you can use the Add To Library option found under the iTunes File menu.

1. **Choose File ⇨ Add to Library.** You are presented with a standard file browser dialog box.

2. **From the file browser, select the media files or folder that you would like to import into iTunes.**

3. **Click OK.**

**Note** iTunes for Windows users offers two options on the File menu: Add File to Library and Add Folder to Library. These function in exactly the same way that the Mac's single Add to Library option does, although you need to select the appropriate option depending on whether you're adding individual files or an entire folder.

# Importing playlists from another application

If you've come from another media-management application, chances are that you've collected more than a few playlists in your time over there. Although iTunes doesn't offer a direct conversion option, if your playlists are in the M3U format, or can be exported into this format (most common media players can do this), then you can import them into iTunes manually.

1. **Make sure the media files on the playlist you are importing are already imported to your library.** If the media files are not already imported, your imported playlist may not function correctly.

2. **Export your playlists into an M3U format from your existing media player.**

3. **In iTunes, choose File ⇨ Library ⇨ Import Playlist.** A file browser dialog box appears.

4. **Browse to and select the saved M3U file on your computer.**

5. **Click OK.** Your M3U file is imported into iTunes as a new playlist with the name of the M3U file.

# What Do I Need to Know about Purchasing Content Online?

Although many iTunes users still get their music the traditional way by purchasing CDs, there are many online music stores available today that offer a massive selection of music and other media content that can be purchased from the convenience of your computer. Not all online media stores are the same, however, and it is important to understand the differences and limitations between them so that you can make an informed purchase and get the most out of your digital media experience.

# Getting the Most Out of the iTunes Store

The first and most obvious source of content for your iPod is the Apple online media store, which you can access directly from within iTunes. The iTunes Store began as a music-only store exclusive to Mac users in the United States. Today, however, it has expanded to support both Mac and Windows users in over 60 countries and includes a wide variety of media content such as music, audiobooks, podcasts, music videos, movies, TV shows, and even games and other applications for your iPod or iPhone. Although using the iTunes Store is not at all necessary for you to enjoy your iPod, it can be a very convenient source of additional content.

## How to set up an iTunes Store account

Although you can browse the iTunes Store and even preview content without setting up an account or being signed in, you need an account to actually purchase anything from the store. To set up an iTunes Store account, you need to specify a payment method. This can be a credit card, a PayPal account (if you're in the U.S.), or an iTunes Store Gift Card or Gift Certificate. This last option is especially useful if you do not have a credit card, because you can actually fund all of your iTunes Store purchases simply using prepaid Gift Cards, which can be purchased at any Apple Store and many other retailers.

To create an account on the iTunes Store, follow these steps:

1. **Chose Store ⇨ Sign In from the iTunes menu.** You should see a dialog box similar to the one shown in figure 2.1.

2.1 The iTunes Store sign-in dialog box

2. **Click the Create New Account button.** The main iTunes window shows a Welcome screen similar to the one shown in figure 2.2.

2.2 The iTunes Store Welcome screen

3. **If you are signing up for an account using a credit card or PayPal account, simply click the Continue button.** If you are signing up using a prepaid iTunes Store Gift Card or Gift Certificate, click the Redeem Gift Card button instead. If you are redeeming a Gift Card or Gift Certificate, you are prompted to enter the code from your card or certificate, which is credited to your account once you have finished the sign-up process.

4. **Fill in your personal information on the remaining screens.** Note that if you have used an iTunes Gift Card or Gift Certificate to create the account, you do not need to specify credit card information.

**Caution**
iTunes Gift Cards and Gift Certificates may only be redeemed at the iTunes Store for the country where they were purchased. This is something to be aware of if you travel to other countries. Gift Cards purchased while abroad may end up being of no use to you once you arrive home.

## Making Allowances

The iTunes Store provides a useful feature for parents who do not want to give their off-spring carte blanche on the iTunes Store by setting up an account with a credit card. Instead, you set up an iTunes Store account normally for yourself, and then set up an allowance under the Buy iTunes Gifts section of the iTunes Store. Your son or daughter receives an e-mail with the allowance amount and instructions on setting up their own iTunes Store account. Once this is set up, on the first of each month the specified amount is automatically billed to your credit card through your own iTunes Store account, and credited to his or her iTunes Store account. The effect is the same as buying a Gift Card for the account, except that the money is added automatically on a monthly basis.

Of course, you can modify or cancel an allowance at any time, and you can still purchase Gift Certificates to supplement the allowance credit for those special occasions when you want to give a bit more.

**Note**

There is a distinction between iTunes Store Gift Cards and Apple Store Gift Cards. Apple Store Gift Cards may be redeemed for Apple product purchases at all Apple Retail Stores and the Apple Store (which is online), but cannot be used on the iTunes Store, although you can purchase an iTunes Store Gift Card from the Apple Store. Likewise, an iTunes Store Gift Card can only be used to purchase media content on the iTunes Store, and cannot be used at the Apple Store or Apple Retail Stores.

# What you can do with content purchased from the iTunes Store

Traditionally, much of the content that you purchase from the iTunes Store is protected by the FairPlay digital rights management (DRM) system from Apple. The bad news is that this puts some limitations on what you can actually do with some of the content you've purchased, but the good news is that the iTunes restrictions are actually some of the most generous of any DRM-laden online media store.

Basically, the restrictions on standard iTunes Store purchases are as follows:

- **You can play back your purchased content through iTunes, on up to five authorized computers.** Note that this limit is based on five computers authorized at any given time, and these authorizations can be moved to other computers, which I discuss a bit later in this chapter.

- **You can transfer your purchased content to an unlimited number of iPods or iPhones if it was transferred from one of your five authorized computers.**

- **You can transfer your purchased content to up to five Apple TV devices.**

- **You can burn individual audio tracks to audio CDs an unlimited number of times.** The only restriction on burning audio tracks is that you can only burn the same playlist a maximum of seven times. This is presumably to prevent mass reproduction of the same CD.

- **You cannot convert an iTunes Store purchase to another format (for example, AAC to MP3), at least, not directly.** You can get around this by burning your purchases to CD and then importing them in your preferred format, but this is a time-consuming process and can result in a potential loss in audio quality as the files are recompressed.

- **You cannot play this content on a non-Apple device.** Apple has not licensed its FairPlay DRM to any third parties.

- **You cannot burn movies, TV shows, or music videos to DVD.**

In 2007, Apple introduced iTunes Plus content to the iTunes Store, which was made available in conjunction with certain music labels that were willing to sell their content without digital restrictions. iTunes Plus content comes in a higher-quality 256 kbps AAC format, and contains no DRM restrictions whatsoever. Purchased tracks are still tagged with your iTunes Store account information for tracking purposes, but you can otherwise use them on any device supporting the AAC format, freely convert them to another format such as MP3, and use them on as many different devices as you please, whether or not they are made by Apple.

iTunes Plus content can be easily identified on the iTunes Store by the small Plus symbol that appears next to the track price, as shown in figure 2.3.

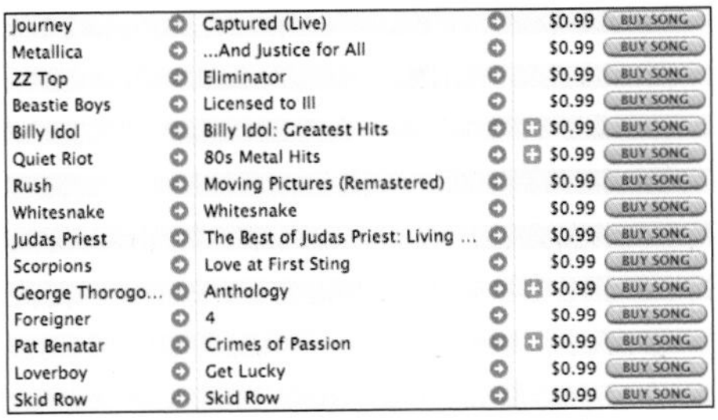

In January 2009, Apple announced that it would be converting the remainder of the iTunes Store music catalog over to the iTunes Plus format, a process which is expected to be completed by mid-2009. Users can also convert their existing traditional iTunes music tracks into the new iTunes Plus format for a nominal per-track fee.

| Artist | | Title | | | Price | |
|---|---|---|---|---|---|---|
| Journey | ⊙ | Captured (Live) | ⊙ | | $0.99 | BUY SONG |
| Metallica | ⊙ | ...And Justice for All | ⊙ | | $0.99 | BUY SONG |
| ZZ Top | ⊙ | Eliminator | ⊙ | | $0.99 | BUY SONG |
| Beastie Boys | ⊙ | Licensed to Ill | ⊙ | | $0.99 | BUY SONG |
| Billy Idol | ⊙ | Billy Idol: Greatest Hits | ⊙ | ✛ | $0.99 | BUY SONG |
| Quiet Riot | ⊙ | 80s Metal Hits | ⊙ | ✛ | $0.99 | BUY SONG |
| Rush | ⊙ | Moving Pictures (Remastered) | ⊙ | | $0.99 | BUY SONG |
| Whitesnake | ⊙ | Whitesnake | ⊙ | | $0.99 | BUY SONG |
| Judas Priest | ⊙ | The Best of Judas Priest: Living ... | ⊙ | | $0.99 | BUY SONG |
| Scorpions | ⊙ | Love at First Sting | ⊙ | | $0.99 | BUY SONG |
| George Thorogo... | ⊙ | Anthology | ⊙ | ✛ | $0.99 | BUY SONG |
| Foreigner | ⊙ | 4 | ⊙ | | $0.99 | BUY SONG |
| Pat Benatar | ⊙ | Crimes of Passion | ⊙ | ✛ | $0.99 | BUY SONG |
| Loverboy | ⊙ | Get Lucky | ⊙ | | $0.99 | BUY SONG |
| Skid Row | ⊙ | Skid Row | ⊙ | | $0.99 | BUY SONG |

2.3 Identifying iTunes Plus content

# Managing your purchasing style

One of the problems with the iTunes Store is that sometimes it's a bit too easy to go on a shopping spree. By default, the iTunes Store uses a one-click purchasing system, which means that as soon as you see something you like, you click the button, and it is immediately purchased, billed to your account, and downloaded to your computer. Although this is very convenient, if you're a compulsive buyer, such convenience may be hard on your monthly credit card bill.

Fortunately, there are some solutions to this problem that you can apply with some very simple changes to how you use iTunes.

## Using the Shopping Cart feature

In most grocery stores, you don't pay for items as you take them off the shelves. Instead, you put them into a shopping cart and then get to see the bad news all at once when you arrive at the checkout counter. At this point, you can either pay the bill as it stands or decide to reduce it by putting a few things back on the shelf.

iTunes offers a similar feature, where instead of buying items the minute you actually click them, they're added to your shopping cart. Then, when you've finished your excursion through the aisles of the iTunes Store, you can go take a look at the shopping cart and decide if you really need to spend that money, or if you want to put a few things back on the shelves.

By default, the Shopping Cart feature is disabled, but you can easily enable it through your iTunes preferences:

1. **Open your iTunes preferences and click the Store tab, as shown in figure 2.4.**

2. **Select the Buy using a Shopping Cart option.** Buy and download using 1-Click is the default.

3. **Click OK.**

Once enabled, you should see a Shopping Cart icon appear in your iTunes Source list, and the buttons on the iTunes Store that used to say Buy have changed to say Add to indicate that these items are added to your shopping cart instead of being purchased outright.

When you're done shopping, simply select the cart from the iTunes Source list on the left to see all of the content you've queued up. It should look something like figure 2.5.

From this listing, you can still buy individual items or click the Buy Now button in the bottom-right corner of the iTunes window to purchase your entire cart.

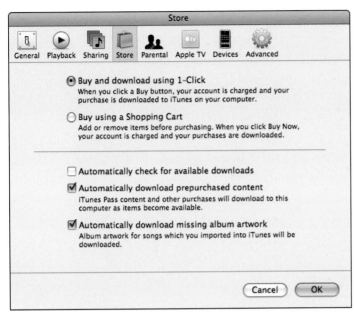

2.4 The Store tab of the iTunes Store preferences dialog box

2.5 The iTunes Store shopping cart

## Creating an iTunes Store wish list

The shopping cart can be a useful feature for individual trips to the iTunes Store, but what if you want to make a listing of items that you might want to purchase at some point in the future, but aren't ready to buy just yet?

Fortunately, another little-known feature of iTunes offers the solution: Create a playlist and add tracks directly from the iTunes Store to create your wish list:

1. **Create a new playlist by choosing File ⇨ New Playlist from the iTunes menu.** An untitled playlist appears in your Source list, with the name selected for editing.

2. **Type in a name for the new playlist and press Enter.** Call it whatever you like.

3. **Visit the iTunes Store, and browse or search for tracks that you would like to add to your iTunes Store wish list.**

4. **Drag-and-drop these tracks from the iTunes Store window to the iTunes playlist that you created in step 1.**

5. **Select the playlist in iTunes, and you should see that the tracks have been added as iTunes Store references, similar to figure 2.6.**

2.6 An iTunes Store wish list

From this wish list, you can listen to the 30-second iTunes Store previews directly and purchase individual tracks as you would directly from the iTunes Store. As an added bonus, once you actually purchase a track from your wish list, it remains listed in the playlist and the iTunes Store entry is simply replaced with the actual track.

# Renting video content from the iTunes Store

In January 2008, Apple announced that it would begin offering movie rentals through the iTunes Store, akin to the video-on-demand services that many cable operators offer. Of course, unlike purchased content, which you get to keep in your iTunes library in perpetuity, rentals by their very nature eventually have to be returned to the store.

The Apple solution to this problem was relatively straightforward. Although you purchase rentals through iTunes in much the same way as any other type of content, these rentals simply expire after a specific time frame. When you rent a movie, you can store it in your iTunes library or on an Apple media device such as an iPod or Apple TV for up to 30 days, after which it is automatically deleted whether you have watched it or not.

Once you actually "break the seal" and start watching a rented movie, it expires in 24 hours, again whether you have actually finished watching it or not. You can, however, watch the movie as many times as you want within that 24-hour period, and, in fact, if you begin watching a movie even one minute before it is due to expire, you are permitted to continue watching it, and even pause, rewind, and fast-forward through the movie. The expiry is enforced only when you actually stop watching the movie, or leave it on pause for an extended period of time.

**Note** Although movie rentals were initially only available on the U.S. iTunes Store, Apple has recently expanded this service to U.K. and Canadian iTunes Store customers. Most notably, users in the U.K. and Canada are given 48 hours to watch their rented movies, instead of the 24 hours available for movies rented in the U.S.

The other major difference in how rentals are handled as compared to purchased content is that a rental can only be stored on a single Apple device at a time. So if you rent a movie on your computer using iTunes and want to watch it on your iPod, you must move it to the iPod. If you later decide that you want to finish watching it on your computer, you must move it back. You must also be connected to the iTunes Store when moving rented content between devices so that the necessary authorization information can be updated.

**Note** Apple TV users with the latest software can rent movies directly from their Apple TV. Note that movies rented on the Apple TV, however, must remain on the Apple TV. They cannot be transferred to iTunes or to other devices.

# Working with Season Passes for TV shows

If you purchase current TV content through iTunes, you may have noticed that some shows have a Season Pass option listed beside them, whereas others merely have an option to buy the season outright.

A Season Pass is a feature of the iTunes Store that is offered for some TV shows that allows you to buy all of the current episodes and future episodes from a given season in a single transaction. When you purchase the Season Pass, all of the available episodes for that season are downloaded immediately. As new episodes become available, they are automatically downloaded to your designated iTunes library, saving you the trouble of having to visit the iTunes Store each week to check for and get the latest episodes.

## Setting iTunes to automatically download new episodes

To get the most out of a Season Pass, you should enable the setting in your iTunes preferences to automatically download prepurchased content as it becomes available:

1. **Open your iTunes preferences and click the Store tab, as shown in figure 2.7.**

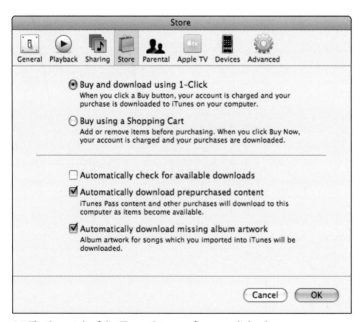

2.7 The Store tab of the iTunes Store preferences dialog box

2. **Select the Automatically download prepurchased content option.**

3. **Click OK.**

As new episodes become available in your Season Pass, they are automatically downloaded to your iTunes library and become available for viewing through iTunes or on any other device you are synchronizing them to.

## Managing your Season Passes

From your iTunes Store account page, you can view a list of your current Season Passes. This screen also allows you to check for any pending episodes that have not yet been downloaded, and control whether or not you receive e-mail notifications when new episodes are available for a given Season Pass.

1. **Choose Store ➪ View My Account from the iTunes menu.**

2. **Type your iTunes Store account name and password when prompted.** You are taken to your iTunes Store account information screen, similar to figure 2.8.

3. **Click Manage Passes.** You are shown a page listing all of your current and completed Season Passes, similar to figure 2.9.

**2.8** An iTunes Store account information screen

**Manage Passes**                                                    🔒 Secure Connection

Below are the Passes you have purchased. To receive an email when new episodes are available for download, make sure that the
Email Notification checkbox next to each Pass is checked.

**Current Passes**

| | |
|---|---|
| Season Pass: *Heroes, Season 1* | ☑ Email Notification |
| Season Pass: *Star Trek: The Original Series (Remastered), Season 1* | ☑ Email Notification |
| Season Pass: *Lost, Season 3* | ☑ Email Notification |
| Season Pass: *Top Chef, Season 3* | ☑ Email Notification |
| Season Pass: *Planet's Funniest Animals, Season 9* | ☑ Email Notification |
| Season Pass: *Stargate Atlantis, Season 3* | ☑ Email Notification |
| Season Pass: *Stargate SG-1, Season 10* | ☑ Email Notification |
| Season Pass: *Saturday Night Live (SNL): 2006/07 Season Sketches*<br>(2 episodes awaiting download) | ☑ Email Notification |

**Completed Passes**

| | |
|---|---|
| Season Pass: *Battlestar Galactica, Season 3* | Completed: 04/17/2007 |
| Season Pass: *24, Season 6* | Completed: 05/31/2007 |
| Season Pass: *House, Season 3* | Completed: 06/29/2007 |

2.9 The Manage Passes screen

4. **Check or uncheck the Email Notification check box to turn e-mail notifications on or off for a given Season Pass.**

5. **If a Season Pass shows any episodes awaiting download, clicking the notification checks for and downloads any missing episodes.**

6. **Click Done to return to the iTunes Store account information screen and save any changes to the Email Notification settings.**

**Note**   You may find that the information on the Manage Passes screen about Season Passes and pending episodes is not entirely accurate. Many Season Passes seem to remain listed as current long after they have ended, and sometimes a Season Pass even shows new episodes available that have already been downloaded. These are simply display issues that should not affect how your Season Passes actually work.

# Purchasing high-definition TV content

With iTunes 8, you can now purchase certain TV shows in high-definition (HD) format from the iTunes Store, where available. These are purchased in the same way as standard-definition (SD) TV shows, except that they are slightly more expensive and include both a 720p high-definition version that you can watch on your computer or your Apple TV, and a standard-definition version that is compatible with your iPhone or video-capable iPod.

When you purchase an HD TV episode, both versions are downloaded to your computer; however, they appear as a single entry in your iTunes library. By default, the HD version is used when watching the episode on your computer or your Apple TV, and the SD version is automatically selected if you choose to sync the TV show to your iPod or iPhone. Selecting HD and SD content for playback in iTunes is discussed in more detail in Chapter 4.

# Subscribing to podcasts from the iTunes Store

With the exception of a few weekly promotional items, much of the content available directly from the iTunes Store comes at a cost. However, the iTunes Store also provides a gateway to a large amount of free content in the form of podcasts.

Podcasts are independently produced programs similar in concept to radio shows and cable access TV shows. Some podcasts are simply produced by individuals, while others are podcast versions of popular radio programs made available by the broadcasters themselves. These days, you can find podcasts on a wide variety of subjects, from arts and music to science and technology to business and finance.

Apple doesn't provide podcasts directly from the iTunes Store. Instead, it simply provides a directory of podcasts to allow you to quickly and effectively locate podcasts that may be of interest.

## Subscribing to podcasts

You search for and subscribe to podcasts through iTunes in much the same way as you purchase music:

1. **Browse the iTunes Store to find a podcast that interests you.** If you click the title of the podcast, you should see a summary screen similar to figure 2.10.

2. **Click the Subscribe button if you would like to subscribe to the podcast to receive new episodes on a regular basis.** The current episode(s) are downloaded immediately, and any new episodes are automatically downloaded as they become available. Some podcasts publish new content very infrequently, while others are updated daily, so be sure you know what you're getting into before subscribing to a podcast.

3. **If you want to download only one or two specific episodes of a podcast, click the Get Episode button beside the specific podcast episodes that you would like to download.** The selected episodes are downloaded immediately, but you are not subscribed to the podcast, and so new episodes are not downloaded unless you revisit this page and select them manually.

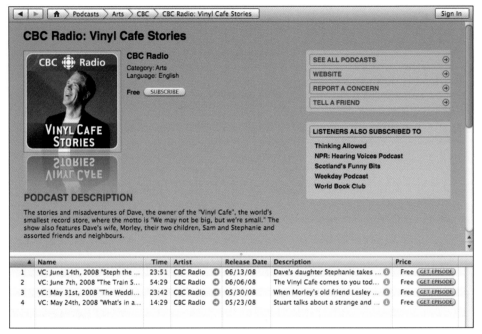

**2.10** A podcast summary screen

## Viewing your podcast subscriptions

You can find a listing of all podcasts that you have downloaded or subscribed to by selecting the Podcasts listing in iTunes.

As shown in figure 2.11, podcasts for which you have downloaded individual episodes have a Subscribe button next to the podcast series title, allowing you to subscribe to the entire podcast if you like. For episodes that have not yet been downloaded, a Get button displays to allow you to manually download these additional episodes, and a Get All button displays to allow you to download all episodes.

To unsubscribe from a podcast, simply delete the podcast series title from this listing in the same way as any other item in your iTunes library. All podcast episodes are removed and iTunes no longer looks for and downloads new episodes. As an alternative, you can keep the podcast series in your library and simply turn off automatic updating as described in the next section.

**2.11** The iTunes Podcasts listing

## Managing podcast download settings

You can set how often iTunes checks for new episodes of any podcasts you're subscribed to, and how many episodes are automatically downloaded, by visiting your iTunes preferences:

1. **Select Podcasts from the iTunes Source list.** The Podcasts listing appears.

2. **Click the Settings button at the bottom of the Podcasts listing screen.** The Podcast Settings dialog box appears, as shown in figure 2.12.

**2.12** The iTunes Podcast Settings dialog box

3. **From the Check for new episodes drop-down menu, select how often you would like iTunes to automatically check for new podcast episodes.** Options are Every hour, Every day, Every week, or Manually.

4. **From the Settings for drop-down menu, select Podcast Defaults to adjust the setting for all current and future podcast subscriptions.** You can also select how many episodes to download when new episodes are available by selecting a specific podcast subscription from this drop-down menu. Managing podcasts is discussed further in Chapter 6.

5. **From the When new episodes are available drop-down menu, select how many new episodes you would like to download.** Options are as follows:

   - **Download all.** Downloads all new episodes that have become available since the last time iTunes checked for new episodes.

   - **Download the most recent one.** Downloads only the most recent episode. Other episodes are still listed under the podcast subscription in iTunes so that you can download them manually if you want them by clicking the Get button from the podcast listing in iTunes.

   - **Do Nothing.** The podcast listing is updated to show the new episodes, but you need to download them manually using the Get button from the podcast listing in iTunes.

# Authorizing and deauthorizing your computer

As I mentioned earlier in this chapter, a significant amount of content purchased from the iTunes Store is protected by digital rights management (DRM), which controls how and where this content may be used. To play back this protected content in iTunes, you must ensure that your computer is authorized for the iTunes Store account that was used to purchase this content.

## Authorizing iTunes on your computer

Normally, when you first purchase content from iTunes on a given computer, that computer is automatically authorized for your iTunes Store account. If you transfer purchased content to another computer, however, you need to specifically authorize it before you can play that content or transfer it further to an iPod or iPhone.

iTunes should normally prompt you to authorize your computer the first time that you attempt to play back a track that requires authorization; however, you can also authorize your computer manually:

1. **Choose Store ⇨ Authorize Computer from the iTunes menu.** An iTunes Store Authorize Computer dialog box appears, as shown in figure 2.13.

2.13 The iTunes Store Authorize Computer dialog box

2. **Enter your iTunes Store account name and password.**

3. **Click Authorize.** Provided you have not already reached your five-computer limit, iTunes should respond with a message that your authorization was successful, and indicate how many authorizations have been used, as shown in figure 2.14.

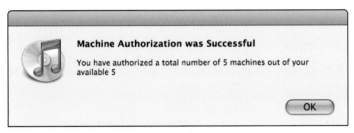

2.14 The iTunes authorization is successful

**Note** Reauthorizing an existing computer does not use up any additional authorizations, provided that the software and hardware configuration has not changed. iTunes still displays a dialog box to indicate how many authorizations have been used, but the number should remain the same each time.

If you are using more than one iTunes Store account on a single computer (for different family members, for example), then you must repeat this process for each additional iTunes Store account that you have purchased content from.

## Deauthorizing iTunes on your computer

Because you are limited to a total of five computers that may be authorized at any given time, you should always deauthorize a computer for your iTunes Store account before selling it or reinstalling your operating system. Deauthorizing a computer is about as simple as authorizing it in the first place:

1. **Choose Store ➪ Deauthorize Computer from the iTunes menu.** The iTunes Store Deauthorize Computer dialog box appears, as shown in figure 2.15.

2.15 The iTunes Store Deauthorize Computer dialog box

2. **Enter your iTunes Store account name and password.**

3. **Click Deauthorize.** iTunes responds with a dialog box indicating that the deauthorization is successful.

**Caution** Always ensure that you deauthorize your computer before reinstalling the operating system, taking it in for service, or performing major hardware upgrades on it. iTunes stores its authorization based on your specific configuration, so any major changes require the computer to be reauthorized as if it were new. Further, because the old configuration is gone, you have no way of deauthorizing the old computer. You could quickly reach your five-computer authorization limit if you regularly reinstall your operating system or upgrade your computer without deauthorizing first.

# Resetting your authorization count

iTunes limits you to a maximum of five computers that may be authorized for an iTunes Store account at any given time. While I explained earlier how you can deauthorize computers, that only works if you still have the computer in your possession, and you have not reinstalled the operating system.

It's not uncommon for iTunes users to get into trouble by not realizing that they need to deauthorize a computer before they reinstall their operating system or perform a major hardware upgrade. Further, even for the most-diligent user, sometimes circumstances are just beyond your control. Sometimes a computer just dies, and there is really no way you can get at it to deauthorize it, and, of course, it's not uncommon for many computer repair shops to just reinstall the operating system on your behalf without realizing that iTunes needs to be deauthorized first.

Fortunately, Apple offers a solution for users who have reached their maximum number of authorizations: Once you have reached your five-computer authorization limit, you can reset your authorization count and all of your authorizations from your iTunes Store Apple Account Information page. Note that once you have done this, any computers that you wish to continue using iTunes on must be reauthorized manually by following the steps earlier in this chapter.

1. **Choose Store ⇨ View My Account from the iTunes menu.**

2. **Type your iTunes Store account name and password when prompted.** You are taken to your iTunes Store Apple Account Information page, similar to figure 2.16.

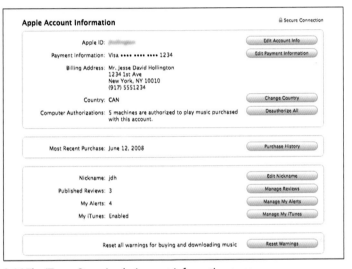

2.16 The iTunes Store Apple Account Information page

3. **Beside Computer Authorizations, you can see information on how many computers are authorized for this account.** If you are at your five-computer limit, a Deauthorize All button appears beside this entry. If this button does not appear, it is because you have not yet authorized five computers.

4. **Click Deauthorize All.** You are prompted to confirm that you want to deauthorize all of your registered computers.

5. **Click Deauthorize All Computers in the confirmation dialog box.** Your authorization count is reset to zero. Note that any computers that you still plan to use with iTunes need to be reauthorized manually.

Keep in mind that you can only do this once per year, and so this should not be considered a practical alternative to deauthorizing your computer manually; however, it can save you the trouble of having to contact iTunes Store customer service if you find yourself in a situation where you've used up all of your authorizations on only one or two computers.

# Using Other Digital Media Stores

While the iTunes Store was among the first online media stores to provide iTunes- and iPod-compatible content, and is still the top online music retailer in the world, it is not the only game in town. Many other online music stores have emerged in the past few years, and with the music industry relaxing its attitude toward DRM restrictions, many of these stores are now iTunes and iPod compatible.

## Types of digital media stores supported

The first and most important thing to keep in mind when shopping around for other online music stores is to look at the format they provide their content in. In the days when almost all online media content was sold with DRM restrictions, the iTunes Store really was the only option for iTunes and iPod users because Apple had not licensed their FairPlay DRM to third parties. The result was that most other online media stores sold music in the Microsoft PlaysForSure Windows Media Audio (WMA) DRM format, which was completely incompatible with iTunes and the iPod.

Although many online media stores are still only providing music in the protected WMA format, the good news is that many of these stores are starting to abandon this format in favor of the more open-standard MP3 format, which includes no DRM protection, and can be played on just about any digital audio player on the market, including software and hardware devices from Apple.

Other online stores are normally accessed through your Web browser, and purchased tracks are downloaded as standard MP3 downloads. These files are then imported into your iTunes library in the same way as any other MP3 file.

Some good examples of online music stores that now sell music in an unprotected MP3 format are Amazon.com, Walmart.com, Napster, Rhapsody, and eMusic.com. Unfortunately most of these are only available to users in the United States at this time.

# Purchasing audiobooks from Audible.com

If you like listening to audiobooks, an alternative source of content to the iTunes Store is Audible.com, one of the first and largest online audiobook providers. In fact, much of the audiobook content that is available on the iTunes Store actually comes from Audible, and is merely resold by iTunes.

Generally for one-time purchases, the prices of audiobooks on Audible are not much different from the iTunes Store. However, for an audiobook enthusiast, Audible offers subscription plans that are economical because you can generally get several audiobooks per month for a fixed monthly price, regardless of individual cost.

Audible's content is protected by its own proprietary DRM similar to content purchased from the iTunes Store, with slightly tighter restrictions: Only two computers can be authorized to play back Audible content.

Purchasing audiobooks from Audible.com is handled through Audible's own Web site, where you sign up for an account independently of your iTunes Store account, and download content directly through your Web browser. For Mac users, Audible content is downloaded directly into iTunes from Audible's Web site. Windows users require an additional Audible Download Manager plug-in, available from Audible's Web site.

**Caution** Your Audible account is authorized separately from your iTunes Store account, and the number of authorized computers is limited to two. As with your iTunes Store authorizations, always ensure that you deauthorize your Audible account by choosing Advanced ➪ Deauthorize Audible Account before selling, upgrading, or performing other maintenance on your computer.

# How Should I Organize My Content?

If you have your iTunes library loaded up with your music, videos, and other content, now you need to know how to make the best use of that content. The best place to start is by organizing it so that you can find it and use it. iTunes is an outstanding media-management application, but getting the most out of it requires that you take the time to properly label and catalog your content and organize it in the way that works best for you.

content, you are probably going to find that the majority of your content is still actually music, a that you spend most of your time working with your music collection.

As I mentioned in Chapter 1, iTunes uses a tag-based system to keep track of your music, rath than relying on a file and folder structure. As a result, it is absolutely essential that your music tagged properly if you are going to get the most out of your iTunes experience. Music import from CDs or purchased from online music stores normally has this information filled in for you, b music from other sources may not. Further, you may find that you don't like the way a particu field is filled in and want to change it to your liking.

## Filling in required tags

For music content, there are three tags that are required for your music to be properly organiz by iTunes and on your iPod. These are the Name, Artist, and Album fields. iTunes organizes yo music, both within its own menus as well as within the underlying file system, based on these thr tags. Although iTunes doesn't force you to fill in the Artist and Album fields, you may find yo music very difficult to locate, particularly on your iPod, if these fields are left blank.

To fill in the artist and album information for a single track, follow these steps:

1. **Select the track that you would like to edit.**

2. **Choose File ⇨ Get Info from the iTunes menu.** A dialog box similar to figure 3.1 appears

3. **Fill in or edit the Name, Artist, and Album fields with the appropriate information.**

4. **Click OK.**

**Genius**

You can also edit name, artist, and album track properties right from the iTunes track listing. Simply click twice (two single clicks — not a double-click) on the field that you want to edit and type in the new information.

## Filling in optional tags

In addition to the standard tags that are required to organize your music, you have probab noticed that there are a lot of additional properties for any given track. Some of these fields a used to aid in sorting and organizing your music, while others are simply for reference purposes

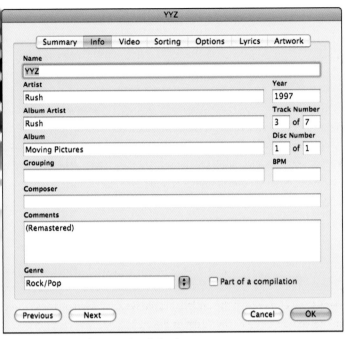

3.1 The iTunes track properties dialog box

- **Year.** This should contain the year the track or album was produced. Most tracks downloaded from CDDB or the iTunes Store contain the album year in this field, regardless of when the original song may have been produced. This can be used for sorting.

- **Album Artist.** This should contain the name of the artist for the album as a whole. This is generally used for albums with guest artists or featured artists to indicate the primary artist for the album. For single-artist albums, it is usually either blank or the same as the Artist field for all of the individual tracks. This is used primarily for grouping and sorting.

- **Track Number.** This would contain the number of the track from a CD or album, and the total number of tracks. This is used primarily for sorting both in iTunes and on the iPod to list tracks in their proper album order when viewing an album listing. If this field is blank, tracks are sorted within each album alphabetically instead of by track number.

- **Disc Number.** For multidisc albums, this field contains the disc number that this track is from and the total number of discs. Like Track Number, it is used primarily for sorting of multidisc albums to ensure that tracks appear in their proper order.

# The Beat Goes In

A very useful field in your iTunes library is the BPM, or Beats Per Minute field. This is often ignored by iTunes users as they either do not understand it, or they simply don't know of any easy way to get information into it. The field itself is used to enter a number representing the tempo of each song expressed as an average number of beats per minute. While you can technically put any number you want in this field, it is most effective when you use numbers that represent the tempo of your music as closely as possible, because you can then easily build Smart Playlists that automatically select music based on tempo — for example you could easily generate an upbeat workout mix or a mix of slow music to relax by.

The trick to making the most use of this is getting valid information into the BPM field. Fortunately, there are a number of third-party tools that can handle this for you by analyzing your music library and updating the field directly. Some of the more popular options include

- **MixMeister BPM Analyzer.** (www.mixmeister.com) A free tool available in both Mac and Windows flavors, this will quickly analyze any set of MP3 files you throw at it and write the results directly into the BPM field. Unfortunately, AAC files are not supported.

- **iTunes-BPM (www.blacktree.com).** Another free tool for Mac users that takes a slightly different approach by simply displaying a window that you click on in time to the beat of the song while actually listening to your music. The result is calculated and added to your iTunes library. The advantage is that it supports any format that iTunes can play, including DRM-protected iTunes Store files. The obvious disadvantage is that it's only slightly less arduous of a task than manually entering values into the BPM field yourself.

- **Tangerine (www.potionfactory.com).** A $25 shareware tool similar in concept to MixMeister BPM, but only available for Mac users. This tool has the advantage of supporting both MP3 and unprotected AAC formats and can automatically read and analyze your iTunes library and write the BPM information directly back in.

- **beaTunes (www.beatunes.com).** A $25 shareware tool for both Mac and Windows that not only performs BPM analysis but can also handle other iTunes library analysis and cleanup functions, such as correcting inconsistent artist names. Also supports both MP3 and unprotected AAC formats.

- **Grouping.** This field is used for classical works to group movements of the same work together during playback. The Grouping in this case would specify the name of the overall work for each movement. For example, if you have a recording of Beethoven's Fifth Symphony, each of the four movements is an individual track with the title of the movement itself as the track number, but all four tracks would contain "Beethoven: Symphony No. 5 in C minor, Op 67" in the Grouping field.

- **BPM.** This field is used to enter the tempo of a track in beats per minute. It is normally blank, and is used primarily for reference purposes and as a criterion for Smart Playlists. Third-party tools are available to assist in entering this information into your tracks.

- **Composer.** This field lists the composer of a work. Depending upon the work in question, this may be the same as the artist, or it may indicate the lyricist, songwriter, or classical composer. Music can be grouped and searched for by composer as another level of organization in iTunes and on the iPod. This is particularly useful for classical music listeners, although many contemporary tracks downloaded from the iTunes Store also contain information in this field.

- **Comments.** This is a free-form field where additional comments may be entered. This is used primarily for reference purposes, although you can also search this field and use it in Smart Playlists.

- **Genre.** This lists the genre of the track in question. You can select from one of the existing genres or simply type in your own.

- **Part of a compilation.** This indicates that this track is part of a multiartist compilation album. This feature is covered in more detail later in this chapter.

While some of the tags stored within your tracks are primarily informational, almost all of them may be searched for within iTunes, providing an easy way to quickly locate groups of tracks based on this additional information. Further, these tags can be used in Smart Playlists to provide a very effective way of selecting and managing the content you listen to. Smart Playlists are discussed in more detail in Chapter 5.

# Tagging multiple tracks simultaneously

Tagging individual tracks is sometimes necessary to get information like track names and numbers correct, but when putting information into common fields such as Album and Artist, it's much more effective to edit multiple tracks at once.

1. **Select the tracks you would like to edit.** As with any other application, you can use the Shift key to select a range of tracks and the ⌘ key (Mac) or Ctrl key (Windows) to select multiple noncontiguous tracks. You can also use ⌘+A (Mac) or Ctrl+A (Windows) to select all of the tracks currently displayed.

2. **Choose File ⇨ Get Info from the iTunes menu.** If this is the first time you have done this, you may receive a prompt asking you if you want to edit the properties for multiple items. If this dialog box appears, click Yes to continue. The Multiple Item Information dialog box appears, as shown in figure 3.2.

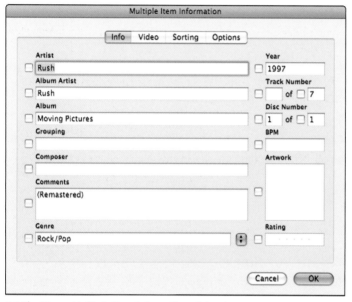

3.2 The iTunes Multiple Item Information dialog box

3. **Fill in the properties that are common to all of the selected tracks.** Note that properties that are the same for all tracks are filled in already, but you can modify them by typing over them.

4. **Ensure the boxes beside any fields you want to modify are checked.** These boxes are checked automatically when you modify a field, but you may need to check the box yourself if you want to clear a field for all of the selected tracks.

5. **Click OK to save your changes.**

**Genius**

If you have a situation where an artist or album appears twice on your iPod or in iTunes, it is probably because there are invisible differences in the artist or album name between the tracks. The most common cause of this is a space character at the end of an artist or album name. To fix this, select tracks from a given artist or album, and then edit the properties of them all together and retype the artist or album name. This ensures the information is the same across all tracks.

# Filtering and browsing your iTunes library

While you can easily sort and search for tracks within your iTunes library from the Music view, this process is made much easier by turning on the Browser view, which allows you to quickly filter your track listing by genre, artist, and album.

To turn on this view, simply choose View ⇨ Show Browser. The iTunes library browser appears at the top of your track listing, similar to figure 3.3.

3.3 The iTunes library browser

With this browser displayed, simply click the information you would like to filter by. The selections in each column work from left to right, so selecting a genre limits the artist listing to only the artists within that genre; likewise, selecting an artist from the second column limits the album listing to only albums by that artist.

**Genius**

You can also press ⌘+B (Mac) or Ctrl+B (Windows) to quickly toggle the iTunes library browser on and off.

The iTunes library browser can be turned on for almost any listing, including any of the categories in your main iTunes library (such as Music, Movies, and TV Shows) or even within your playlists. Note that the Browser view is set separately for each category; for example, you can have it turned on for your Music listing, but off for your TV Shows.

**Genius**

If you are editing all of the tracks for an artist or album, speed up the track-selection process by selecting the artist or album from the iTunes Browser view so you can change the information for all tracks by that artist or in that album. There is no need to select the individual tracks, and you can even select multiple artists or albums in this manner to edit all of the tracks together.

# Organizing compilation albums

Some of the albums that are in your iTunes library may not have tracks that are all performed by the same artist. These are called *compilations*, and include such albums as movie soundtracks and compilations of music from an era or a theme (such as a Best of the '60s album). Because iTunes and the iPod group music primarily by artist, it can be inconvenient to have a bunch of one-hit wonders cluttering up your artist list, and of course this can also make these albums more difficult to locate.

The solution is to mark these albums as part of a compilation on their track properties, and then tell iTunes and your iPod to group your tracks based on these compilation settings.

## Marking tracks as part of a compilation

To mark tracks as belonging to a compilation, follow these steps:

1. **Select the tracks you would like to edit.** As with any other application, you can use the Shift key to select a range of tracks and the ⌘ key (Mac) or Ctrl key (Windows) to select multiple noncontiguous tracks. You can also use ⌘+A (Mac) or Ctrl+A (Windows) to select all of the tracks currently displayed.

2. **Choose File ⇨ Get Info from the iTunes menu.** The Multiple Item Information dialog box appears.

3. **Click on the Options tab, as shown in figure 3.4.**

4. **From the Part of a compilation drop-down menu, select Yes.** Note the check box that appears to the left of this field, indicating that it is going to be changed for all selected tracks.

5. **Click OK to save your changes.**

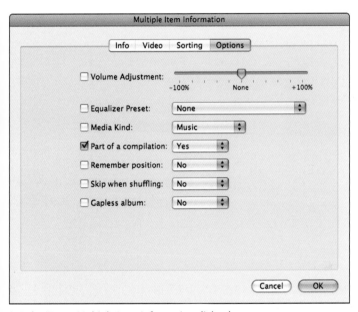

3.4 The iTunes Multiple Item Information dialog box

## Setting iTunes to group compilations

Once you have marked your tracks as part of a compilation, you need to tell iTunes to actually use this field and group your tracks accordingly.

1. **Open your iTunes preferences and click the Advanced tab, as shown in figure 3.5.**

2. **Click the check box beside the Group compilations when browsing option.**

3. **Click OK.** When browsing the iTunes library, a Compilations option should now appear at the top of the Artists listing. Selecting this option displays a list of all compilation albums in the album listing. Further, artists who exist only on compilation albums are not displayed in the Artist listing.

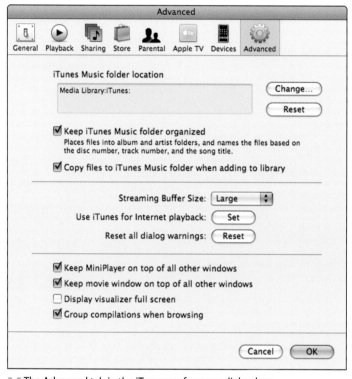

3.5 The Advanced tab in the iTunes preferences dialog box

# Adjusting the column headings

iTunes provides a default column listing to get you started, but you can actually view almost any one of the track properties discussed earlier in this chapter within the normal iTunes Column view, and you can even sort by any of these properties simply by sorting on the appropriate column heading.

To add or remove a column, follow these steps:

1. **Select the listing in the iTunes Source list that you would like to modify.** You may choose either a category from the main iTunes library (such as Music, Movies, or TV Shows) or a playlist. View options are set individually for each listing.

2.  **Choose View ⇨ View Options from the iTunes menu.** The View Options dialog box appears, similar to figure 3.6.

3.  **Select the columns that you would like to be displayed.**

4.  **Click OK.**

---

**View Options**

♫ Music

**Show Columns**

| | | |
|---|---|---|
| ☑ Album | ☐ Episode ID | ☐ Show |
| ☑ Album Artist | ☐ Equalizer | ☐ Size |
| ☑ Album Rating | ☐ Genre | ☑ Skip Count |
| ☑ Artist | ☐ Grouping | ☐ Sort Album |
| ☐ Beats Per Minute | ☐ Kind | ☐ Sort Album Artist |
| ☐ Bit Rate | ☑ Last Played | ☐ Sort Artist |
| ☐ Category | ☐ Last Skipped | ☐ Sort Composer |
| ☐ Comment | ☑ Play Count | ☐ Sort Name |
| ☐ Composer | ☑ Rating | ☐ Sort Show |
| ☑ Date Added | ☐ Release Date | ☑ Time |
| ☐ Date Modified | ☐ Ringtone | ☑ Track Number |
| ☐ Description | ☐ Sample Rate | ☑ Year |
| ☑ Disc Number | ☐ Season | |

( Cancel )    ( OK )

---

3.6 The iTunes View Options dialog box

Once the additional columns have been added, you can reorder them simply by dragging the column headings to the left or right on the listing. Note that the Name column must always remain on the far left side, however.

**Genius**

You can also add and remove columns simply by right-clicking the column headings and choosing the columns from the contextual menu.

# Sorting your library

You probably already know how to perform basic sorting on your iTunes library: Simply click the column headings you would like to sort by, and that's about it. However, iTunes also offers a few hidden sorting options to help you get a bit more control over how your tracks are sorted.

## Album by Artist and Album by Year

The Album column in iTunes actually hides a little-known option. Clicking the Album column heading toggles the heading from merely Album to either Album by Artist or Album by Year. The column itself contains the same information, but the nature of how your tracks are sorted changes.

- **Album.** This simply sorts your track listing alphabetically by album name. This is the default when sorting on the Album column.

- **Album by Artist.** This sorts your track listing first alphabetically by artist, and then alphabetically by album within each artist. iTunes is also clever enough to recognize albums with multiple artists and compilations based on the value of the appropriate tags, and sorts these separately at the bottom of your track listing.

- **Album by Year.** This first sorts your track listing alphabetically by artist, and then groups each album within each artist by the year of release, based on the Year tag. If you have tracks in the same album with different years, they are sorted based on the oldest track.

Because iTunes doesn't otherwise offer the ability for secondary or multicolumn sorting, this feature provides a couple of practical predefined sorting and grouping options.

## Overriding sorting for individual tracks

When sorting information in your library, iTunes normally sorts numbers and letters separately. Further, as of iTunes 7.3, Apple made the decision to change the default behavior to always sort numbers at the bottom of a listing, rather than at the top. This change confused many iTunes users, as it seems to differ from how most other computer applications work, but it can be easily overridden by specifying individual sorting values for your tracks.

For example, say you have the album *2112* by the band Rush. By default, if you sorted by album, iTunes sorts these tracks at the very bottom of your album listing, as the album name starts with a number. You could change the album tag to read "Twenty One Twelve" and the album would sort correctly based on the phonetic pronunciation of the album, but, of course, no self-respecting Rush fan could ever possibly do such a thing.

Instead, iTunes provides the ability to enter different tag information to be used only for sorting purposes, so that you can spell out exactly how you want your tracks sorted without affecting how the information is shown in iTunes or on your iPod.

1. **Select an individual track or group of tracks from an album or artist that you would like to modify.**

2. **Choose File ⇨ Get Info from the iTunes menu.** The iTunes track properties dialog box appears.

3. **Choose the Sorting tab from the top of the dialog box.** The Sorting options are displayed, as shown in Figure 3.7.

3.7 The Sorting tab of the iTunes track properties dialog box

4. **Enter text based on the way you would like the track sorted into the appropriate Sort field.** In figure 3.7, you can see "Twenty One Twelve" has been entered in the Sort Album field. This tells iTunes to sort this track internally based on this value, but the album name is still displayed as 2112.

5. **Click OK.** The selected track is sorted based on the new value in the Sort fields, but is still displayed with the appropriate information.

# Using the Grid and Cover Flow views

In addition to the standard track listing view, iTunes offers two other ways of viewing your iTunes library: Grid view and Cover Flow view.

You can select these views either by choosing them from the iTunes View menu or by clicking the View buttons found in the top-right corner of the iTunes window.

The Grid view, shown in figure 3.8, displays your tracks in a grid layout grouped by album, artist, genre, or composer, with the album artwork shown for each category.

3.8 The iTunes Grid view

You can switch to a different grouping by clicking the buttons shown at the top of the screen. Further, when viewing by categories such as artist or genre, moving your mouse over the artwork scrubs through the covers within each category (for example, all covers for a specific artist or within a specific genre). Sorting is also available in Grid view from the iTunes View menu, or by right-clicking the category headings.

The Cover Flow view, shown in figure 3.9, is similar in concept to the Grid view, in that it is intended to group your tracks and display them in their respective albums. The Cover Flow view provides an experience similar to that of flipping through a CD rack. You can change the columns and sort order that are displayed below the Cover Flow browser, but it works best when sorted by the Album column in order to keep your tracks grouped together. Note that the iTunes library browser is not available in Cover Flow view.

**3.9** The iTunes Cover Flow view

**Note** When browsing your TV shows or podcasts in Grid view, a number is also shown over each item grouping to indicate the number of new items in each category.

**Genius**

The Cover Flow view offers one additional cool feature. With the Cover Flow view active, choose View ⇨ Full Screen from the iTunes menu to switch to a full-screen Cover Flow view. This looks absolutely stunning on a large screen such as an Apple LED Cinema Display, and can be great for letting your friends browse through your music collection when throwing a party.

# Rating tracks and albums

Rating tracks in iTunes is a fun and easy way to mark those songs that you particularly like versus those that you plan to delete. At a basic level, you can rate any track by clicking in the rating column in your iTunes track listing. The main advantage of ratings is their use in building effective Smart Playlists, which are discussed in more detail in Chapter 5.

## Rating tracks while listening to them in iTunes

Although you can rate a track simply from the iTunes track listing, this can be too much trouble if you're listening to iTunes in the background while working on something else. Although a number of third-party tools have been written to assist with this, the reality is that iTunes itself offers the basic tools for rating tracks right in your Dock or System Tray.

To rate a song while you're listening to it in iTunes, follow these steps:

1. **Right-click on the iTunes icon on your Dock (Mac) or System Tray (Windows).**
2. **Choose Rating from the context menu.**
3. **From the Rating sub-menu, select the number of stars you would like to assign to the currently playing song.**

## Rating albums

With iTunes 7.4, Apple added the ability to rate entire albums in addition to individual songs. An Album Rating column can be added to the iTunes track listing to show the album rating on each track, or you can see the album rating shown directly under the album artwork when using the Album view, as shown in figure 3.10.

If you have not set a specific rating for an album, a default rating is assigned based on an average of all rated tracks within that album. This is shown in the form of unfilled stars to indicate that it is an automatically generated rating as opposed to one that you have specifically assigned yourself. Note that tracks with no rating are not counted in this average, and so an album with ten tracks of which one has been given a five-star rating shows a five-star default rating for the entire album.

To set your own rating on an album, simply click the number of stars you want to assign. Ratings you assign yourself are shown as solid black stars, in the same way as track ratings are shown. When you assign a rating to an album, any unrated tracks within that album are assigned the album rating as a default, again shown as hollow stars instead of solid black stars.

3.10 Album ratings as shown in the Album view

# Adding lyrics to your music

If you're a person who likes to sing along with your iPod, or wants to take a look at those lyrics that you can't quite make out when listening to a song, then you may want to consider adding lyrics to your songs in iTunes. While the feature doesn't do much for you in iTunes itself, adding lyrics to your tracks ensures that while you're on the go with your iPod or iPhone, you can easily pull up the lyrics for whatever song you happen to be listening to.

## Adding lyrics manually

If you're only concerned with adding lyrics to a few of your favorite tracks, you can do this manually in iTunes without any third-party tools. There are many sources on the Internet where you can find lyrics for your favorite songs, and Google is a good place to start looking. Once you've found the lyrics, you can just paste them straight into the track in iTunes:

1. **Select the track you want to add lyrics to.**

2. **Choose File ⇨ Get Info to display the track properties.**

3. **Choose the Lyrics tab to see the lyrics tag field, shown in figure 3.11.**

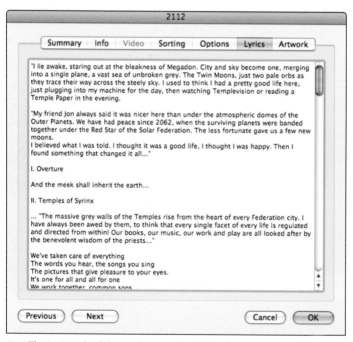

3.11 The Lyrics tab of the track properties dialog box

4. **Either type in the lyrics, or paste them in from your system Clipboard.**

5. **Click OK to save the lyrics.** The lyrics are attached to the track, and synchronized with your iPod or iPhone for viewing on the go.

## Adding lyrics automatically

While adding lyrics manually works for a few tracks here and there, if you're serious about lyrics, you'll want to look at a third-party tool that can scour the Internet for lyrics on your behalf, and add them to your tracks.

For Mac users, the simplest of these tools is the Sing That iTune! dashboard widget, which can be found from a quick search on the Apple downloads site at www.apple.com/download. This widget installs on your Mac OS X dashboard and automatically looks up and adds lyrics to songs in your iTunes library as you play your songs back in iTunes.

A version of the Sing That iTune! dashboard widget is also available for Windows users as a Yahoo! widget that performs the same function. Another Yahoo! widget that can be used for this is iTunes Companion. You can download Yahoo! widgets from widgets.yahoo.com.

A number of full-featured, standalone applications are also available that can look up lyrics and add them to your tracks as a group. iLyrics (http://senthilkumar.googlepages.com/ituneslyricsimporter) is a free application for Windows users that works quite well for this purpose. A free application that can do this for Mac users is GimmeSomeTune (www.eternalstorms.at/gimmesometune).

**Note**

A number of older applications are also available to download lyrics; however, many of these do not work properly as they have not been updated for the latest version of iTunes. Always ensure that you get a relatively current version of any iTunes companion software to ensure maximum compatibility.

# Organizing Video Content

While iTunes started out as being "all about the music," these days there is much more to iTunes than just music content. Limited video support was first added to iTunes 5.0 in 2004, but little was done with it until the release of the fifth-generation iPod with video in the fall of 2005. From that point on, video support in iTunes and on the iTunes Store has simply exploded, and iTunes has now become almost as adept at handling your videos as it is with your music collection.

## Types of video content

iTunes organizes your video content into three general categories:

- **Movies.** As far as the iTunes Store is concerned, this category applies to feature-length films. Realistically, however, it can just as easily represent any video clip you have imported into iTunes. It is the default category for any newly imported video content, and the most generic category of the three.

- **TV Shows**. As the name implies, this category is used for TV content. Content in this category is generally organized by typical TV show information such as a show name, season, episode name, and episode number.

● **Music Videos.** This category identifies music videos, and is organized in much the same way as your music is. Album, artist, and track name fields are all used here, and you can find your music videos in your Music section in iTunes, listed right alongside your audio music tracks by the same artists.

# Tagging video content

As with the music in your iTunes library, your video files must be properly tagged in order for iTunes and your iPod to properly organize your content so that you can easily find it.

Video tracks have the same basic tag information as audio tracks, and this information is edited in much the same way. However, there are also some video-specific fields that apply to different types of video content, not the least of which is the content type itself.

Any videos that you import into your iTunes library are automatically tagged as Movies by default. To change the video kind to either TV Show or Music Video, follow these steps:

1. **Select the individual video track or group of tracks that you would like to modify.**

2. **Choose File ⇨ Get Info from the iTunes menu.** The standard track properties dialog box appears.

3. **Select the Options tab, as shown in figure 3.12.**

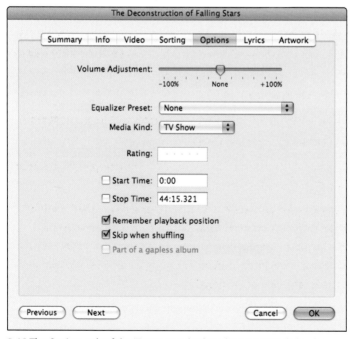

3.12 The Options tab of the iTunes standard track properties dialog box

4. **From the Media Kind drop-down menu, choose Movie, Music Video, or TV Show.**

5. **Click OK.** Depending on the video type, there may be additional fields that need to be filled in for the content to be organized and to display properly.

## Organizing movies

Movies are the simplest video content to tag and organize in iTunes. They are displayed in the Movies section, and organized simply by the standard track name field. Other tags such as genre can be filled in to provide more sorting options, but these are completely optional.

## Organizing TV shows

TV shows, on the other hand, are much more complex to deal with properly in iTunes, and if the necessary fields aren't filled in, you may not be able to even see your TV shows listed on your iPod.

To fill in the proper TV show information, follow these steps:

1. **Select the individual TV show or group of shows that you want to modify.**

2. **Choose File ➪ Get Info from the iTunes menu to open the track properties dialog box.**

3. **Select the Info tab, as shown in figure 3.13.**

4. **Type the name of the specific episode in the Name field, as shown in figure 3.13.**

5. **Optionally, fill in the Artist, Album Artist, and Album fields.** The convention for these fields is to type the show name in the Artist field, and the show name and season number in the Album field. These fields are not strictly necessary for proper organization; however, TV shows purchased from the iTunes Store use this standard, and it is therefore a good idea to fill these fields in for consistency.

6. **Select the Video tab, as shown in figure 3.14.**

7. **Fill in the following fields in the video properties, using figure 3.14 as an example:**

   - **Show.** Type the name of the TV show (for example, the TV series).

   - **Season Number.** Type the season number. iTunes uses this to group episodes into their appropriate seasons in iTunes and on the iPod and Apple TV.

   - **Episode ID.** Type the production episode ID or simply the episode number. This field is optional and may be left blank. It is used primarily for reference purposes, but is also used for sorting in the absence of the Episode Number field. You can type both letters and numbers in this field, as it is intended to follow a studio production-numbering system, which varies between different TV shows.

3.13 The Info tab of the iTunes TV Show track properties dialog box

3.14 The Video tab of the iTunes TV show video properties dialog box

- **Episode Number.** Type the number of the episode within the season, or within the series. Content purchased from the iTunes Store normally numbers episodes on a per-season basis; however, you can use a numbering system for the entire series here if you prefer. This field is simply used to sort episodes within each season. This field accepts numeric values only.

  - **Description.** Optionally, you may type a description for the TV show that you would like to see appear on the Apple TV or in iTunes. This field is not yet used on the iPod or iPhone.

8. **Click OK to save your changes.**

## Organizing music videos

Music videos are tagged in the same way as music tracks are. They are organized by artist and track name and shown in the Music section of your iTunes library, right alongside your audio tracks. Refer to the section on organizing music content earlier in this chapter for more information.

# Adding more information to your videos

Although there are a number of video-related fields that iTunes can happily display for you, such as release date and content rating, it does not provide a way to actually put information into these fields yourself. These fields are regularly used by content purchased from the iTunes Store, but iTunes provides no way for users who want to encode their own content to fill in this information.

Fortunately, around the time that iTunes began supporting video content, an open-source tool known as AtomicParsley (www.atomicparsley.sourceforge.net) was released to handle updating the metadata directly within the underlying video files. AtomicParsley is a command-line tool and can be cumbersome to use, but a number of tools have been developed to provide a graphical interface for AtomicParsley.

For Mac users, Lostify (www.lostify.com), Parsley is Atomically Delicious (www.them.ws/pad) and MetaX (www.kerstetter.net) are both good options to handle these tasks for you, as well as modify some of the advanced metadata. The best part of all is that these tools are free.

For Windows users, TVTagger (http://tvtagger.wordpress.com) can perform a similar set of functions.

Note as well that Mac users can also take advantage of AppleScript, which provides another set of options for tagging videos in iTunes. You can find more on AppleScript in Chapter 15.

Some of the extra information that you may want to add to your own videos include

- **Content Rating.** This field allows you to specify an MPAA-style content rating for your movies or TV shows, such as PG-13 or TV-MA. These ratings are primarily for display purposes within iTunes, but can be used to enforce parental controls on the Apple TV, and may therefore be very important if you are an Apple TV user with children in the house. Note that this field currently cannot be set using AppleScript.

- **Release Date.** Although this field is largely informational, it is displayed on the Apple TV, and some users may want to have accurate release dates for their movies and TV shows. Note that this field currently cannot be set using AppleScript.

- **Cast and Crew.** This is a multivalued field that allows you to specify actors, directors, writers, and other principal movie credits. This is completely optional, but like Release Date, it is displayed on the Apple TV. This information is also displayed in iTunes beneath the Long Description. Note that this field currently cannot be set using AppleScript.

Many of the third-party tools mentioned earlier can fill in other information such as the TV network, copyright notices, encoding tool, and even rating annotations. These fields are not presently used in any meaningful way by iTunes or any of the Apple media devices.

# Adding Artwork to Your Media

At one time, most of us were merely content to actually listen to our music, and with the early iPod models it was considered a bonus just to have a screen. Of course, this all began to change when Apple began putting color screens on its iPods a few years ago. Suddenly, with that shiny color screen, you wanted to see more than just the title of the song on a white background, and the ability to add and display album artwork came to iTunes and the iPod.

Recent versions of iTunes should show your album artwork automatically unless you have turned this feature off. If so, just choose View ⇨ Show Artwork from the iTunes menu to turn it back on. You can also press ⌘+G (Mac) or Ctrl+G (Windows) to toggle the artwork display on and off.

**Note**

iTunes 8 has the album artwork pane on automatically and there is no longer a menu option to turn it off. The ⌘+G (Mac) or Ctrl+G (Windows) keyboard command is now used to toggle the artwork column in the normal list view in iTunes 8.

**Genius**

By default, iTunes shows the artwork for the currently selected item, but here's a hidden trick: Click the words *Selected Item* that appear above the artwork, and iTunes toggles between showing artwork for the selected item or the item now playing.

# Where to find album artwork

Of course, if you purchase your music from the iTunes Store, it comes complete with artwork already provided, and there's rarely any need to change this. However, because you have probably ripped a large portion of your music from your own CD collection, you're likely going to need to fill in some of your own album artwork for these tracks.

There are a number of sources on the Internet where you can find album artwork, with the most obvious being online CD stores such as Amazon.com and Walmart.com. Depending on how and where you plan to use your album artwork, you may be concerned about getting the highest-resolution artwork images possible. This is especially important if you plan to display artwork on a device such as the Apple TV. You should go with an absolute minimum resolution of 600 × 600 for this purpose (which is the same resolution of artwork found in content purchased from the iTunes Store).

If you're only displaying artwork on an iPod screen or a lower-resolution computer screen, the resolution is going to be considerably less important, and you can probably get away with resolutions of around 200 × 200.

If you're concerned about getting the highest resolution possible and you have the original CD and a scanner, you can also scan in the artwork yourself to a JPEG file and add it from there.

**Note**

Keep in mind that album artwork takes up additional space within your media files. The additional space requirements are relatively small compared to the size of each track, but it can add up, so this is something to consider when adding higher-resolution album artwork. Expect to see about a 40K to 100K increase in size per file when adding artwork.

# Adding album artwork manually

Although there are several ways in iTunes to add album artwork to a track, the simplest way is by using drag-and-drop:

1. **Locate the artwork that you want to add.** Note that if you are finding artwork on the Internet, there is no need to actually download the file to your computer — simply leave the browser window open on that page.

2. **Locate and select the track(s) that you would like to add artwork to.** Note that if you are adding artwork to an entire album, you can simply select the album from the iTunes library browser.

3. **Ensure the artwork panel is displayed in the bottom-left corner of your iTunes window, as shown in figure 3.15.** Choose View ⇨ Show Artwork if it is not displayed.

3.15 The iTunes album artwork panel

4. **Drag the artwork image from your Web browser, or the image file from the Finder or Windows Explorer, directly into the artwork panel.** The artwork is added to all of the selected tracks. Note that if you are adding artwork to large media files such as video content for the first time, iTunes may take a few minutes to actually process the artwork, because it must be written into the actual files.

Note that this method adds to any existing artwork that is already in your tracks, and secondary artwork images are generally of no use other than taking up space. If you have existing artwork in more than one track and want to replace it with the artwork you're adding, you need to use the Multiple Item Information dialog box instead:

1. **Locate the artwork that you want to add.** Note that if you are finding artwork on the Internet, there is no need to actually download the file to your computer — simply leave the browser window open on that page.

2. **Locate and select the tracks that you would like to add artwork to.** Note that if you are adding artwork to an entire album, you can simply select the album from the iTunes library browser.

3. **Choose File ⇨ Get Info to open the Multiple Item Information dialog box.**

4. **Drag the artwork image from your Web browser, or the image file from the Finder or Windows Explorer, directly into the Artwork panel in the Multiple Item Information dialog box.** A thumbnail of the artwork is displayed, as shown in figure 3.16.

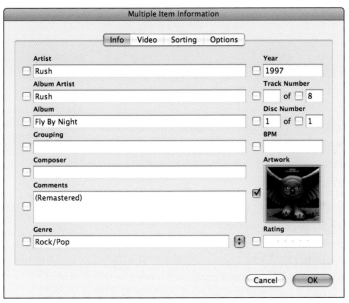

3.16 Adding album artwork using the Multiple Item Information dialog box

5. **Click OK to save your changes for all selected tracks.** The added artwork replaces any artwork that was already in these tracks. Note that if you are adding artwork to large media files such as video content for the first time, iTunes may take a few minutes to actually process the artwork, because it must be written into the actual files.

**Genius**

You can also use the system Clipboard to add artwork. Simply copy the artwork to the Clipboard from your browser, and then paste it in to the artwork panel. To accomplish this in the main iTunes window, right-click and choose Paste from the context menu. In the Multiple Item Information dialog box, click the artwork pane to highlight it, and then press ⌘+V (Mac) or Ctrl+V (Windows) to paste in the content of the Clipboard.

# Getting album artwork automatically

With iTunes 7, Apple recognized that many users had large libraries of content that they had added from their own CDs and other sources. Further, because the iTunes Store had such a large existing repository of music, it only made sense that the artwork for that music be made available to iTunes users to add to their own tracks. The result was a new feature in iTunes to automatically search the iTunes Store for any missing artwork on your tracks and automatically add it for you.

Although this feature is a very useful addition, it is not without its limitations:

- **You must have an iTunes Store account in order to use this feature.** Album artwork is completely free, but you need to set up an iTunes Store account as discussed in Chapter 2, because you are accessing the iTunes Store to get the artwork. This can be a serious limitation for some users, as you need to use either a credit card or an iTunes Store Gift Card in order to set up an account. Note that if you are only getting album artwork, however, your credit card is not charged.

- **You can only get artwork for content that is currently available on the iTunes Store.** If the iTunes Store doesn't have the album, then of course it doesn't have the artwork either, and so you'll still have to add artwork to all those Beatles albums manually.

- **Your tracks must be properly tagged.** iTunes uses the album and artist name to find artwork, and although it tries to work around common naming discrepancies such as disc number suffixes on album names, the reality is that if you don't have your music tagged reasonably well, iTunes isn't going to be able to find the artwork that belongs to a given album or track.

- **Beware of generic album names.** Because the album name is used for matching artwork to your tracks, generic album names can sometimes cause problems. Common examples of this are album names like "Greatest Hits" and "Singles," which could easily apply to more than one artist.

## How Album Artwork Is Stored

If you've used another media-management application, you may be familiar with the idea of album artwork being stored as a separate FOLDER.JPG file within your music folder structure. iTunes does not use this method, nor does it even read a FOLDER.JPG file to get album artwork. These files are ignored by iTunes completely, and if you've migrated your music library from another application, you can safely delete any JPEG files within your iTunes music folder structure.

Instead, iTunes embeds any album artwork you add manually directly into the tags within the actual file. This has the advantage of ensuring that the artwork remains with the file, regardless of where it may be located in the future — there's no corresponding FOLDER.JPG file that you have to worry about keeping around with your music. The disadvantage is that this increases the size of your files slightly, because the artwork is stored in each track rather than as one file for an entire album. This size increase is generally negligible, however, compared to the overall size of your media files. Even at 128 kbps, a 5-minute MP3 file should be approximately 5MB in size. Artwork generally adds between 40K and 100K, for an increase of around 1 percent of the overall file size.

- **You can only get album artwork for music tracks.** Other types of content such as movies, TV shows, audiobooks, and podcasts are not included, even if the iTunes Store has that content available.

- **Despite its best efforts, iTunes doesn't always get it right.** Obscure albums and tracks might be mismatched and have incorrect album artwork added to them. Note that iTunes only adds artwork to tracks that don't already have artwork, and so you don't need to be concerned about losing any existing artwork that you've added yourself. However, you may find some odd images on those obscure little single tracks that have otherwise been sitting unnoticed in your library for a while.

You can have iTunes scan your entire library for album artwork, or just search for artwork for selected tracks.

To have iTunes scan your entire iTunes library for missing artwork, follow these steps:

1. **Choose Advanced ⇨ Get Album Artwork from the iTunes menu.** iTunes begins scanning your entire library for missing artwork. The status is shown at the top of your iTunes window, similar to figure 3.17.

**3.17** The iTunes Processing Album Artwork status screen

2. **Once the scan completes, iTunes displays a status message listing any tracks that it could not find artwork for, similar to figure 3.18.**

3. **Optionally, click the Save button to save this listing to a text file for later review.** A standard file browser dialog box appears, requesting a name and location to save this file. This can be useful if you want a listing of tracks that you need to find artwork for manually.

4. **Click OK.**

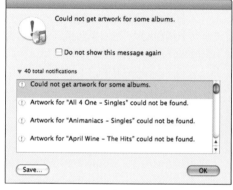

**3.18** An iTunes listing of artwork that could not be found

If you want to only search for artwork for a few selected tracks, follow these steps:

1. **Select the track(s) that you want to find artwork for.**

2. **Right-click your selection and choose Get Album Artwork from the context menu.** iTunes begins scanning for artwork for the selected tracks. Note that you must use the context menu for this. The Get Album Artwork option on the Advanced menu always searches your entire iTunes library for artwork, regardless of any tracks you may have selected. Once the scan completes, iTunes displays a status message listing any tracks that it could not find artwork for.

3. **Optionally, click the Save button to save this listing to a text file for later review.** A standard file browser dialog box appears, requesting a name and location to save this file. This can be useful if you want a listing of tracks that you need to find artwork for manually.

4. **Click OK.**

iTunes also searches for album artwork automatically whenever you import a CD or add tracks to your library from other sources.

**Note**

When adding artwork automatically using iTunes, this artwork is stored in a separate cache rather than being embedded within your actual media files. This means that if you move your media files to another iTunes library on another computer, the artwork is not moved with them. However, because you can presumably download the artwork from iTunes again, this is normally not a serious concern.

# How Do I Play My Content in iTunes?

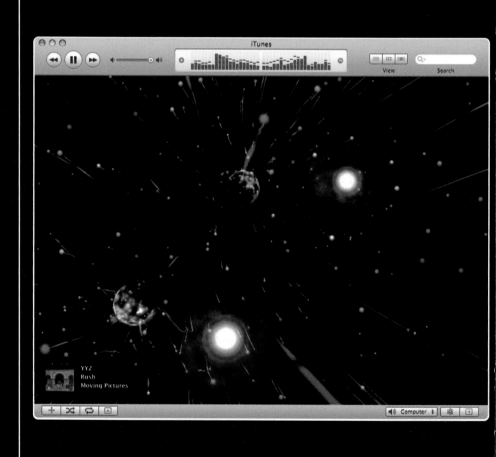

Although many users only discover iTunes when they purchase an iPod, you can use iTunes very effectively as your primary media player on your computer and as a hub for your digital entertainment. iTunes provides many advanced features for listening to your music, audiobooks, and podcasts, and even watching your video content.

other types of content, it remains quite true to its origins. The main playback features in iTunes are still very much focused toward listening to your music, and iTunes offers a number of advance features for getting the most enjoyment out of your listening experience.

# Using Party Shuffle

Although most users just listen to their music by selecting a playlist and track, iTunes offers a more effective way of handling music playback through the Party Shuffle feature. Unlike the traditiona way of playing back music in iTunes, the Party Shuffle list creates a dynamic playlist of music based on some simple criteria that you select, and allows you to queue up tracks for playback without having to resort to continuously modifying your existing playlists.

To get started with Party Shuffle, follow these steps:

1. **Select Party Shuffle from the iTunes Source list.** A Party Shuffle playlist is displayed. At the bottom of the Party Shuffle playlist, you should see a set of options for managing your Party Shuffle selections, similar to figure 4.1.

Source: JDH Mix    Display: 5 recently played songs, and
Play higher rated songs more often    25 upcoming songs    Refresh

4.1 The iTunes Party Shuffle settings

2. **From this section, choose the playlist that you would like Party Shuffle to select its tracks from.** You can select any of your iTunes playlists or the Music heading at the top to tell Party Shuffle to select from your entire music library.

3. **In the Display section, choose the number of recently played songs and upcoming songs that you would like to be shown in the Party Shuffle list.**

4. **Optionally, you may also choose to have higher-rated songs played more often in the Party Shuffle process by checking the Play higher rated songs more often option.**

5. **Click the Play button to begin playback of the first selected track in the Party Shuffle playlist.**

When using Party Shuffle, iTunes plays back the tracks in the order in which they are listed in the Party Shuffle listing, selecting new tracks at random from the specified playlist as needed. Unlike playing from a normal playlist, however, iTunes keeps the selection bar in the same location and refreshes the list of upcoming tracks based on the number of tracks you've selected to be displayed.

You can remove or reorder tracks in the Party Shuffle playlist in the same way as you would for any other playlist to control which tracks are played by iTunes and in which order. Additionally, however, you can also add new tracks to the Party Shuffle play order from anywhere in your iTunes library, regardless of whether or not they're in the selected playlist.

To add tracks to a Party Shuffle playlist, follow these steps:

1. **Select the track(s) that you would like to add to the Party Shuffle playlist.**

2. **Right-click on the selected track(s). The contextual menu shown in figure 4.2 appears.**

3. **Choose Add to Party Shuffle to add the selected track(s) to the end of the current Party Shuffle list, or Play Next in Party Shuffle to add the selected track(s) immediately after the currently playing Party Shuffle track.** Choosing a track and selecting Play Next in Party Shuffle while the Party Shuffle list is not being played back begins the Party Shuffle playlist with the selected track. Any other music that you may be listening to from another playlist stops playing in favor of the Party Shuffle playlist.

4.2 Choosing the Play Next in Party Shuffle option

# Using Sound Check

If you have collected music from a variety of different sources, you may find that some albums are naturally louder in volume than others. While this is not normally a problem when listening to one album at a time, it can quickly become annoying when working with playlists or shuffling your tracks from multiple albums.

**Genius**

You can also add tracks to the Party Shuffle playlist simply by dragging-and-dropping them onto the Party Shuffle playlist as you would for any other iTunes playlist.

iTunes provides a solution for solving this problem through the Sound Check option. When you enable this option, iTunes analyzes the volume levels on any tracks already in your library and additional tracks that you import, and adjusts the volume to attempt to provide a balanced listening experience.

The Sound Check feature is enabled globally in your iTunes library through your iTunes preferences:

1.  **Open your iTunes preferences and click the Playback tab, as shown in figure 4.3.**

2.  **Click the check box beside Sound Check.**

3.  **Click OK.** The first time you enable Sound Check, iTunes scans through your existing library to analyze any tracks that do not yet have Sound Check information stored in them. This may take anywhere from a few seconds to several minutes, depending upon how large your iTunes library is. Any new tracks that you add to your library while Sound Check is enabled are analyzed during import to have their appropriate Sound Check information added.

**Genius**

iTunes does not actually change the volume of each track; instead, it merely adds an adjustment value that is read by iTunes and other Apple media devices to dynamically adjust the volume during playback. Turning off Sound Check does not remove this value; rather, it merely tells iTunes to ignore it.

**Note**

Although the iPod, iPhone, and Apple TV also support Sound Check, the option must be enabled individually for each device that you want to use it on, as well as in iTunes.

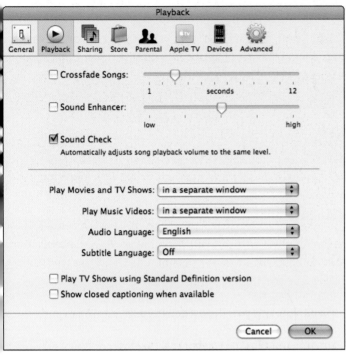

4.3 The Playback tab of the iTunes preferences dialog box

# Using Crossfade

For your listening enjoyment, iTunes can also crossfade between songs when playing back music from your iTunes library. This feature has iTunes fade-down at the end of the currently playing track and fade-up into the next, providing a smooth transition between certain types of music.

To enable the Crossfade feature, follow these steps:

1. **Open your iTunes preferences and click the Playback tab, as shown in figure 4.4.**

2. **Click the check box beside Crossfade Songs.**

3. **Drag the slider to set the crossfade interval from 1 to 12 seconds.** Longer intervals begin the fade-out earlier in the first track and take longer to fade in during the second track.

4. **Click OK.**

**Note**

Crossfade is only supported in iTunes and on the fourth-generation iPod nano. Other iPod models, the iPhone, and Apple TV do not support this feature.

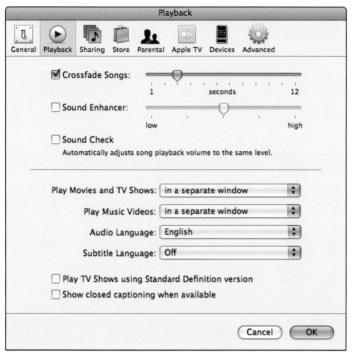

4.4 The Playback tab of the iTunes preferences dialog box

# About gapless playback

In iTunes 7, Apple introduced a long-awaited gapless playback feature, allowing albums that had been recorded with no silence between tracks to also be played back without gaps in iTunes and on the iPod. Common examples of gapless albums include live concert recordings, certain types of mix albums, and some classical works.

**Note**  iPod models prior to the fifth-generation iPod do not support gapless playback.

iTunes automatically analyzes your music during import to determine gapless playback information, and no special effort is required on your part to enable gapless playback, although there are a couple of important points that should be noted about when and how gapless playback works:

● **iTunes plays tracks without gaps only if they were originally recorded that way.** Don't expect all of your music to play without gaps; also note that tracks added into iTunes from sources other than the original album CD or the iTunes Store may not match up correctly for gapless playback.

● **iTunes does not play tracks back without gaps unless they are being played in their proper order.** Gapless playback is disabled when shuffle is turned on, for example.

● **Gapless playback and crossfade playback cannot be used together on the same tracks.** If crossfade playback is enabled, then gapless tracks must be marked in iTunes to override the Crossfade feature when playing back these tracks.

You can mark individual tracks in iTunes as belonging to a gapless album to override the Crossfade feature when playing these tracks:

1. **Select the track that you would like to mark for gapless playback.**

2. **Choose File ⇨ Get Info from the iTunes menu.** The iTunes track properties dialog box appears.

3. **Choose the Options tab from the top of the dialog box.** The track options are displayed, as shown in figure 4.5.

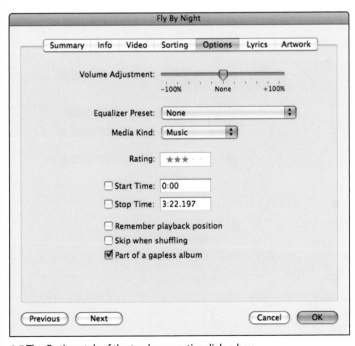

4.5 The Options tab of the track properties dialog box

4. **Click the check box beside Part of a gapless album.**

5. **Click OK.**

**Note**

The Part of a gapless album setting is only to override crossfade playback, and is not required for gapless playback otherwise.

To mark multiple tracks in iTunes as belonging to a gapless album, follow these steps:

1. **Select the tracks that you would like to mark for gapless playback.** As with any other application, you can use the Shift key to select a range of tracks and the ⌘ key (Mac) or Ctrl key (Windows) to select multiple noncontiguous tracks. You can also use ⌘+A (Mac) or Ctrl+A (Windows) to select all of the tracks currently displayed.

2. **Choose File ⇨ Get Info from the iTunes menu.**

3. **Choose the Options tab from the top of the dialog box.** The track options are displayed, as shown in figure 4.6.

4. **From the Gapless album drop-down menu, choose Yes.**

5. **Click OK.**

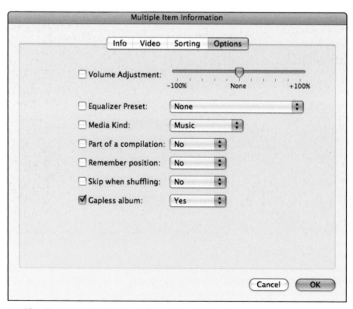

4.6 The iTunes Multiple Item Information dialog box

# Using the iTunes Visualizer

If you listen to a lot of music in iTunes and have your computer in a common area where you can see it while you're listening to your music, the iTunes Visualizer can provide a very handy way to jazz up your listening experience by providing on-screen visuals to the beat of your music.

To turn on the iTunes Visualizer, simply choose View ⇨ Turn on Visualizer from the iTunes menu while listening to your music, and the normal iTunes track list is replaced with a visual kaleidoscope that moves to your music, similar to figure 4.7.

In addition, you can switch to a full-screen view of the Visualizer by choosing View ⇨ Full Screen once you turn on the Visualizer. If you would always like to see the Visualizer in full-screen mode, you can also easily adjust this in your iTunes preferences.

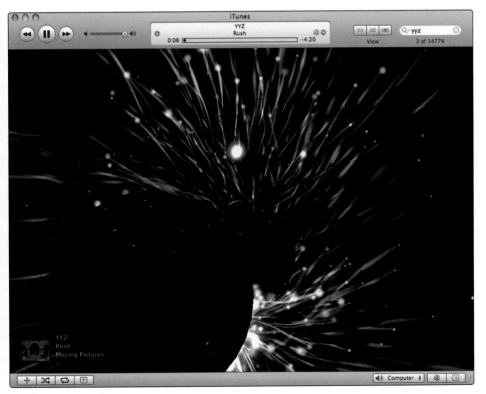

4.7 The iTunes Visualizer

**Note** iTunes 8 has introduced a greatly enhanced Visualizer compared to previous versions of iTunes. It's definitely worth checking out if you haven't seen it already. If, however, you still prefer the old iTunes Classic Visualizer, you can switch back to the old one easily enough from the View ⇨ Visualizer menu.

1. **Open your iTunes preferences and click the Advanced tab, as shown in figure 4.8.**

2. **Click the check box beside Display visualizer full screen.**

3. **Click OK.**

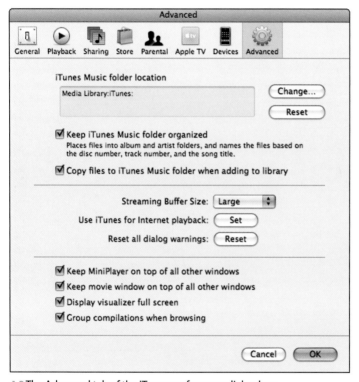

4.8 The Advanced tab of the iTunes preferences dialog box

**Note** Third-party visualizers are available to be installed into iTunes as well. Each of these third-party visualizers has its own specific visualizer options.

# Listening to Internet Radio in iTunes

In addition to playing your own imported media content, iTunes can also play streaming Internet Radio right in your iTunes player. A variety of Internet Radio sources are predefined in iTunes, and you can also open any standard MP3/M3U/PLS Internet Radio stream.

To begin listening to Internet Radio in iTunes, follow these steps:

1. **Click on the Radio category in the iTunes Source list.** A list of genres is shown in the main iTunes window, similar to figure 4.9.

4.9 A list of iTunes radio genres

**Genius**

The selection of radio stations in iTunes can be somewhat limited compared to what's available on the Internet. If you're really into Internet Radio, be sure to check out the iRADIOmast iTunes plug-in at www.iradiomast.com, which adds thousands of additional radio stations right into your iTunes radio list.

2. **Double-click the radio genre you would like to listen to.** The genre heading expands to show a list of available stations within that genre, with a bit-rate and a description shown by each, as shown in figure 4.10.

3. **Double-click a station to begin streaming audio from it.**

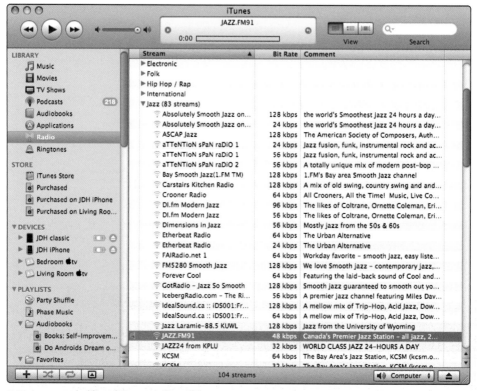

**4.10** An expanded list of iTunes radio stations

Note the bit-rate shown beside each individual station entry. As with audio files that you import yourself, each Internet Radio station has a bit-rate at which it "broadcasts" its programming. The higher the bit-rate, the higher the quality, but the more Internet bandwidth that is required. If you're on a low-speed Internet connection, such as dial-up, you should stick with streams of 48 kbps or lower.

You can also improve performance on lower-speed Internet connections by increasing the streaming buffer size in your iTunes preferences:

1. **Open your iTunes preferences and click the Advanced tab.**

2. **Choose Large from the Streaming Buffer Size drop-down menu as shown in figure 4.11.** Other choices include Small and Medium. It is only necessary to use a smaller streaming buffer size if your computer has limited memory capacity.

3. **Click OK.**

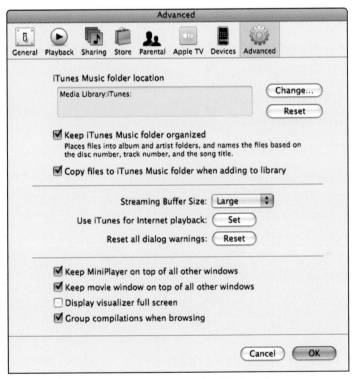

4.11 Choose a size form the Streaming Buffer Size drop-down menu.

**Genius**

You can also add your favorite radio stations into iTunes playlists to keep track of them and play them from there. Simply drag-and-drop a stream from the Radio listing directly into a playlist. You can even sync this playlist to an Apple TV to get access to your favorite radio stations from there.

# Streaming to remote speakers with AirTunes

If you're like many iTunes users, chances are that your computer doesn't live in the most conven-ient place in your home for using it as a digital jukebox. While you can, of course, take your music with you on an iPod and play it through portable speakers, iTunes offers another option to listen to your music throughout your house.

The AirTunes feature in iTunes allows you to stream any audio playing from within iTunes to remote speakers connected to either an Airport Express base station or an Apple TV. Playback is still managed and controlled through iTunes in the same way you would listen to music on your computer, but the actual sound is sent over your home network to a remote device.

If you have an Airport Extreme or Apple TV on your network, setting up AirTunes is simply a matter of telling iTunes to look for these remote devices.

1. **Open your iTunes preferences and click the Devices tab.**

2. **Click the check box beside Look for remote speakers connected with AirTunes to enable this setting, as shown in figure 4.12.**

4.12 The Devices tab in the iTunes preferences dialog box

3. **Optionally, click the check box beside Disable iTunes volume control for remote speakers if you do not want your volume adjustments in the iTunes application to be passed on to the remote speakers.**

4. **Optionally, click the check box beside Allow iTunes control from remote speakers to control whether or not commands like Play, Pause, Previous Track, Next Track, and so on, are passed back from the remote device to control playback in iTunes.** When this is enabled, playback can be controlled from the Apple TV with the standard Apple TV remote, or from an Airport Express with an optional remote control accessory.

5. **Click OK.**

**Caution**

You need to ensure that AirTunes is also enabled on any client devices that you want to use with iTunes. This is normally enabled on the Apple TV and Airport Express by default, and so it's unlikely to be a problem unless you had specifically turned it off when you set up these devices.

Once iTunes has been told to look for remote speakers in the preferences, a drop-down menu option appears in the bottom-right corner of the iTunes window showing the currently selected set of speakers, similar to figure 4.13.

Clicking this option brings up a list of speakers that you can stream your music to. A Multiple Speakers option is also available to stream your music to more than one set of AirTunes speakers at once — a nice way to provide music to your entire household.

4.13 The AirTunes speaker selection drop-down menu

**Genius**

If you're using an iPhone or iPod touch with the v2.x firmware, you can also download the free Remote application from the iTunes App Store. This allows you to use your iPhone or iPod touch as a remote control for iTunes from anywhere in your house — a feature that can be very useful when combined with AirTunes.

# Playing Videos in iTunes

In recent years, iTunes has evolved far beyond its humble roots as a simple music playback application, and now supports the storage, organization, and playback of video content as well. In addition to streaming your videos to an Apple TV, or loading them up on an iPod or iPhone, iTunes can also act as a very capable video player.

## Playing videos in a window versus full-screen

By default, iTunes plays your videos in a window, which is fine if you're just previewing the occasional video, or want to play something on the side while you're working, but it's not really great for turning that 30-inch Cinema Display into a small home entertainment system.

You can change any video while it's playing to use different screen sizes simply by selecting the appropriate option from the iTunes View menu. However, it may be more useful to set the defaults for how you would normally like your videos played:

1. **Open your iTunes preferences and click the Playback tab.**

2. **From both the Play Movies and TV Shows drop-down menu and the Play Music Videos drop-down menu, choose how you would like each of these types of videos displayed. In figure 4.14, in a separate window is selected for both. The options are**

   - **In artwork viewer.** Videos play back in the artwork panel in the bottom-left corner of the iTunes window. The artwork viewer is automatically displayed when you begin playing a video if it is not already enabled.

   - **In the iTunes window.** Videos play back in the main iTunes window, occupying the full window. When a video ends, the normal iTunes window content returns.

   - **In a separate window.** Videos play back in a separate window. When a video ends, the window closes automatically.

   - **Full screen.** Videos play back full screen. When a video ends, you are returned to your normal screen view.

   - **Full screen (with visuals).** Videos play back full screen. If you are playing a mixture of videos and music, however, iTunes remains in full-screen mode and displays the iTunes Visualizer for normal music tracks, rather than returning to the normal iTunes view. This can be particularly useful for mixing music videos with normal music tracks in a party setting.

3. **Click OK.**

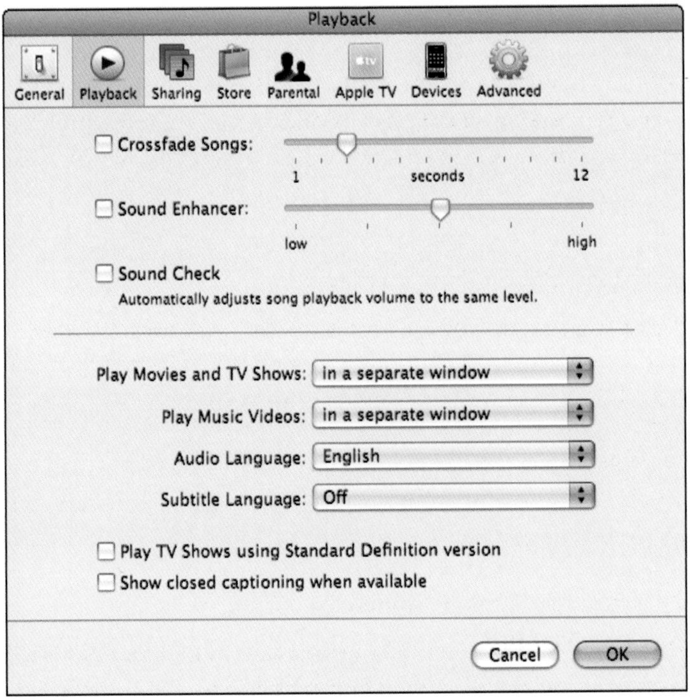

4.14 The Playback tab of the iTunes preferences dialog box

# Selecting high-definition or standard-definition TV shows

As discussed in Chapter 2, with iTunes 8 you can now download high-definition (HD) TV shows from the iTunes Store. These shows actually come with both an HD version to watch on your computer or your Apple TV and a standard-definition (SD) version for viewing on your iPod or iPhone.

By default, iTunes 8 shows you the high-definition version of a TV show whenever one is available. However, if you prefer, you can choose to view the standard-definition version instead. This may be particularly useful if you're using a slower computer or video card that has problems rendering the higher-resolution HD content.

When browsing your iTunes library, you can identify high-definition TV shows by a small HD-SD badge that appears next to them, as shown in figure 4.15. From this listing, you can set an individual episode to play the standard-definition version instead of the HD version:

1. **Right-click the HD episode that you would like to watch in standard definition.** A context menu appears.

4.15 An iTunes HD TV show listing

2. **From the context menu, choose Version ⇨ Standard Definition (SD) as shown in figure 4.16.** Note that no specific visual feedback is provided to indicate which version is presently selected, although you can confirm your selection by bringing up the context menu again. The selected version is indicated with a check mark.

If you have a slower computer that does not meet the minimum system requirements to play back HD TV content, you may want to set iTunes to play back all of your TV shows in standard definition by default. You can adjust this globally under your iTunes playback preferences.

1. **Open your iTunes preferences and click the Playback tab.**

2. **Click the check box beside Play TV Shows using Standard Definition version as shown in figure 4.17**.

3. **Click OK.**

4.16 The iTunes HD-SD Version context sub-menu

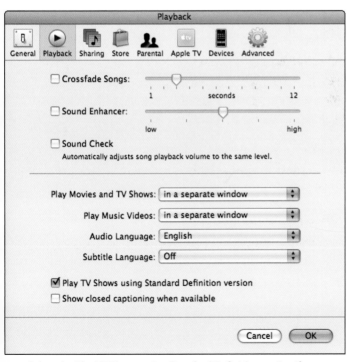

4.17 Select the Play TV Shows using Standard Definition option if your
computer doesn't meet HD requirements.

# Using chapter markers in videos

Recent versions of iTunes have also introduced support for chapter markers within video files, similar to those found on commercial DVDs. Most of the movies that you purchase from the iTunes Store include these preset chapter markers, and you can also add them into videos that you convert yourself. For more on converting your own videos, see Chapter 9.

When playing back a video in iTunes that includes chapter markers, a Chapters menu appears on the iTunes menu bar, and a chapter selection icon is shown on the playback controls overlay. Clicking the Chapters menu or chapter selection icon displays a list of chapters in the currently playing video, similar to figure 4.18.

4.18 The iTunes Chapter selection menu

Note that chapters may or may not include titles and thumbnails, depending on how they were encoded. Some videos offer titles or descriptions for each chapter, while others simply list text such as "Chapter 01."

**Note**

The iPhone and iPod touch also provide chapter support as of firmware v1.1.3 for these devices. Selection of chapters works in much the same way as it does in iTunes.

# Selecting alternate audio tracks

iTunes 7 also provides support for selecting alternate audio tracks from video files that are encoded with more than a single track. This is normally used to provide multilanguage support for movies and TV shows from the iTunes Store.

If a video file has alternate audio tracks, you can select a different track while you are playing that video, by choosing Controls ⇨ Audio & Subtitles from the iTunes menu. Note that this option only displays alternate audio tracks if there are any available in the currently playing track.

You can also configure which language track is selected by default when playing back a video that supports your preferred language:

1. **Open your iTunes preferences and click the Playback tab.**

2. **Select your preferred audio track language from the Audio Language drop-down menu as shown in figure 4.19.** Video files that include the selected language use this instead of their default language track.

3. **Click OK.** Video content that does not include your preferred language plays back in its default language.

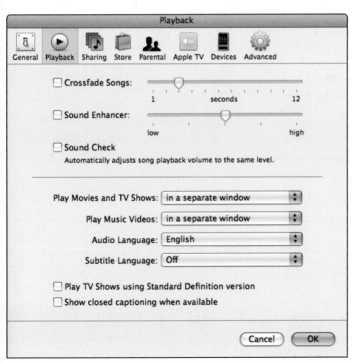

4.19 Selecting your language of choice from the Audio Language drop-down menu

# Enabling subtitles and closed captioning

You can enable subtitles and closed captioning in your video files where available. *Closed captioning* is used to provide text for dialog and other descriptive text for hearing-impaired users. In addition to the dialog itself, closed captioning normally includes descriptive text for other audio cues within a movie or TV show. *Subtitles* are normally used to provide alternate-language translations for movies and TV shows, and therefore generally only include text for the actual dialog.

There are two types of subtitles that are used in digital video. *Soft subtitles* refer to subtitles that are stored in a separate track and can be toggled on or off. *Hard subtitles* are embedded in the main video track, and cannot be turned off. iTunes does not specifically care about hard subtitles, as these are simply part of the video image displayed by iTunes.

At this point, there are no consumer-grade tools to encode your own content with soft subtitles, and so this is primarily intended for content that you have purchased from the iTunes Store. Most of the video-conversion tools discussed in Chapter 9 can convert closed-captioning tracks from DVDs that include them, however.

Closed captioning and subtitles can be enabled during playback by selecting Controls ⇨ Audio & Subtitles from the iTunes menu. Note that this item only displays these options if the current track has been encoded with subtitles or closed captions.

You can choose to have iTunes display subtitles or closed captioning by default when playing back videos:

1. **Open your iTunes preferences and click the Playback tab.**

2. **Select your preferred subtitle language or turn the feature off  from the Subtitle Language drop-down menu, as shown in figure 4.20.** When playing back videos that have subtitles in the selected language, those subtitles are automatically enabled. If subtitles are not available in the selected default language, no subtitles are shown.

3. **Click the check box beside Show closed captioning when available to have iTunes automatically display closed captions for any movies that have them available.**

4. **Click OK.**

**Genius**

You can search for movies that include closed captioning in the iTunes Store by selecting the Power Search link from the iTunes Store page and selecting Movies.

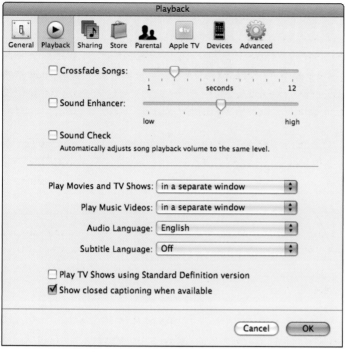

**4.20** You can turn off Subtitles in the Playback tab of the iTunes preferences.

# How Do I Use Playlists to Manage My Library?

If you have even a medium-sized iTunes library, sooner or later you're going to want to find ways to make sense of it all and keep your favorite items more accessible. Like most digital media-management applications today, iTunes solves this problem by allowing you to organize your music and other media content into playlists. However, iTunes also takes it a step beyond this by providing playlists that you can manually manage, Smart Playlists that can automatically maintain themselves, and Genius playlists that automatically pick a collection of music for you.

# Using Standard Playlists

For the purposes of our discussions here, a *standard playlist* is simply a normal playlist in iTunes that you create by adding and managing the content manually. Tracks only appear in standard playlists if you add them, and are only removed if you remove them. For most beginning iTunes users, standard playlists are the easiest starting point, and iTunes offers a lot of features even in these seemingly basic lists.

## Sorting and manually reordering tracks in playlists

You probably already know the basics about how to create and maintain your standard playlists, but what you may not realize is that you also have a number of options for sorting the content in these playlists to help further organize your music.

Basic sorting is handled in a playlist in much the same way that it is handled anywhere else in your iTunes library:

1. **Select the playlist you would like to sort from the iTunes Source list.**

2. **Click the column heading that you would like to sort by.** The selected column heading is highlighted with blue shading to indicate that iTunes is now using that column for its sorting, as shown in figure 5.1.

3. **Click the same column heading again if you would like to reverse the sort order.**

You can also manually reorder the tracks in any given playlist simply by highlighting a track and dragging it up or down within your playlist.

5.1 Sorting an iTunes playlist, here by album

You may sometimes find that you cannot manually reorder a playlist. Try as you might, the tracks just don't want to move when you drag them. This is a common pitfall that many iTunes users run into, and the key is that you cannot manually reorder a playlist if you've already sorted it on another column. You must first return the playlist to its natural unsorted order:

1. **Select the playlist you would like to reorder from the iTunes Source list.**

2. **At the top of the playlist, click the unnamed column heading on the left side.** This column heading is highlighted with blue shading to indicate that iTunes is now using that column for its sorting, as shown in figure 5.2. The playlist is returned to its natural unsorted order, and you can then drag-and-drop the tracks up and down within the playlist to reorder them as desired.

5.2 Sorting an iTunes playlist using the unnamed column

**Note**  Any sort order you apply to a playlist in iTunes is also transferred to the corresponding playlist on your iPod, iPhone, or Apple TV.

# Saving the play order

Sometimes it can be useful when reorganizing the content of your playlists to begin with a specific sort order, and then reorder the tracks further from there. Although iTunes does not allow you to manually reorder tracks unless the playlist is unsorted, you can save the displayed sort order as the playlist's natural unsorted play order:

1. **Select the playlist you would like to reorder from the iTunes Source list.**

2. **Sort the playlist as desired by clicking one of the column headings.**

3. **Right-click the playlist in the iTunes Source list.** A contextual menu appears, similar to figure 5.3.

4. **Choose Copy To Play Order from the contextual menu.**

5. **Return the playlist to its natural sort order by clicking the unnamed column heading on the left.** The playlist should remain in the same order that it was previously sorted in, and you may now drag-and-drop the tracks into a new order as desired.

5.3 The playlist contextual menu

**Genius**

You can also permanently shuffle a playlist by using the same method. Simply turn on Shuffle mode in iTunes as you normally would for a given playlist, and then use the Copy To Play Order option to save the shuffled playlist order as the default for that playlist.

# Finding out which playlists contain a given track

Once you have a large number of playlists set up, it can often be useful when browsing your library to find out which playlists contain a given track. iTunes makes this quite simple:

1. **Highlight the track that you would like to search playlists for.** You can select a track from the main iTunes library, or from any of your existing iTunes playlists.

2. **Right-click the highlighted track.** iTunes displays a contextual.menu.

3. **From the contextual menu, choose Show in Playlist.** iTunes displays a sub-menu with a list of playlists that contain the highlighted track, similar to figure 5.4.

4. **Optionally, you may select one of the displayed playlists from the sub-menu to switch to that particular playlist and display the highlighted track within that playlist.**

The Add to Playlist option on the same context menu can be used as a shortcut to quickly add the selected track to an existing playlist. This can be much faster than dragging-and-dropping when you have a large number of playlists in your iTunes library.

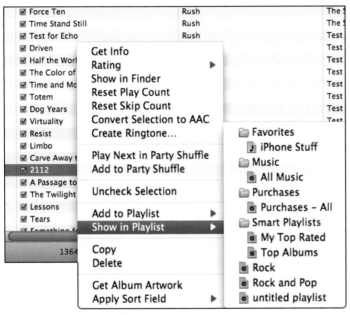

**5.4** The Show in Playlist sub-menu

# Organizing playlists into folders

iTunes 7 introduced the ability to organize your playlists into folders within the iTunes library. Originally, these folders served little purpose other than as a means for organizing a large number of playlists in your iTunes library. However, with some of the recent iPod models and the Apple TV, your folder structure is also replicated on your device.

To create a playlist folder in iTunes, follow these steps:

1. **Choose File ➪ New Folder from the iTunes menu.** A new playlist folder appears in the iTunes Source list with a default name highlighted and the insertion point ready to type a new name.

2. **Type a name for the playlist folder.**

3. **Press the Enter key.**

To create new playlists within your playlist folders, simply ensure that the playlist folder is high-lighted before creating a new playlist. You may also drag-and-drop existing playlists into playlist folders to reorganize them.

Playlist folders may also contain other playlist folders.

# Using Smart Playlists to Manage Music Content

One of the more powerful features of iTunes is the Smart Playlists feature. In addition to creating standard playlists that you manage, iTunes also allows you to create Smart Playlists that automatically select content based on a set of criteria that you specify.

Think of a Smart Playlist as a saved search: You specify the criteria that you would like iTunes to search for, and each time you access that playlist, it dynamically builds a list of tracks that meet those criteria. At a basic level, you could create a Smart Playlist that simply selects tracks from your favorite artist or genre; however, iTunes takes even this a step further by monitoring other information about your tracks, such as the number of times you've played each track, the date and time that you last played each track, and even the number of times and last date and time that you skipped a track. Further, you can also apply a rating to each track and to albums as a whole. All of this additional information that iTunes keeps track of makes Smart Playlists an extremely powerful and useful feature for dynamically organizing your media library.

## Creating a basic Smart Playlist

At the most basic level, you can create a Smart Playlist simply to make a quick list of tracks by your favorite artist:

1. **Choose File ⇨ New Smart Playlist from the iTunes menu.** The Smart Playlist dialog box appears, as shown in figure 5.5. Notice that the default criteria are set to Artist and contains, and the cursor is placed in the empty criteria field.

2. **Type the name of the artist you would like the Smart Playlist to match.** iTunes auto-completes the field as you type based on artists in your library to help ensure that you spell the artist's name correctly.

5.5 The Smart Playlist dialog box

3. **Click OK.** The Smart Playlist appears in your iTunes Source list with a default name high-lighted in editing mode.

4. **Type a new name for the Smart Playlist, if desired, or simply press the Enter key to accept the default name.**

When you select the Smart Playlist, you should see a listing of all tracks by the selected artist. If you later add new tracks from the same artist, they are automatically included in this Smart Playlist.

This is a very simple example of a Smart Playlist. The real power of this feature comes from your ability to specify multiple criteria within a Smart Playlist. Any of the track properties discussed in Chapter 3 can be used as criteria for your Smart Playlist, in addition to some other special properties that are discussed a little bit further on in this chapter.

For example, say you are throwing a party and you want to build a playlist of jazz tracks, but only those from a certain era. You could do this by creating a Smart Playlist that selects tracks based on both the genre and the year, similar to the one shown in figure 5.6. Note that the Plus button is used to add additional criteria to a Smart Playlist.

5.6 A Smart Playlist with multiple criteria

By default, Smart Playlists match all of the specified criteria. You can create a playlist that matches any one of the specified criteria simply by changing the drop-down menu that appears in the first line of a Smart Playlist dialog box as soon as you add more than one criteria to "any" instead of "all." For example, the Smart Playlist shown in figure 5.7 includes all classical and all jazz tracks, or more precisely, all tracks where the genre contains classical *or* the genre contains jazz.

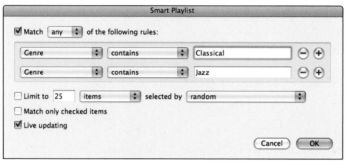

5.7 A Smart Playlist with multiple criteria ("Match any")

You can also easily edit an existing Smart Playlist:

1. **Select the Smart Playlist that you want to edit from the iTunes Source list.**

2. **Choose File ⇨ Get Info from the iTunes menu.** The Smart Playlist dialog box appears with the current Smart Playlist settings displayed.

3. **Edit the Smart Playlist as desired.**

4. **Click OK.**

Smart Playlists can be built using any of the information that is stored in iTunes for your tracks, which really allows you to fine-tune your Smart Playlists, provided that your media files have been tagged properly and you therefore have this information in your database. The more information you put into your tracks, the more creative you can be with your Smart Playlists. For example, fields like Beats per Minute (BPM), if filled in, can be used to select music of a certain tempo — which can be useful for creating dynamic workout mixes, for example.

## Using ratings and play counts in a Smart Playlist

So far, you have looked at creating Smart Playlists by filtering on relatively static criteria such as artist name and genre. Although this can be useful in an ever-changing library, you don't necessarily gain a huge advantage over standard playlists by doing this. After all, you can just as easily search for these tracks yourself and add them to a normal playlist.

Where the real power of Smart Playlists starts to kick in, however, is in the ability of iTunes to use your actual listening patterns as criteria to build your Smart Playlists. Under the hood, iTunes keeps track of your basic listening habits, updating information as you listen to your music (or watch your videos). iTunes monitors how many times you've listened to a given track, the date and time that you last listened to it all the way through, and even how many times you've skipped over a track without listening to the end, as well as the date and time you last did that. This all occurs regardless of whether you listen to your tracks directly in iTunes or on your iPod, iPhone, or Apple TV.

Some of the additional information that iTunes keeps track of is

- **Date Added.** This is the date that the track was added to your iTunes library.

- **Date Modified.** This is the date that the track information was last modified.

- **Play Count.** This is the number of times the track has been played, either in iTunes or on any iPod, iPhone or, Apple TV that is synchronized with the current iTunes library. A track is considered "played" if you have listened to the very end of the track.

- **Last Played.** This is the date and time the track was last played. The same rules apply as for the Play Count field.

- **Skip Count.** This is the number of times the track has been skipped, either in iTunes, or on your iPod, iPhone, or Apple TV. A track is considered "skipped" if you listen to between 2 seconds and 30 seconds of the current track and skip ahead to the next track. Note that skip count tracking is only supported on newer iPod, iPhone, and Apple TV models with the latest firmware updates.

- **Last Skipped.** This is the date and time the track was last skipped. The same rules apply as for the Skip Count field.

**Note**    Play count, last played, skip count and last skipped are only transferred from your iPod to your iTunes library if you are using automatic synchronization. More on iPod synchronization is discussed in Chapter 7.

Further, iTunes gives you the ability to rate your tracks as you are listening to them. Tracks begin with no rating at all, but you can assign a rating from one to five stars on a track-by-track basis, and even rate entire albums.

All of this information can be used as criteria to build very dynamic Smart Playlists that can help keep your content fresh by allowing you to select tracks based on your listening habits rather than simply using a conglomeration of artists and genres. This can be best illustrated by a few practical examples of some useful Smart Playlist ideas.

For the first example, suppose that you want to create a Smart Playlist that includes all of your rock tracks that you've listened to at least once. A Smart Playlist similar to the one shown in figure 5.8 could be used.

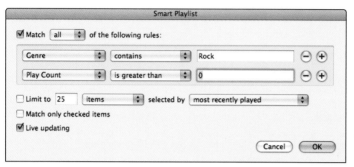

5.8 This Smart Playlist selects rock tracks that you have listened to at least once.

Although such a Smart Playlist might be useful to review the tracks that you've listened to (perhaps to go back through and rate them), it is likely going to include far too many tracks to be of much use as a listening playlist. If you've been rating your tracks, why not add an additional criteria to select only those that you obviously like? Figure 5.9 shows a slight modification to your Smart Playlist to limit the criteria to only tracks with a rating higher than three stars.

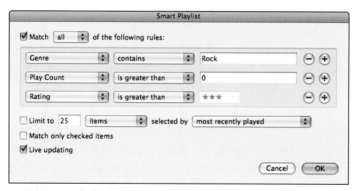

5.9 This Smart Playlist selects favorite rock tracks listened to at least once, with a rating higher than three stars.

This gets you a bit closer to a useful listening playlist, but it might risk becoming repetitive after a while, because if you've recently listened to a given track, you may not want to hear it again right away. One other simple addition to monitor the last-played date can easily solve that problem. For example, you can exclude any tracks that have been played in the past seven days, as shown in figure 5.10.

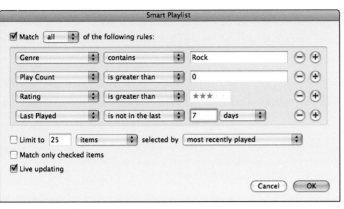

**5.10** This Smart Playlist selects favorite rock tracks listened to at least once but not in the past seven days.

Now you have a truly dynamic Smart Playlist. As you listen to tracks in the playlist, they are automatically removed (because the last played date is updated), but automatically reappear seven days later. Any new rock tracks you listen to for the first time and rate with four or five stars also automatically appear in the playlist seven days after you've last listened to them.

**Caution**

Pay close attention when using greater-than or less-than criteria in your Smart Playlists. There is no match for greater-than or equal-to, and so you must always specify a criteria one number higher or lower than you want to include. For example, to include all tracks played at least once, you must use greater-than and type **0** in the field.

# Limiting the number of tracks in a Smart Playlist

Sometimes it can be useful to limit the number of tracks that you include in a Smart Playlist. For example, if you have a lot of music in a given genre, you may not want your Smart Playlist to include the entire selection of music from that genre. This might be due to a desire to limit the amount of listening time, or to create a playlist of music that can fit on a limited-capacity iPod.

iTunes offers the ability to easily limit the number of items selected in a Smart Playlist by either total duration (in minutes or hours) or size (in MB or GB), or simply based on a specified number of items:

1. **Choose File ➪ New Smart Playlist from the iTunes menu.** The Smart Playlist dialog box appears.

2. **Fill in your Smart Playlist criteria as desired.**

107

3. **Click the check box beside Limit to.**

4. **From the first drop-down menu to the right, choose the units you would like to use when limiting this Smart Playlist.** Your options are minutes, hours, MB, GB, or items.

5. **To the left of the drop-down menu, type in the number of units you would like to limit this Smart Playlist to, based on the unit selected in Step 4.**

6. **From the Selected By drop-down menu, choose how you would like iTunes to prioritize tracks for this Smart Playlist.** Because you are limiting the number of tracks, this option is used to specify which tracks are selected first. Options include alphabetically by Album, Artist, Genre, or Name, by highest or lowest rating, by how often or how recently tracks have been played, or by how recently tracks were added to iTunes.

7. **Click OK.**

For example, if you are throwing an '80s-themed party and want to select three hours of your favorite '80s tunes that are relatively short (in order to keep the music flowing), choosing the Smart Playlist criteria shown in figure 5.11 could do the trick.

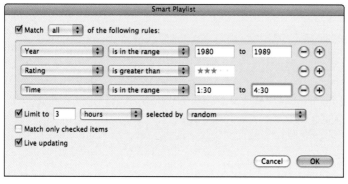

5.11 A Smart Playlist limited by time

Limiting Smart Playlists can also be useful for controlling how much content is transferred to your iPod. This can be particularly useful for rotating the content on your iPod to keep it fresh when combined with Smart Playlists that track the last-played date. For example, if you want to keep only 4GB of jazz music on your iPod, but limit it to your favorite tracks that you have not recently listened to, choosing the Smart Playlist criteria shown in figure 5.12 could be used.

If you configure your iPod to only sync this particular playlist, then tracks that do not meet the criteria are removed from your iPod on the next sync with iTunes and replaced with new tracks. This allows you to effortlessly rotate the music stored on your iPod, which can be particularly useful for lower-capacity iPods. iPod synchronization is discussed further in Chapter 7.

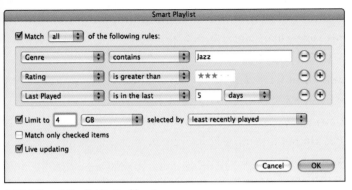

**5.12** A Smart Playlist limited by size

Other criteria that can be very useful if you have a recent model iPod are the skip count and date last skipped. When you've just started playing a track and then suddenly decide to skip ahead to the next track, the skip count and date last skipped fields are updated. These fields can be used to filter out those tracks that you may not really feel like listening to. The example criteria shown in figure 5.13 expands on the previous Smart Playlist examples, but also excludes all tracks that you have skipped in the past two days.

**5.13** A Smart Playlist limited by size, excluding recently skipped tracks

This can be very handy to keep the same tracks from coming up repeatedly, particularly in a relatively short Smart Playlist. Skipped tracks end up being excluded in favor of other tracks that you have neither listened to nor skipped recently.

109

# Nesting Smart Playlists

One of the limitations of Smart Playlists is that there is no way to specify complex criteria within a single Smart Playlist. Say, for example, that you want to create a Smart Playlist that contains all music from the Rock *or* Pop genres that is rated five stars and that you haven't listened to in at least three days. This is not possible to do with a single Smart Playlist, as you can only match either "all" of the criteria, or "any" of the criteria, but you cannot mix both of these conditions.

Fortunately, there is a way to work around this by nesting Smart Playlists. One of the criteria that you can use in a Smart Playlist is whether or not a track is included in another playlist. This other playlist can be a standard playlist, a playlist folder, another Smart Playlist, or even a main library category such as "Music" or "Movies."

To build a Smart Playlist for this example, first build an intermediate Smart Playlist that includes all music in the Rock and Pop genres, as shown in figure 5.14.

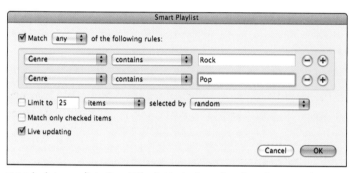

5.14 An intermediate Smart Playlist including all rock and pop music

Then, using the criteria from the scenario described earlier, build your final Smart Playlist, selecting "Playlist" as one of the criteria with the intermediate playlist selected, and the rating and last-played dates included, as shown in figure 5.15.

Multiple playlists can be used as criteria, and playlists can be nested multiple levels deep (so playlists can depend on playlists which depend on other playlists, and so on). This can be used to create extremely powerful sets of playlists with very complex criteria.

**Caution** If you plan on transferring nested Smart Playlists onto your iPod, iPhone, or Apple TV, you must transfer all of the intermediate Smart Playlists as well to get live updating on the device.

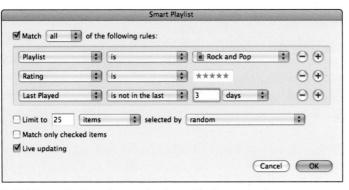

5.15 A Smart Playlist using another Smart Playlist as criteria

**Genius** Intermediate Smart Playlists that are created only for nesting purposes can clutter up your iTunes library. To keep them out of the way, you can either store them in their own playlist folder, or name them with a Z prefix so that they sort alphabetically at the bottom of your playlists.

# Removing tracks from Smart Playlists

Because Smart Playlists are dynamically generated, you cannot remove a track manually from most Smart Playlists. If a track meets the criteria for a Smart Playlist, it is always included and there's no sense in removing it because it would just reappear anyway.

The exception to this is Smart Playlists set to limit items with a random selection. In this case, you can remove an entry from a Smart Playlist as you would from any other playlist by highlighting it and pressing the Delete key. The selected track is removed from the playlist and replaced with another random track. This can be a useful way to refresh the content in a random Smart Playlist.

# Using Genius Playlists

iTunes 8 introduced a new feature called Genius that can help you automatically build lists of songs from your iTunes library that naturally go well together in the same playlist. This is done based on analyzing your music library and tastes and comparing it to information available at the iTunes Store and from other iTunes 8 Genius users. This produces better results than simply analyzing sound patterns in your tracks because iTunes is actually looking at a very large statistical sample of what other iTunes users are purchasing and listening to.

# Enabling the Genius feature

Because the Genius feature works by analyzing your music collection against the Apple iTunes database, it requires that iTunes submit information about your music collection to Apple. Due to the privacy concerns involved with this, Apple has taken an opt-in approach where you must specifically enable and sign up for the Genius service. Note that even though your iTunes library information is stored anonymously, an iTunes Store account is required to use the Genius feature.

When you run iTunes 8 for the first time, a Genius Sidebar appears at the right side of your iTunes window, as shown in figure 5.16.

**5.16** The iTunes Genius Sidebar

This sidebar provides you with a brief explanation of the Genius feature and buttons to either enable the feature or hide the sidebar entirely.

**Note**
If you have hidden the Genius Sidebar previously, it can be turned back on from the iTunes View menu.

To enable the Genius feature, follow these steps:

1. **Click the Turn on Genius button in the Genius Sidebar.** An iTunes Store sign-in screen appears to begin the Genius setup process, as shown in figure 5.17.

5.17 The iTunes Genius setup screen

2. **Sign in to your iTunes Store account and click the Continue button.** You may also create a new iTunes Store account from this screen if you do not already have an existing account. More information on the iTunes Store can be found in Chapter 2. Once you have successfully signed in to your iTunes Store account (or created a new one), iTunes presents you with the Genius terms and conditions, similar to figure 5.18.

3. **Once you have reviewed the Genius terms and conditions, click the check box indicating your acceptance and click the Continue button.** iTunes begins gathering information about your iTunes library and sends this information to the Apple iTunes servers for analysis. You should see a status screen similar to figure 5.19.

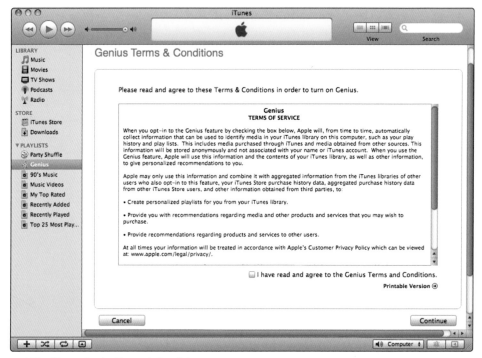

**5.18** The iTunes Genius Terms & Conditions page

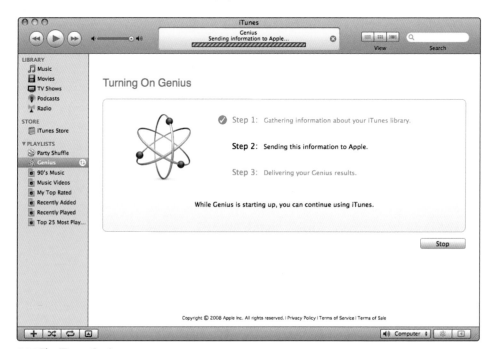

**5.19** The iTunes Genius status screen

Depending on the size of your iTunes library and the speed of your computer and Internet connection, the process of gathering information and sending it to Apple can take anywhere from a few minutes to slightly upwards of an hour. This process occurs in the background, however, and so you can continue using iTunes while this is occurring. Once the process has completed, iTunes displays a screen confirming that Genius has been turned on, similar to figure 5.20.

Should you later decide that you want to turn the Genius feature off for any reason, you can do so by choosing Store ➪ Turn Off Genius from the iTunes menu.

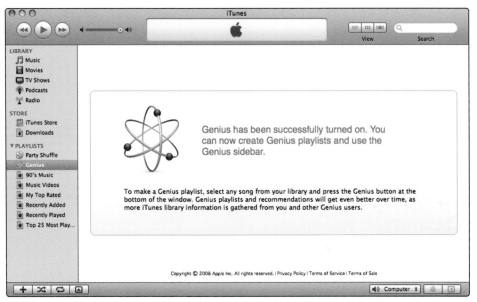

5.20 The iTunes Genius confirmation screen

**Note** You can also turn Genius on from the iTunes Store menu, or by selecting the Genius playlist entry below Party Shuffle on the left side of the iTunes window.

# Creating Genius lists

Once the Genius feature has been enabled, you are ready to begin creating Genius lists based on your music collection. To create a Genius list, follow these steps:

1. **Select a music track from your library that you would like to base your Genius list on.**

**2. Click the Genius button in the bottom-right corner of the iTunes window, as shown in figure 5.21.**

iTunes attempts to locate 24 additional tracks in your iTunes library to accompany the selected track and place them together in your Genius list, as shown in figure 5.22.

5.21 The iTunes Genius button

5.22 A generated iTunes Genius list

By default, iTunes limits a new Genius list to 25 tracks, including the track on which the playlist is based. You can adjust this limit to 50, 75, or 100 tracks by using the Limit to drop-down menu at the top of the Genius list.

From the Genius list, you can begin playing your tracks or sort and reorder them as you would with any other playlist. You can also refresh the content to select a different group of tracks by clicking the Refresh button at the top of the Genius list.

**Note** The current Genius list is only stored in iTunes — it is not transferred to other devices unless you save it as a playlist (which is covered in the next section).

The content of the most recently built Genius list remains available under the Genius entry immediately below Party Shuffle in the iTunes Source list.

If iTunes is unable to successfully build a Genius playlist, it notifies you with a dialog box similar to figure 5.23.

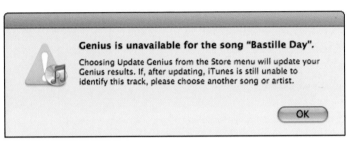

**Genius is unavailable for the song "Bastille Day".**

Choosing Update Genius from the Store menu will update your Genius results. If, after updating, iTunes is still unable to identify this track, please choose another song or artist.

OK

**5.23** iTunes Genius is unavailable for the selected track

This problem normally occurs either because your Genius information is out of date or you simply do not have enough matching tracks in your own iTunes library. As the dialog box suggests, you can ensure your Genius results are up to date by choosing Store ⇨ Update Genius from the iTunes menu. If you have done this and iTunes still fails to build a Genius listing for the selected track, then the likely reason is that you simply do not have enough matching music tracks. This often occurs in very small iTunes libraries (for example, with less than 500 tracks), but can also occur even in a larger library if you're trying to build a Genius list from a more obscure track.

## Saving your Genius list as a playlist

For quick Genius compilations, you can simply begin playing your music directly from the Genius listing. If you've found a particular collection that you'd like to keep, however, you can also easily save your Genius listing as an iTunes Genius playlist:

1. **Create a Genius listing, as described in the previous section.**

2. **From the Genius listing, click the Save Playlist button at the top-right corner, as shown in figure 5.24.**

iTunes creates a new playlist in your library with the name of the original track with which the Genius list was created. This playlist is shown with a Genius icon beside it, rather than the standard playlist icon, similar to figure 5.25.

5.24 Using the iTunes Genius Save Playlist button

This Genius playlist can be renamed or moved into a folder in the same manner as any other playlist. Within the Genius playlist, you can also change the number of tracks selected or refresh the playlist content in the same way as you would for the main Genius list. Changes made within a Genius playlist are saved automatically to that playlist.

Genius playlists can also be synced to your iPod, iPhone, or Apple TV, and even updated and managed directly on those newer devices that provide support for the Genius feature.

# Using Genius recommendations

In addition to building Genius lists and playlists, iTunes 8 also uses the Genius feature to highlight songs that you may be missing from your collection and offer recommendations for other similar music that is available on the iTunes Store. This is similar to the iTunes Mini-Store found in previous versions, but is far more accurate and flexible.

5.25 The iTunes Genius playlist is indicated by the Genius icon

**Note**

Older iPod models that do not have Genius support can still use Genius playlists — they are simply synced to the device as a standard playlist.

Once the Genius feature is enabled, the Genius Sidebar displays a listing of recommendations based on the currently selected track, highlighting albums and missing tracks by the same artist first, and then showing recommendations for similar music from other artists. Figure 5.26 shows an example.

From the Genius Sidebar, you can click a track or album name to visit the iTunes Store page for that track, or click the Buy or Add button beside each track to directly purchase it or add it to your shopping cart (depending on your iTunes Store preferences).

You can also preview tracks directly from this listing by clicking the musical note button that appears to the left of each title.

Finally, clicking the arrow that appears beside the Recommendations heading takes you to an iTunes Store listing of all recommended tracks.

5.26 Recommendations made by the iTunes Genius feature

**Note** You can toggle the Genius Sidebar on and off from the iTunes View menu or by clicking the arrow button at the bottom-right corner of the iTunes window to the right of the Genius button.

# How Do I Manage Podcasts and Audiobooks?

Although the majority of your iTunes media content is likely to consist of music, iTunes also provides support for two other categories of audio content: audiobooks, which are basically digital versions of books on tape, and podcasts, which are episodic content covering a wide range of interesting topics. Although at a basic level these are both just audio content, there are some specific features that are relevant for managing these types of content.

# Managing Podcasts

Podcasts differ from most other audio content in that they are normally imported automatically as part of a series that you subscribe to, and you're therefore managing a series of podcast episodes as a collection, rather than on an individual track-by-track basis.

## Subscribing to podcasts from outside of the iTunes Store

Most podcasts are available through the catalog maintained by the iTunes Store, but you may still find the occasional podcast that is not in the iTunes catalog for whatever reason, or you may want to subscribe to private podcasts from friends or family members.

Keep in mind that even if you find a podcast listed on another Web site, it may still be available through the iTunes Store, and many of these podcasts have a direct link somewhere on their Web page that automatically takes you to their podcast in the iTunes Store.

Further, many podcasts also have a direct iTunes link on their page that calls up your own iTunes application to automatically subscribe to the podcast.

However, if you find a podcast on the Internet that does not have an iTunes subscription link anywhere on the page, then you can subscribe to this podcast manually:

1. **Find the URL for the podcast on the podcast's Web page.** If the URL isn't visible, you can sometimes find it listed as an RSS subscription link from the podcast listing.

2. **Copy this URL to your Clipboard by choosing Edit ➪ Copy from your browser's menu.**

3. **In iTunes, choose Advanced ➪ Subscribe to Podcast from the iTunes menu.** A URL entry dialog box appears, as shown in figure 6.1.

4. **Paste the URL from your Clipboard into the URL dialog box by choosing Edit ➪ Paste from the iTunes menu.**

6.1 The Subscribe to Podcast URL entry dialog box

5. **Click OK.** You are taken to the Podcast listing in iTunes, and the newly added podcast appears and begins downloading the most recent episode or episodes.

   All Podcasts within iTunes are managed in the same way, regardless of how you subscribe to them.

# Setting how many podcast episodes to keep

Once you have subscribed to a podcast, iTunes automatically downloads new episodes of that podcast as they become available. By default, however, iTunes also keeps all of the old episodes of each podcast, regardless of whether you have listened to them or not. If you have a podcast that updates on a daily basis, you can quickly accumulate a lot of podcasts that may no longer be relevant yet are taking up space on your computer.

Fortunately, iTunes can perform some housekeeping for you in this regard by automatically removing old podcast episodes. To adjust how many episodes of each podcast iTunes keeps, follow these steps:

1. **Select Podcasts from the iTunes Source list.** The Podcasts listing appears, as shown in figure 6.2.

6.2 The iTunes Podcasts listing screen

2. **Click the Settings button at the bottom of the Podcasts listing screen.** The Podcast Settings window appears, as shown in figure 6.3.

3. **From the Settings for drop-down menu, select the individual podcast subscription that you would like to adjust the settings for, or select Podcast Defaults to adjust the default settings for all podcasts.**

4. **If you have selected an individual podcast subscription, click the check box beside the Use Default Settings option to clear it and permit you to override the podcast default settings. The two drop-down menus at the bottom of the dialog box become active.**

6.3 The iTunes Podcast Settings window

5. **From the Episodes to keep drop-down menu, choose how many episodes you would like iTunes to retain for each podcast:**

- **All episodes.** iTunes does not automatically delete any podcast episodes. All episodes are retained by iTunes unless you delete them manually.

- **All unplayed episodes.** iTunes automatically deletes all podcast episodes that have been listened to at least once, based on the play count field. Podcasts that you have not listened to all the way through are not deleted, regardless of age or number of podcasts.

- **Most recent episode.** Only the most recent episode is retained. iTunes automatically deletes all older podcast episodes as each new episode is downloaded.

- **Last <X> episodes.** Only the most recent 2, 3, 4, 5, or 10 episodes are retained. iTunes automatically deletes any episodes above this number as each new episode is downloaded.

6. **Click OK.**

# Exempting specific podcast episodes from automatic deletion

You can exempt specific podcast episodes from automatic deletion by iTunes on an individual basis. This can be useful if you have a specific favorite episode that you want to keep, but still want iTunes to automatically manage and clean up your other podcast episodes. To exempt a specific episode from automatic deletion, follow these steps:

1. **In the iTunes podcast listing, right-click the individual episode that you would like to exempt from automatic deletion.** A contextual menu appears.

2. **From the context menu, choose Do Not Auto Delete, as shown in figure 6.4.** If the option Allow Auto Delete is shown instead of Do Not Auto Delete, this indicates that the podcast has already been set as exempt from automatic deletion. Clicking the Allow Auto Delete option resets the podcast to being automatically deleted according to your default podcast-retention setting in iTunes.

**Genius**

You can change the automatic-deletion status for all episodes of a given podcast by right-clicking the podcast title and selecting either Allow Auto Delete or Do Not Auto Delete. Choosing either option from the context menu resets all episodes in the current podcast to the selected value, overriding any individual per-episode selections.

| Podcast | Time | Release Date ▼ | Descr |
|---|---|---|---|
| ▼ CBC Radio 3 Podcast   SUBSCRIBE | | 06/09/08 | |
| ☑ The Sleepless Nights – Allyson Got Robbed | 4:29 | 06/09/08 | New |
| ▶ CBC Radio: Comedy Factory | 8:31 | 07/23/08 | If a |
| ▶ CBC Radio: Editor's Choice | 12:55 | 07/27/08 | Edit |
| ▼ CBC Radio: Toronto This Week | | 07/25/08 | Torc |
| ☑ Reuniting Owners and Bicycles; After the East-End Explosion; Cemetary Workers on Strike; a Nur... | 34:33 | 07/25/08 | Hun |
| ☑ Toronto Soccer Splash; Baby Angelica Update; Downtown Chickens; Kids, Parents and Summer C... | 29:48 | 07/18/08 | Meta |
| ☑ Models at risk?; Storm too much for Toronto sewers; Rising corn prices hit livestock industry | 26:41 | 07/11/08 | How |
| ☑ Talking  trash in Toronto; Toronto police officers arrested in grow–up bust | 25:04 | 07/04/08 | Pay- |
| ☑ How safe is Toronto?; Shooting victim buried; New nukes for Darlington: and tip from psychic le... | 33:07 | 06/20/08 | Polic |
| ☑ Thumbs down to new download rules; and apologizing for residential schools: is it enough? | 28:19 | 06/13/08 | Meta |
| ☑ End of the line: GM to close truck plant in Oshawa | 27:58 | 06/06/08 | Plan |
| ☑ Cell phone use banned while driving?; Gun ranges si | 23:06 | 05/30/08 | Onta |
| ☑ Making Toronto's schools safer; Paralympian cleared | 22:09 | 05/23/08 | A ne |
| ☑ Toronto relief for disaster victims in Burma and Chir | 29:39 | 05/16/08 | Torc |
| ▶ CBC Radio: Vinyl Cafe Stories | 24:24 | 07/25/08 | The |
| ▼ CityNews Webcast | | 07/28/08 | You |
| ☑ CityNews WebCast PM – July 28 | 6:15 | 07/28/08 | CAW |
| ☑ CityNews WebCast AM – July 28 | 4:20 | 07/28/08 | Clea |
| ☑ CityNews Webcast – July 27 | 5:56 | 07/27/08 | Mult |
| ☑ CityNews Webcast – July 26 | 4:24 | 07/26/08 | One |
| ☑ CityNews Webcast PM – July 25 | 5:39 | 07/25/08 | Raid |
| ☑ CityNews Webcast AM – July 25 | 3:19 | 07/25/08 | The |
| ☑ CityNews Webcast PM – July 24 | 6:27 | 07/24/08 | The |
| ☑ CityNews Webcast AM – July 24 | 4:39 | 07/24/08 | The |
| ☑ CityNews Webcast PM – July 23 | 5:48 | 07/23/08 | Recc |
| ☑ CityNews Webcast AM – July 23 | 4:22 | 07/23/08 | Torc |
| ▶ Hidden Universe HD: NASA's Spitzer Space Telescope | 5:12 | 06/13/08 | This |
| ▶ iLounge Library | | 06/01/08 | Dow |
| ▶ Interesting Thing of the Day | | 06/11/08 | An c |
| ▶ MacBreak (AppleTV)   CLEAN | 4:51 | 02/14/08 | The |
| ▶ ReGenesis : ReMixed | 15:52 | 06/11/06 | An a |
| ▶ The Tudors | 6:50 | 05/29/08 | Bypa |

Context menu:
- Update Podcast
- Get Info
- Show Description
- Rating ▶
- Show in Finder
- Reset Play Count
- Reset Skip Count
- Convert ID3 Tags...
- Convert Selection to AAC
- Play Next in Party Shuffle
- Add to Party Shuffle
- Uncheck Selection
- Mark as Not New
- Do Not Auto Delete
- Add to Playlist ▶
- Copy
- Delete
- Get Album Artwork
- Apply Sort Field ▶

6.4 A podcast contextual menu

# Managing Audiobooks

One of the first new types of content other than music to appear in iTunes were audiobooks, spoken versions of books narrated and available to be listened to through iTunes or on your iPod. Although an audiobook is really just another audio file, it differs from a music file in that it is usually quite a bit longer — sometimes several hours. it provides support for bookmarking so that iTunes and your iPod can remember where you left off, and is often divided into chapters.

## Converting and importing your own audiobooks

Audiobooks compatible with iTunes and the iPod may be purchased in digital form either from the iTunes Store or from Audible.com. These come encoded in an iTunes-ready format, with chapter markers and the ability to bookmark their playback position already included. They also very nicely show up under the Audiobooks category in iTunes.

You may have obtained audiobooks from other sources, however, and want to add these features to your own audiobooks. Unfortunately, if you simply import these audiobooks into your iTunes library, they are catalogued alongside your normal music files — they do not appear in the Audiobooks section, nor do they automatically remember their playback position.

An additional advantage of ensuring your audiobooks are properly categorized is that you can vary their playback speed when listening to them on your iPod or iPhone. Normal music tracks do not provide this feature.

Although previous versions of iTunes required you to jump through some manual hoops in order to get your own files imported as audiobooks, the great news is that iTunes 8 now provides the ability to set any audio file as an audiobook.

1. **Locate the file or group of files in your iTunes library that you would like to set as audiobooks.**

2. **Select File ➪ Get Info from the iTunes menu.** The file information dialog box appears.

3. **Select the Options tab from the file information dialog box, as shown in figure 6.5.**

4. **From the Media Kind drop-down menu, choose Audiobook.**

5. **Click OK.**

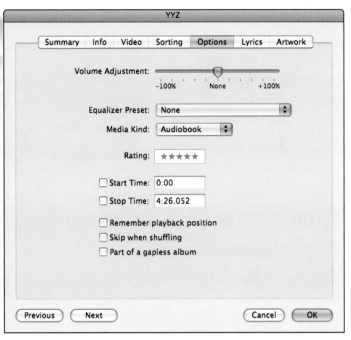

6.5 The Options tab of the iTunes file information dialog box

Some audiobooks that you obtain from other sources may consist of multiple files, with each chapter divided into its own MP3 file, for example. Although you can import these files individually into your iTunes library and listen to them as you would any other file, you may want to merge these tracks together and convert them into a proper audiobook for a better listening experience. Although there are numerous tools available on the Internet that can join MP3 files together, there are some tools that also allow you to turn these files into a proper audiobook in the process.

For Mac users, I recommend checking out Audiobook Builder by Splasm Software at www.splasm.com. Windows users should look at MarkAble from iPodSoft at www.ipodsoft.com. Both of these tools provide the ability to join separate audiobook files together, convert them into an iTunes-ready audiobook format, and import them directly into your iTunes library.

You can also add chapter markers to your own audiobooks with these third-party tools. Audiobook Builder for the Mac includes this capability, while MarkAble provides this feature through a companion product called Chapter Master.

# Importing audiobooks from CD

Another common source of audiobooks is from CDs that may be purchased from bookstores or borrowed from your local library. Because your iPod is a far more convenient device than a portable CD player, you may want to import these audiobooks into iTunes so that you can listen to them on your iPod. When borrowing audiobook CDs from your local library, you should check your library's policies concerning the conversion of borrowed material into other formats.

Most audiobooks on CD, however, come as multiple-track CDs, and by default are imported into iTunes as separate tracks. Although you can certainly join up these tracks later, iTunes offers a very useful built-in feature for merging tracks from a CD during import:

1. **Open your iTunes preferences and click the General tab, as shown in figure 6.6.**

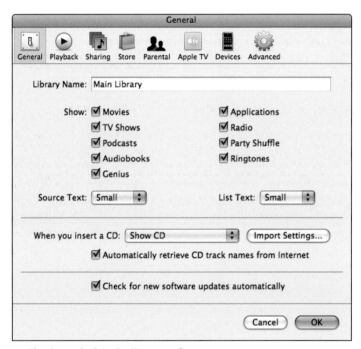

6.6 The General tab in the iTunes preferences

2. **From the When you insert a CD drop-down menu, choose Show CD.**

3. **Click OK.**

4. **Insert the CD into your computer's CD drive as you normally would.**

5. **A CD track listing appears, as shown in figure 6.7.**

6.7 An iTunes CD track listing

6. **Click the first track in the CD track listing.**

7. **Choose Edit ⇨ Select All from the iTunes menu.** All tracks are selected.

8. **Choose Advanced ⇨ Join CD Tracks.** iTunes indicates that the selected tracks are going to be imported as a single track, as shown in figure 6.8.

9. **Click the Import CD button in the bottom-right corner of the iTunes window.**

6.8 iTunes indicating joined tracks

When the import is completed, a new single track appears in your iTunes library, representing the content of the entire CD.

**Caution** If the Join CD Tracks option is not available, ensure that you are not sorting your CD track listing. Only contiguous tracks may be joined together by iTunes, and the CD track listing must therefore be left unsorted.

**Genius** The Join CD Tracks option may be used to join any two or more contiguous tracks on a CD during import. To join only specific tracks, simply select those tracks before choosing the Join CD Tracks option.

# Setting tracks to remember their playback position

One of the benefits of audiobooks is that iTunes remembers and stores the playback position in each file when you stop listening to it. This means that you can stop listening anywhere in a track and then pick up again later on, exactly where you left off. Further, this playback position is also transferred between devices, so if you listen to an audiobook on your iPod, and then sync it to iTunes, this bookmark is transferred to your iTunes library, and then from there to any other device on which that file is stored, such as an Apple TV.

Audiobooks purchased from the iTunes Store or Audible.com are always set to remember their playback position by default. If you have imported your own audiobooks from other sources, however, you must specifically tell iTunes to remember the playback position in these tracks. You can set the *Remember playback position* option manually on any audio track in your library:

1. **Select the track that you would like to remember the playback position for.**

2. **Choose File ⇨ Get Info from the iTunes menu.**

3. **In the iTunes track information dialog box, click the Options tab.** The track options are displayed.

4. **Click the check box beside Remember playback position to enable this option as shown in figure 6.9.**

5. **Click OK.**

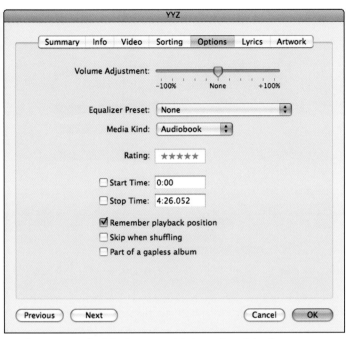

6.9 The Options tab of the iTunes track information dialog box

**Note**

If you select the track options for an audiobook purchased from the iTunes Store or Audible.com, the Remember playback position option is forced on and cannot be changed. This is normal, as this setting cannot be disabled for audiobook files.

# Setting audiobooks to be excluded from shuffled playback

Another feature common to audiobooks is that they are not included in shuffled playback, because it wouldn't make much sense to start into a reading of *The Da Vinci Code* in the middle of your hip-hop party.

As with the Remember playback position option, this is a mandatory setting for audiobooks from the iTunes Store or Audible.com, but you can apply this setting to your own imported audiobooks or any other track in your library:

1. **Select the track that you would like to skip when shuffling.**

2. **Choose File ⇨ Get Info from the iTunes menu.**

3. **In the iTunes track information dialog box, click the Options tab.** The track options are displayed.

4. **Click the check box beside Skip when shuffling to enable this option as shown in figure 6.10.**

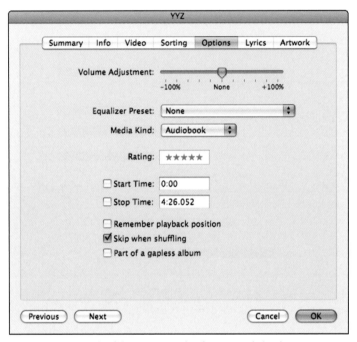

6.10 The Options tab of the iTunes track information dialog box

5. **Click OK.**

**Note**

If you select the track options for an audiobook purchased from the iTunes Store or Audible.com, the Skip when shuffling option is mandatory and cannot be changed. This is normal, as this setting cannot be disabled for audiobook files.

# How Do I Manage the Content on My iPod?

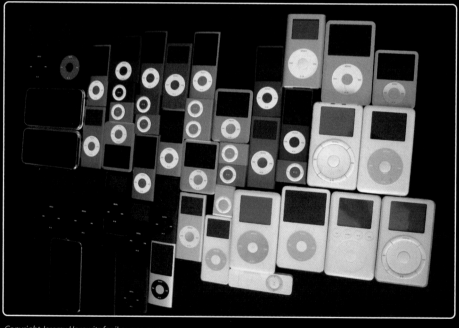

# Identifying Your iPod Model

The iPod was first introduced to the world back in 2001 as a 5GB audio-only media player. Since then, it has evolved dramatically from those humble beginnings, with ever-increasing capacity, support for storing and displaying photos and video content, and a myriad of accessory options and new features.

With a wide variety of different iPod devices now available, it's important to understand the difference among the various iPod models so that you understand what types of content and features are supported by the different iPods.

Current iPod models are divided into four basic categories:

- **iPod classic.** This iPod, shown in figure 7.1, is the device that likely first comes to mind when you hear the term iPod. It is the direct evolution of the original iPod. Prior to 2007, this was known simply by the name iPod, and each new model was referred to using a generation designation. The original iPod that was released in 2001 is now referred to as the first-generation, or 1G, iPod, while the last model to simply bear the name iPod was the fifth-generation, or 5G, iPod. The iPod classic is considered by most to be the sixth-generation iPod. All of these models include hard drives of various sizes and have the same basic dimensions and form factor. The fourth-generation iPod was the first model to support photo playback and TV output, while the fifth-generation iPod introduced video playback. Support for iPod Games was added in a firmware update for the fifth-generation iPod. Today, the current iPod classic, or sixth-generation iPod, comes as a single 120GB model. Although last year's 80GB and 160GB models can still be found with an identical design, they do not include the latest features of the 2008 120GB model, such as Genius list support.

- **iPod nano.** The iPod nano, shown in figure 7.2, was introduced in 2005 as the first flash memory-based digital audio player from Apple. It was intended as a replacement for the iPod mini, which was a smaller version of the original iPod models. The transition to using flash memory instead of hard drives allowed Apple to build a much thinner iPod at the same capacities as the previous iPod mini. The iPod nano is also sometimes referred to by generation designations, and there have been four models of iPod nano as of this writing. The fourth-generation iPod nano is available in 8GB and 16GB capacities, although a limited number of 4GB units were also sold outside of the United States. Only the third- and fourth-generation iPod nano models support video playback and iPod Games.

**7.1** iPod classic

**7.2** iPod nano (with video)

● **iPod shuffle.** In 2005, Apple also introduced a small, portable, screenless iPod known as the iPod shuffle, shown in figure 7.3. The idea behind the iPod shuffle is that you load it up with a selection of your favorite music and just listen to it as it plays, either in a random or sequential order. The original iPod shuffle resembled a white USB flash drive. The current second-generation iPod shuffle has taken on a significantly different design, connecting to your computer through a special dock that plugs into the headphone port. Current models are available in 1GB and 2GB capacities.

Copyright Jeremy Horwitz for iLounge.com

**7.3** iPod shuffle

● **iPod touch.** Released about three months after the debut of the Apple iPhone, the iPod touch, shown in figure 7.4, bears more resemblance to the iPhone than it does to its iPod brethren. The iPod touch is very similar to the iPhone without the phone features, and otherwise uses the same operating system and interface; current firmware includes features like a calendar, e-mail client, and even a Web browser. This makes it part personal digital assistant (PDA), part media player. There have been two models of iPod touch released to date, and while the first generation of iPod touch was little more than a stripped-down iPhone, the current model has begun to provide some new and unique features of its own, such as built-in support for the Nike+ sport kit.

Copyright Jeremy Horwitz for iLounge.com

**7.4** iPod touch

One other model of iPod that you may own or occasionally encounter is the iPod mini. This was a smaller version of the fourth-generation iPod, with 4GB and later 6GB capacities. Other than the smaller form factor and lower capacity, it supported the same basic feature set as the 4G iPod. Although a very popular iPod model at the time, it was discontinued and replaced by the iPod nano in 2005.

The most important distinction between iPod models for the purposes of this book is based on the types of content that each iPod model supports and some of the restrictions on that content. For the most part, when you connect an iPod model to your computer, iTunes simply hides any options that are not available on that particular iPod model. Therefore, if you find that certain tabs or options are missing as you read through this chapter, the most likely reason is that your particular iPod does not support those features.

Further, there is normally a correlation between features added to new versions of iTunes and the iPods released around the same time. For example, the new Genius feature in iTunes 8 (discussed in Chapter 5) is also supported directly on the fall 2008 iPod models. With the exception of the iPhone and iPod touch, Apple rarely provides firmware updates to bring these features to older iPod models.

# Managing Music and Video Content on Your iPod

Although today's iPods have evolved into more than just media players, the ability to play back music and video content remains the primary purpose of the iPod for most users. Unlike many other portable media players on the market, the iPod is designed to work hand-in-hand with the iTunes application on your desktop computer, based on the concept that you manage your music content in the form of a main library on your computer, and then carry around some or all of it on your portable device by synchronizing your iPod with your iTunes library.

## Synchronizing your content to your iPod automatically

By design, iTunes is intended to manage all of the content on your iPod through automatic synchronization. In this default mode, you simply connect your iPod to your computer and iTunes detects it and mirrors the state of your computer's library onto your iPod. Any tracks you have added to iTunes since the last synchronization are transferred onto your iPod, and any tracks you have removed from your iTunes library are removed from your iPod.

Further, during automatic synchronization, certain data is transferred back from your iPod into your iTunes library. This includes information such as the play count and last played date information for any tracks you've listened to on your iPod, and the rating information for any tracks you have rated directly on the iPod.

If you are using an iPod that is large enough to store your entire iTunes media library, there is rarely any need to be concerned about your automatic synchronization settings. iTunes handles this automatically for you, and your iPod simply mirrors your entire iTunes library.

However, if your library is larger than the capacity of your iPod, you may want to adjust some settings to choose which content from your library is synchronized with your iPod. If iTunes detects that you are trying to synchronize a library larger than your iPod's capacity, it offers to handle this for you by automatically creating a playlist of selected items, as shown in figure 7.5.

Generally, iTunes' choices in building this playlist are somewhat random, and are not likely to reflect your own preferences. Rather than relying on iTunes to simply build a random playlist of music from your library, you can build your own playlists and simply select those playlists for synchronization to your iPod:

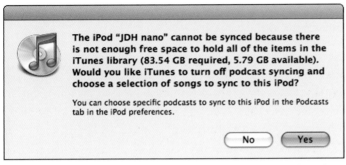

The iPod "JDH nano" cannot be synced because there is not enough free space to hold all of the items in the iTunes library (83.54 GB required, 5.79 GB available). Would you like iTunes to turn off podcast syncing and choose a selection of songs to sync to this iPod?

You can choose specific podcasts to sync to this iPod in the Podcasts tab in the iPod preferences.

No     Yes

7.5 The iTunes warning dialog box when syncing a library larger than the iPod's capacity

1. **Create a playlist or series of playlists containing the content you would like to synchronize to your iPod.** Note that Smart Playlists that limit content by MB or GB sizes are ideal for this purpose — this is discussed more in Chapter 5.

2. **Connect your iPod to your computer.**

3. **Select your iPod from the iTunes Devices list on the left side of the iTunes window.** You see a Summary screen for your iPod, similar to figure 7.6.

7.6 iPod Summary screen

4. **From the tabs that appear at the top of the iPod Summary screen, click the Music tab.**
The screen switches to your music sync settings, similar to figure 7.7.

7.7 iPod music sync settings

5. **Click the check box beside Sync music if it is not already checked.**

6. **Click the radio button beside Selected playlists to choose to synchronize only selected playlists to your iPod.**

7. **From the list of playlists, click the check box beside each playlist that you created in Step 1 that you would like to sync to your iPod.**

8. **Optionally, click the check box beside Include music videos if your playlists contain music videos that you would like transferred to your iPod.** This option is only displayed if your iPod model supports video playback.

9. **Click the Apply button in the bottom-right corner of the iTunes window.** iTunes saves the settings for your iPod and begins synchronizing the selected content.

**Genius**

When building playlists for synchronization to your iPod, you can confirm the size of the content in each playlist by looking at the bottom of the iTunes window. The size is shown in number of songs, total playing time, and capacity.

Note that the iPod shuffle behaves a bit differently from all of the other iPod models. Instead of providing automatic synchronization of your entire library or only selected playlists, in the case of the iPod shuffle, you select one playlist that the iPod shuffle automatically fills its content from. When you connect the iPod shuffle to your computer, it simply transfers as many tracks from this playlist as possible onto the iPod shuffle. To configure your iPod shuffle, follow these steps:

1. **Connect your iPod shuffle to your computer.**

2. **Select your iPod shuffle from the iTunes Devices list on the left side of the iTunes window.** You see a Settings screen for your iPod shuffle, similar to figure 7.8.

7.8 iPod shuffle Settings screen

3. **From the tabs that appear at the top of the iPod shuffle Settings screen, click the Contents tab.** The screen switches to your iPod shuffle content settings, similar to figure 7.9.

143

**7.9** iPod shuffle Contents screen

4. **In the Autofill from drop-down menu, located at the bottom of the Contents screen, choose the playlist that you would like to fill your iPod shuffle from.** You may also choose Music to simply autofill your iPod shuffle using your main iTunes library, rather than limiting the content to a specified playlist.

5. **Other options you can decide to use include:**

   ● **Replace all items when Autofilling.** Click this check box to enable iTunes to replace any existing content on the iPod shuffle with content from the selected playlist. If this option is not checked, iTunes adds the content of the selected playlist to the content already on the iPod shuffle.

   ● **Choose items randomly.** Click this check box if you want iTunes to determine if it fills the iPod shuffle with the playlist content in its original playlist order or randomly.

   ● **Choose higher rated items more often.** Click this check box if you would like iTunes to give preference to higher-rated items when filling the iPod shuffle.

6. **Click the Autofill button to begin filling the iPod shuffle.**

## iTunes Phones

Prior to the introduction of the iPhone, Apple established a partnership with Motorola to add iPod-like functionality to Motorola's cellular phones.

The first of these to be introduced was the Motorola ROKR E1 in mid-2005, followed later by the Motorola RAZR V3i — an iTunes version of Motorola's very popular RAZR V3 series phones. These devices operated like normal Motorola phones, but instead of the generic MP3 player that other Motorola phones included, these phones had an iTunes application, providing iPod-like functionality.

Synchronization of an iTunes Phone was handled over the phone's USB v1.1 interface, and iTunes basically treated the phone in the same way as the iPod shuffle. However, these phones had an artificial limit of 100 tracks, regardless of the size of memory card used in the phone.

The iTunes Phones were never hugely popular, mostly due to their slow USB interface, 100-track limitation, and proprietary headphone connectors. However, they did represent the first foray by Apple into an iTunes-integrated phone solution, and were not a bad companion solution for those iPod users who simply wanted to carry around a few music tracks on their phone.

**Genius**

The iPod shuffle provides one other unique option. On the Settings tab, you can click the check box beside Convert higher bit rate songs to 128 kbps AAC to have iTunes automatically convert any higher-quality songs in your iTunes library to a smaller size. This helps to fit more songs on the iPod shuffle.

# Managing content on your iPod manually

When using automatic synchronization, iTunes takes the approach that your iPod is simply an extension of your main iTunes library — a portable device that you carry your content around on when away from your desktop computer. As a function of this iTunes-iPod relationship, your iPod becomes associated with your main iTunes library. Connecting your iPod to a different iTunes library yields a warning that your iPod is associated with a different iTunes library and informs you that you must erase all of the current content on your iPod in order to sync with this second library, similar to the message shown in figure 7.10.

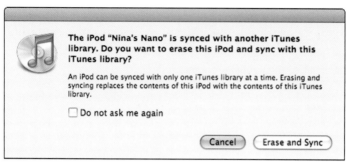

**The iPod "Nina's Nano" is synced with another iTunes library. Do you want to erase this iPod and sync with this iTunes library?**

An iPod can be synced with only one iTunes library at a time. Erasing and syncing replaces the contents of this iPod with the contents of this iTunes library.

☐ Do not ask me again

( Cancel )   ( Erase and Sync )

7.10 iPod synchronization warning

This is necessary because an iPod in automatic synchronization mirrors the content in a single iTunes library. You therefore cannot synchronize the same iPod to a second iTunes library without mirroring that library instead, thereby removing all of the content from the first iTunes library and replacing it with the content from the second library.

Fortunately, for users who want to synchronize their iPod to more than one computer, iPod offers the ability to manage the audio and video content on their iPod manually, rather than using automatic synchronization. In this mode, instead of the iPod acting as an extension of your main iTunes library, it acts as its own separate library that you manage directly from iTunes.

In a manual configuration, it is not even necessary to maintain an actual iTunes library on your computer — iTunes merely becomes the conduit by which you transfer your audio and video content onto the iPod, and once transferred, this content does not need to remain in your iTunes library.

**Caution** Although you can use manual management to store your music and video content exclusively on your iPod, this is not recommended. The iPod is a portable device that can be lost, stolen, or damaged, and is therefore not a good place to store the only copy of your music. If you're not going to keep your music on your computer, at least ensure that it's backed up somewhere else.

To set your iPod to manage the audio and video content on it manually, follow these steps:

1. **Connect your iPod to your computer.** If you are connecting your iPod to a new iTunes library, you are prompted with the warning dialog shown in figure 7.10.

2. **If a warning dialog box appears, simply click the Cancel button.** Your iPod remains connected to your iTunes library, but no automatic synchronization occurs.

3. **Select your iPod from the iTunes Devices list on the left side of the iTunes window.** You see a Summary screen for your iPod.

4. **Click the check box beside Manually manage music and videos, as shown in figure 7.11.** Note that on older iPod models that do not support video, this simply reads Manually manage music.

5. **Click the Apply button in the bottom-right corner of the iTunes window.**

7.11 iPod Summary screen with Manually manage music and videos checked

**Note** When an iPod is in manual mode, changes made on the iPod, such as rating, play count, and last-played information, are not transferred back to your iTunes library. This information is stored only on the iPod.

Once your iPod has been set to manual mode, it no longer automatically syncs with any iTunes library unless you disable this setting. Even if you connect the iPod to another iTunes library, it remains in manual mode. Any content that was synchronized to your iPod manually remains on your iPod, including any playlists, but the iPod is treated as a completely separate library while in manual mode.

**Caution** Placing your iPod in manual mode requires that you manually eject it from your computer before you physically unplug it. This is done by clicking the small Eject symbol that appears next to the iPod in your iTunes Devices list. Failing to eject the iPod properly may cause corruption of your media and other content. Note that this restriction does not apply to the iPod touch or the iPhone.

To add content to your iPod manually, simply drag-and-drop that content directly onto your iPod icon in the iTunes Devices list on the left side of your iTunes window. You can also transfer playlists from your iTunes library onto your iPod by simply dragging-and-dropping them onto the iPod icon in the same way as you do for music and video content.

**Note** The iPod shuffle always behaves as if it is in manual mode for the purposes of content management. There is no manual mode setting for the iPod shuffle, as you can drag-and-drop content to it at any time.

To modify or remove content from a manually managed iPod, you must first expand the iPod to show its content by clicking the small triangle to the left of your iPod icon, as shown in figure 7.12.

You can then select content directly on the iPod from within iTunes as you would for your main library. Most of the same iTunes library-management functions are available while managing an iPod's content manually, including the ability to update track information and delete tracks.

Keep in mind that not all content is managed manually on an iPod. The manual-management option only applies to audio and video content. Individual podcast episodes can be added to your iPod manually, or you can still choose to synchronize whole podcast subscriptions automatically while still managing the rest of your iPod content manually. Other types of content, such as photos, iPod Games, contacts, and calendars, are always synchronized automatically if enabled.

7.12 Managing content of an iPod (here called JDH classic) manually

**Note** You can only manage the content on an iPhone manually from a single computer. The iPhone does not appear in manual mode when you connect it to another iTunes library, and you cannot enable manual mode on a second library without erasing your iPhone content.

# Synchronizing checked items

You can also control which items are synchronized to your iPod through the use of the check boxes that appear beside your items in your iTunes library. By default, iTunes synchronizes all items to your iPod, regardless of whether they are checked or unchecked in your iTunes library. You can easily change this on a per-iPod basis, however.

To set your iPod to manage the audio and video content on it manually, follow these steps:

1. **Connect your iPod to your computer.**

2. **Select your iPod from the iTunes Devices list on the left side of the iTunes window.** You see a Summary screen for your iPod.

3. **Click the check box beside Sync only checked songs and videos.** Note that on older iPod models that do not support video, this simply reads Sync only checked songs, as shown in figure 7.13.

4. **Click the Apply button in the bottom-right corner of the iTunes window.**

7.13 iPod Summary screen with the Sync only checked songs option enabled

Note that when you enable this option, any items on your iPod that are not checked in your iTunes library are removed from the iPod during the sync operation that occurs immediately after clicking the Apply button.

**Note** Unchecked songs do not play back in iTunes either, unless you specifically select them by double-clicking them. This method of iPod management can therefore be useful to exclude items that you do not want to listen to anyway, such as seasonal or holiday music. However, using specified playlists is the recommended option for syncing an iPod that is smaller than your iTunes library.

# Synchronizing movies

If you are using a video-capable iPod model, you can also control which movies and TV shows are transferred to your iPod in a similar manner. In this case, however, you can either build playlists as you would for music, or you can simply select specific movies and TV shows directly.

To select which movies you would like to synchronize to your iPod, follow these steps:

1. **Connect your iPod to your computer.**

2. **Select your iPod from the iTunes Devices list on the left side of the iTunes window.**

3. **Click the Movies tab (iPod) or the Videos tab (iPhone).** The screen switches to your movie sync settings, similar to figure 7.14.

7.14 iPod movie sync settings

4. **Click the check box beside Sync movies if it is not already checked.**

5. **If you are using an iPod classic or iPod nano, click one of the following radio buttons:**

   - **All movies.** iTunes synchronizes all movies in your iTunes library to your iPod.

   - **Unwatched movies.** Use the drop-down menu to specify either all or recent movies. iTunes synchronizes all movies, or the specified number of the most recent movies that you have not yet watched, as determined by the play count in iTunes.

   - **Selected.** Use the drop-down menu to specify either movies or playlists. iTunes synchronizes either the individually selected movies or all of the movies listed in the selected playlists. The listing below this dialog box updates to reflect either a listing of movies or a listing of playlists.

6. **If you have chosen Selected movies or Selected playlists, click the check boxes beside the movies or playlists that you would like to synchronize to your iPod.** Movies you have not yet viewed are displayed with a blue dot next to the movie title. Note that on the iPod touch and iPhone, you can only sync Selected movies.

7. **Click the Apply button in the bottom-right corner of the iTunes window.** iTunes saves the settings for your iPod and begins synchronizing the selected content.

# Synchronizing TV shows

The process for selecting specific TV shows is quite similar, although in this case, you are selecting a show as an entire series and setting the number of episodes of each show that you would like to sync. To select which TV shows you would like to synchronize to your iPod, follow these steps:

1. **Connect your iPod to your computer.**

2. **Select your iPod from the iTunes Devices list on the left side of the iTunes window.**

3. **Click the TV Shows tab (iPod) or the Videos tab (iPhone).** The screen switches to your TV Shows sync settings, similar to figure 7.15.

4. **Click the check box beside Sync if it is not already checked.**

5. **From the drop-down menu beside the Sync option, choose the number of episodes of the selected TV shows that you would like to sync to your iPod.** Your choices are all episodes, a specified number of recent episodes, all unwatched episodes, or a specified number of either least-recent or most-recent unwatched episodes.

151

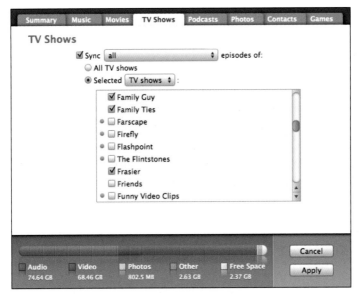

7.15 iPod TV Shows sync settings

6. **Click one of the following radio buttons:**

   - **All TV shows.** iTunes synchronizes all TV shows, subject to the number of episodes specified in step 5.

   - **Selected.** Use the drop-down menu to specify either TV shows or Playlists. iTunes synchronizes either the individually selected TV shows or all of the TV shows in the selected playlists, again subject to the number of episodes specified in Step 5.

7. **If you have chosen Selected TV shows or Selected playlists, click the check boxes beside the TV shows or playlists that you would like to synchronize to your iPod.**

8. **Click the Apply button in the bottom-right corner of the iTunes window.** iTunes saves the settings for your iPod and begins synchronizing the selected content.

**Genius**

The TV Show synchronization settings in iTunes apply to all episodes of each selected show, and therefore may not provide the level of control that you want. The use of Smart Playlists with criteria for play count and limits based on date added, can be a much more flexible way to control the synchronization of TV shows.

# Transferring rented movies

Introduced to the iTunes Store in January 2008, movie rentals are a special case due to the time-based restrictions that are placed on them by iTunes.

The first point you should keep in mind is that only the more recent models of iPod support the playback of rented movies. This includes the iPod classic, iPod nano (with video), iPod touch, and iPhone. All of these iPod models must also be running firmware released after January 2008 to provide rental playback support. Most notably, however, the fifth-generation iPod, which introduced video playback into the iPod family, does not support the playback of rented content, regardless of the firmware version. If you are using an unsupported iPod model, the rental options simply do not appear in your iPod synchronization settings.

The main area in which managing rented content on an iPod differs from other types of content is that it can only reside in a single place at a time. When you transfer rented content from your iTunes library onto your iPod, it is moved rather than copied. If you want to transfer your rented content to another iPod or Apple TV, you must move it back from whatever device it is on, and then move it back to the new device.

To transfer rented content to and from your iPod, follow these steps:

1. **Connect your iPod to your computer.**

2. **Select your iPod from the iTunes Devices list on the left side of the iTunes window.**

3. **Click the Movies tab (iPod) or the Videos tab (iPhone).** The screen switches to your movie sync settings. If you have any rented content in your iTunes library or on the currently selected iPod, it appears at the top of this section, similar to figure 7.16.

4. **In the In your iTunes library column on the left side, click the Move button beside the movies that you would like to transfer to your iPod.** The titles move to the iPod column, indicating that they are selected for transfer to your iPod.

5. **Optionally, in the iPod column, click the Move button beside any movies that you would like to transfer back to your iTunes library.** The titles move to the iTunes column, indicating that they are selected for transfer back to iTunes.

7.16 iPod movie rental transfers

6. **Optionally, you may also click the Delete button beside any movies on your iPod that you would simply like to delete from your iPod without transferring back to your iTunes library.** The titles disappear, indicating that they are selected for deletion.

7. **Click the Apply button in the bottom-right corner of the iTunes window.** iTunes transfers the selected movies to and from your iPod, and removes any movies you've marked for deletion.

No transfers or deletions occur until you actually click the Apply button. If you have made a mistake and do not want to commit your changes, you may simply click the Cancel button instead.

**Note** You must be connected to the Internet and logged in to the iTunes Store with the account that was used to purchase the movies that you are transferring. iTunes updates the authorization keys each time a movie is transferred to a new device to ensure that the rental time restrictions can be properly enforced.

# Managing Podcasts on Your iPod

Although podcasts are actually just audio and video files like any other track, the subscription nature of podcasts makes them a special case for synchronization to your iPod. Unlike most of your media content, podcasts tend to show up automatically in your iTunes library, and you most likely want to ensure that you have your latest podcasts ready to take with you on your iPod.

As a result, podcast synchronization has more in common with synchronizing TV shows. You choose which podcasts you want stored on your iPod and how many episodes of each that you want to keep:

1. **Connect your iPod to your computer.**

2. **Select your iPod from the iTunes Devices list on the left side of the iTunes window.**

3. **Click the Podcasts tab.** The screen switches to your Podcasts sync settings. See figure 7.17.

4. **Click the check box beside Sync if it is not already checked.**

5. **From the drop-down menu beside the Sync option, choose the number of episodes of the selected podcasts that you would like to sync to your iPod.** Your choices are

   - **All episodes.** iTunes syncs all available podcast episodes from your iTunes library.

   - **<X> most recent episodes.** iTunes syncs the most recent 1, 3, 5 or 10 episodes that you specify.

   - **All unplayed episodes.** iTunes syncs all unplayed episodes of each selected podcast from your iTunes library. An unplayed episode, in this case, is a podcast episode that you have not finished listening to, as indicated by the play count field.

   - **<X> most/least recent unplayed.** iTunes syncs the specified number of either most-recent or least-recent unplayed episodes that you specify from your iTunes library.

   - **All new episodes.** iTunes syncs all new episodes of each selected podcast from your iTunes library. A new episode, in this case, is a podcast episode that you have not started listening to, as indicated by the blue dot that appears beside it in the iTunes Podcast listing.

   - **<X> most/least recent new.** iTunes syncs the specified number of either most-recent or least-recent new episodes that you specify.

6. **Click either All podcasts or Selected podcasts to choose which podcast subscriptions you want transferred to your iPod.**

7. **If you have chosen Selected podcasts, click the check boxes beside the specific podcasts that you would like to synchronize to your iPod.**

8. **Click the Apply button in the bottom-right corner of the iTunes window.** iTunes saves the settings for your iPod and begins synchronizing the selected content.

**Note**

The settings on the Podcasts tab are not affected by the iPod manual-management mode. This means that you can still sync your podcasts onto your iPod automatically while managing the rest of your audio and video content manually. Alternatively, individual podcast episodes can still be transferred to the iPod using manual mode.

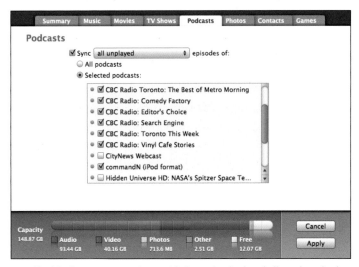

**7.17** iPod Podcasts sync settings, with Sync checked and all unplayed selected from the drop-down menu

# Syncing Photos to Your iPod

Support for photos was introduced to the iPod family in late 2004 when Apple introduced its first iPod with a color screen: the iPod photo. This was basically a fourth-generation iPod with a color screen and added photo support. Every iPod model released since that time has included support for displaying photos.

Synchronization of photos to your iPod is one of the more offbeat features of iTunes, because iTunes does not provide any way to actually manage or even display photos. Rather, iTunes acts simply as a conduit to transfer photos onto the iPod from another application such as iPhoto or simply from a folder of photos on your computer.

Specifically, iTunes recognizes the photo album structure from either iPhoto or Aperture on your Mac, or from Adobe Photoshop Album or Photoshop Elements on your Windows PC. If you are not using any of these applications, you can still point iTunes to a folder on your computer, and it uses the first level of sub-folders to represent your photo albums on your iPod.

To configure photo synchronization for your iPod, follow these steps:

1. **Connect your iPod to your computer.**

2. **Select your iPod from the iTunes Devices list on the left side of the iTunes window.**

3. **Click the Photos tab.** The screen switches to your Photos sync settings.

4. **Click the check box beside Sync photos from if it is not already checked.**

5. **From the drop-down menu beside the Sync photos from option, choose where you would like to sync your photos from.** Compatible applications such as iPhoto (as shown in figure 7.18) or Adobe Photoshop Elements are listed if these are installed on your computer. Alternatively, you may select a predefined folder such as Pictures (Mac) or My Pictures (Windows) to sync from, or select the Choose Folder option to specify your own folder anywhere on your computer.

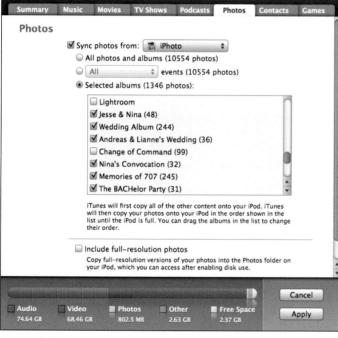

**7.18** iPod Photos sync settings with Sync photos from selected and iPhoto selected as the sync location

6. **Click either All photos and albums or Selected albums to choose which photos you would like synchronized to your iPod.** If you are syncing from a photo-management application, the albums from that application appear here. If you are syncing from a folder, each of the first-level sub-folder names appear as albums. Note that iTunes provides a count of the number of photos that are selected for synchronization.

7. **If you have chosen Selected albums, click the check box beside the selected photo album or folders that you would like to synchronize to your iPod.** Note the number beside each album or folder showing the number of photos that it contains. Unchecking previously selected albums tells iTunes to remove these from your iPod on the next sync. You can also drag the albums in the list to change the order in which they appear on your iPod.

8. **If you are using an iPod classic or iPod nano, you can click the check box beside Include full-resolution photos to place a copy of the original photo on the iPod as well during synchronization.** Photos transferred to the iPod are resized by iTunes during transfer into an iPod-optimized format, which is usually much smaller than the original photo size. This option places a copy of the original photo onto the iPod that can be accessed from the iPod in disk use mode.

9. **Click the Apply button in the bottom-right corner of the iTunes window.** iTunes saves the settings for your iPod and begins synchronizing the selected content.

**Genius**

If you are using iPhoto '08 and iTunes 7.4 or later, you may also opt to synchronize a specified number of recent iPhoto Events to your iPod rather than albums. The Events option appears on the Photos tab as long as the appropriate versions of iPhoto and iTunes are installed.

Note that there is no manual-management option for photos — they are always automatically synced with your iPod. The key point to remember about photo synchronization is that this is a synchronization process, rather than simply a transfer. Each time you connect your iPod, iTunes checks your photo application or photo folders, and any photos or albums that are no longer available are removed from your iPod. You must therefore leave the photos on your computer in order for them to remain on your iPod.

Although you can turn off synchronization and leave the photos on the iPod, you must re-enable synchronization to add additional photos, and of course, if you re-enable synchronization, any photos that are no longer on your computer are removed from your iPod.

## The iPod Photo Cache

Whenever iTunes synchronizes photos to your iPod, it goes through an optimization process to sync these photos into resolutions appropriate for display on the iPod. In fact, several different sizes of each photo are stored on the iPod, optimized for each of the possible display modes — thumbnail view, on the iPod screen, on the TV output, and so forth. In some situations, this may actually mean that a photo can take up more space when transferred to the iPod than the original photo did on your computer.

In fact, the average size of a single photo on the iPod classic is approximately 900KB. This is in addition to any space taken up by the full-resolution version of the image (if you choose to sync that as well).

More importantly, however, iTunes also creates an iPod Photo Cache to store these optimized versions on your computer, so that if you ever need to transfer them back onto your iPod, or onto another similar iPod model, it can save the time of having to go through the optimization process again. The problem is that for a large photo library, this iPod Photo Cache folder can grow very large, taking up needless space on your computer. At 900KB per photo, you can see how even 1,000 photos set for synchronization to your iPod would consume close to 1GB of storage space.

Further, because different iPod models store different resolutions of the photos, the iPod Photo Cache can grow even larger if you're syncing the same photos to multiple iPods.

Unfortunately, there's not much you can do about this folder while still syncing photos. If you delete it, iTunes simply re-creates it on the next iPod sync. About the only option if you're critically low on disk space is to disable photo synchronization to your iPod entirely. In this case, you can still leave any existing photos on your iPod, but they become static content — iTunes does not synchronize them with anything on your computer. Once photo sync is disabled, you can delete the iPod Photo Cache folder with impunity. The catch? If you ever want to add any additional photos to your iPod, you'll have to turn sync back on and allow the cache folder to be re-created and wait through the time-consuming photo optimization stage as well.

# Syncing Games to Your iPod

Although iPods had offered a few basic built-in games for some time, in September 2006, Apple expanded these capabilities by announcing downloadable games support for the fifth-generation iPod, as part of a firmware update and product refresh.

At that time, Apple began selling iPod games through the iTunes Store. Users could purchase iPod games for $4.99 USD, and then transfer these games onto their iPods in the same way as any other type of iTunes-purchased media content.

Game support was later continued on the 2007 iPod classic and iPod nano (with video) products, and the very recent release of the iTunes App Store for the iPhone and iPod touch has created a whole new generation of iPod expansion software.

**Caution**    Apple makes absolutely no guarantees that games purchased for the current-generation iPod will be compatible with any future iPod models. Fifth-generation iPod owners were surprised last year when Apple released the new iPod classic and iPod nano (with video), and none of the games previously purchased for the 5G iPod worked on the newer models. Apple's response was that users had to repurchase the same games if they wanted them for the newer models.

Synchronizing games to your iPod is handled in much the same way as other types of content:

1.  **Connect your iPod to your computer.**

2.  **Select your iPod from the iTunes Devices list on the left side of the iTunes window.**

3.  **Click the Games tab.** The screen switches to your Games sync settings.

4.  **Click the check box beside Sync games if it is not already checked.**

5.  **Click either All games or Selected games to choose which games you would like synchronized to your iPod.** Selected games is selected in figure 7.19.

6.  **If you have chosen Selected games, click the check box beside the selected games that you would like to synchronize to your iPod.** Unchecking previously selected games tells iTunes to remove these from your iPod on the next sync.

7.  **Click the Apply button in the bottom-right corner of the iTunes window.** iTunes saves the settings for your iPod and begins synchronizing the selected content.

Games must always be automatically synchronized to your iPod. There is no manual-management option available.

**Caution**   Removing a game from your iPod also removes any saved information such as preferences or high scores. iTunes does not provide any way of backing this information up, nor does it retain it on the iPod after you remove the game.

**7.19** iPod Games sync settings with Sync games and Selected games selected

# Enabling Disk Use on Your iPod

Many users of higher-capacity iPods find that they have much more space available on their iPod than their actual media content occupies. Rather than letting that space go to waste, the traditional iPod models support a Disk Use feature that allows you to access your iPod simply as an external hard disk. In this mode, you can save other files on it and basically use the iPod as a portable storage device. Note that this mode is not supported on the iPhone or the iPod touch, as these devices use a different synchronization protocol that does not rely on disk use.

To enable disk use on your iPod, follow these steps:

1. **Connect your iPod to your computer.**

2. **Select your iPod from the iTunes Devices list on the left side of the iTunes window.** You see a Summary screen for your iPod, similar to figure 7.20.

3. **Click the check box beside Enable disk use.** Note that if the Manually manage music and videos option is enabled, disk use is forced on and the check box is unavailable.

4. **Click the Apply button in the bottom-right corner of the iTunes window.**

**7.20** iPod Summary screen with Enable disk use selected

**Caution** Enabling disk use on your iPod requires that you manually eject it from your computer before you physically unplug it. This is done by clicking the small Eject symbol that appears next to the iPod in your iTunes Devices list. Failing to eject the iPod properly may cause corruption of your media and other content.

In reality, the traditional iPod models always present themselves as an external USB mass storage device. In fact, this is how iTunes updates information on the iPod as well. What the Enable disk use option actually does is to simply tell iTunes to not automatically eject the iPod following an automatic sync operation. Instead, the iPod remains connected so that you can continue to access it as an external storage device, and then simply eject it yourself when you are done with it. However, you can connect your iPod to any computer that is not running iTunes, whether disk use is enabled or not, and it always appears as an external storage device, because iTunes is not present to automatically eject it.

**Note** If you have a Mac-formatted iPod, you cannot access it from a Windows PC, as Windows is not able to read the Mac HFS+ file system without additional software. If you really need to access a Mac-formatted iPod in Windows, MacDrive from MediaFour (www.mediafour.com) is a $50 software application that allows Windows 2000/XP/Vista to read Mac-formatted disks, including the iPod.

# Syncing Calendars and Contacts to Your iPod

In addition to its use as a media player, you can also use your iPod for viewing your calendar and contacts on the go.

The traditional iPod models (iPod classic and iPod nano) provide read-only support for this information. You can store and view your contacts and calendars on the iPod, but you cannot change or modify them, nor does iTunes sync any of this information back to your computer — it's strictly a one-way relationship.

The iPhone and iPod touch, on the other hand, allow full editing of your contacts and calendars on the device itself, and full two-way synchronization with iTunes. Further discussion on these features on the iPod touch and iPhone takes place in Chapter 11.

You can synchronize your contacts onto your iPod either from Address Book in Mac OS X, or from Windows Address Book or Outlook 2003 or later in Windows. Calendars can be synchronized from iCal on the Mac, or from Outlook 2003 or later in Windows.

Contact and calendar synchronization is configured in your iPod sync settings in iTunes:

1. **Connect your iPod to your computer.**

2. **Select your iPod from the iTunes Devices list on the left side of the iTunes window.**

3. **Click the Contacts tab.** The screen switches to your Contacts/Calendars sync settings, similar to figure 7.21.

4. **Click the check box beside Sync Address Book contacts if it is not already checked.** Windows users must also choose the application to sync their contacts from in the drop-down list menu beside the Sync option. Only those applications installed on your computer are shown.

5. **Click either All contacts or Selected groups to choose which contacts you would like synchronized to your iPod.**

6. **If you have chosen Selected groups, click the check box beside each of the groups that you would like to synchronize to your iPod.**

7. **Click the check box beside Include contacts' photos if you would like to include your contact photos on your iPod.** Note that this option is not available for all models of iPod or all contact applications.

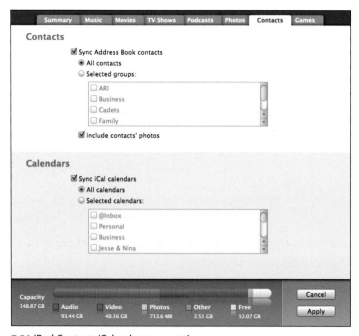

7.21 iPod Contacts/Calendars sync settings

8. **Click the check box beside Sync iCal Calendars if it is not already checked.** Windows users must have Outlook 2003 or later installed for this option to be available.

9. **Click either All calendars or Selected calendars to choose which calendars you would like synchronized to your iPod.**

## Manually Copying Contacts and Calendars

Contact and calendar information is stored on the iPod in the open standard vCard and vCal formats. If you are using an application that is not supported by iTunes, or simply want to do a quick one-time transfer of contact information, you can easily do this by accessing the appropriate folders on the iPod in disk use mode:

1. **Enable disk use on your iPod.**

2. **Export your contact information into a vCard format (VCF file), or your calendar information to a vCal/iCal format (VCS or ICS file).**

3. **Open your iPod in Finder (Mac) or Windows Explorer (Windows).**

4. **Locate the Contacts folder, and copy your VCF file from step 2 into this folder.**

5. **Locate the Calendars folder, and copy your VCS or ICS file from step 2 into this folder.**

6. **Eject the iPod from your computer.**

Note that the information does not need to be combined into a single VCF/VCS/ICS file. The iPod reads all of the VCF files from the Contacts folder or all of the VCS/ICS files from the Calendars folder and combines them to display as a single contact or calendar list. Therefore, you can even drop VCF files that you receive as Contact Cards directly onto the iPod's Contacts folder to take them with you.

10. **If you have chosen Selected calendars, click the check box beside each of the calendars that you would like to synchronize to your iPod.**

11. **Click the Apply button in the bottom-right corner of the iTunes window.** iTunes saves the settings for your iPod and begins synchronizing the selected content.

# Storing Notes on Your iPod

The iPod also provides support for rudimentary notes that can be displayed on the go. However, iTunes does not provide any way of updating, syncing, or managing these. You must add them directly to the iPod's Notes folder in disk use mode.

The notes themselves are simple text files, and may be up to 4KB in length per file. The iPod also supports a basic HTML-style tagging system within notes that can be used to build rudimentary menus, link notes together, and even link to media content on your iPod.

More information on how to build complex notes can be found in the Apple iPod Notes Feature Guide, which you can download from http://developer.apple.com/ipod.

# Using Multiple iPods on One Computer

Many iPod users start out with a single iPod and iTunes library, and before they know it, everybody in the family has one. Or, perhaps they're simply adding an iPhone to their existing iPod collection.

A common question as a result of using multiple iPods is how to use more than one iPod on a single computer. Many users become very concerned about having to set up an alternate iTunes library, or how to figure out which content goes onto which iPod, and so forth.

However, the answer is really as simple as "plug it in." iTunes knows the difference between your iPods. Each iPod you connect gets its own independent synchronization settings, and is treated completely as its own device. Settings that you configure on one iPod are specific to that iPod and do not affect any of your other iPods.

In fact, given enough USB ports or USB hubs, you can even connect multiple iPod devices at once. Figure 7.22 ends this chapter on the

7.22 Synchronizing multiple iPods

rather light note of a single iTunes library with three iPhones, an iPod classic, two iPod nanos, two iPod shuffles, two Apple TVs, and an iTunes Phone all synchronizing to the same iTunes library simultaneously.

I'm not quite sure what the upper limit is of the number of iPods that can be synced with a single iTunes library simultaneously, but I suspect you would run out of USB connections before you reach it.

**Note**    If you plan to use multiple iPods on one computer but do not want to share a single music library, be sure to check out Chapter 13 for information on how you can create multiple iTunes libraries on a single computer.

# How Do I Get the Most Out of My iPod?

Once you have your media content organized in your iTunes library and transferred onto your iPod, you're ready to enjoy listening to your music and audiobooks and watching videos while on the go. The iPod is a pretty intuitive device, and so basic operation isn't likely to be much of a problem, but there are some hidden inner workings and tricks to the iPod that you may not be aware of.

# How Content Is Organized on the iPod

The first important thing to understand is that content is organized on the iPod based on the information contained within each track. The iPod doesn't care about things like filenames or folders any more than iTunes does, and so when you're browsing the content on your iPod, you are accessing it based on the information contained within the headers, or tags, and not based on what you may have named the file before you imported it into iTunes.

Internally, the iPod uses a database to keep track of where your media files are stored on the device and to catalog them by information such as artist, album, name, and genre. For the most part, this database is only read by the iPod — the information contained in it is written by iTunes when you sync your content to the iPod.

This is also the reason why you cannot just connect the iPod to any computer and copy files directly onto it in disk use mode: The iPod doesn't know about files that aren't listed in its database, and you need iTunes to update that database and tell it where those files are.

Organizing your content in iTunes is discussed more in Chapter 3.

# Rating Content on the Go

One of the more useful organizational features on the iPod is the ability to rate your audio content while you are listening to it. Your media files begin their lives in iTunes and on your iPod with no rating at all — it's up to you to set one, and whatever rating you give your tracks is synchronized between your iTunes library and your iPod in both directions. This means that any ratings you set on the iPod are transferred back to your iTunes library the next time you sync your iPod.

**Note** Although video tracks have a rating field, this field is not accessible from the iPod. You must adjust video ratings in iTunes.

You can only rate tracks on the iPod while you are actually listening to those specific tracks. The method for doing this differs slightly, depending on your iPod model. To rate tracks on an iPod classic or iPod nano, follow these steps:

1. **Ensure the track that you want to rate is currently playing.**

2. **From the Now Playing screen on the iPod, press the center SELECT button twice.** The second press brings up the rating screen for the current track, similar to figure 8.1.

3. **Scroll using the iPod click wheel to adjust the number of stars from one to five.**

4. **Press the center SELECT button to return to the normal Now Playing screen.** Note that you may also simply leave the iPod at the rating screen — it times out and returns to the Now Playing screen after a few seconds of inactivity.

You can also adjust the rating on the iPod touch and iPhone, although the method is slightly different:

1. **Ensure the track that you want to rate is currently playing.**

2. **On the Now Playing screen, locate the album button in the top-right corner, as shown in figure 8.2.**

8.1 iPod classic rating screen

8.2 iPhone Now Playing screen

171

**Note**

3. **Tap the album button.** The album cover art flips over and is replaced by a track listing, as shown in figure 8.3.

4. **Tap the position representing the number of stars you would like to assign to the current track.**

5. **Tap the album button in the top-right corner again to return to the Now Playing screen.**

Ratings assigned on the device take effect immediately, making this a useful way to select tracks through the use of Smart Playlists based on their rating. These ratings transfer back to iTunes during the next sync operation.

**8.3** iPhone album track listing and rating screen

**Caution**

If you are managing the content on your iPod or iPhone manually, ratings do not transfer back to your master library. In this case, your ratings exist only on the device. Further, switching back to automatic sync may result in these ratings being lost. Some third-party tools are available to transfer these ratings to your library in manual mode. These are discussed in Chapter 10.

# Using Shuffle Settings Effectively

Listening to all of your albums and playlists in sequential order can get a bit dull, but fortunately, the iPod supports a few different shuffle modes to mix things up a bit.

You may notice that your iPod classic or iPod nano have a Shuffle Songs option right on the main menu. Selecting this menu option starts playing back the entire content of your iPod at random, with the exception of those tracks such as audiobooks and podcasts that have been specifically excluded from shuffled playback. On a device like the iPod nano, which is loaded only with your favorite tracks, this can be a very handy option, but it loses a lot of its practicality when you're dealing with a 160GB iPod classic with a wide variety of music, because there's no way to specify any one genre or type of music to play back. If you have a wide variety of content, you probably won't find much use for this option unless you really do enjoy mixing it up between genres like reggae, rock, jazz, and classical.

## Configuring shuffle settings on the iPod classic and iPod nano

Fortunately, the iPod offers more shuffle options, and so if you don't need the Shuffle Songs option on the main menu, then you can easily remove it:

1. **From your main iPod menu, select the Settings option.** The settings menu is displayed.

2. **From the Settings menu, select the Main Menu option.** A listing of menu items is displayed. On an iPod classic or iPod nano (with video), a series of check marks appears beside those options that are presently shown on the main menu. On older iPods, this is instead represented by the words ON and OFF, where ON indicates that an item is displayed on the main menu, and OFF indicates that it is not.

3. **Using the click wheel, scroll down until you see Shuffle Songs.** This appears near the bottom of the menu listing, as shown in figure 8.4.

8.4 iPod classic main menu settings

4.  **Press the center SELECT button to toggle the Shuffle Songs option off.** The check mark disappears, or the word ON toggles to OFF, depending on the iPod model you are using.

5.  **Press the MENU button on the iPod several times until the main menu reappears.** The Shuffle Songs option is no longer shown.

Instead of going for the global shuffle option, you may prefer to shuffle your music a bit more selectively. This is done by turning on the iPod's general Shuffle setting, at which point any set of tracks you select, be it a playlist, album, artist, or genre, are played back randomly. To enable Shuffle mode, follow these steps:

1.  **From your main iPod menu, select the Settings option.** The Settings menu is displayed.

2.  **From the Settings menu, scroll to the Shuffle option, as shown in figure 8.5.**

3.  **Press the center SELECT button to toggle between the three available shuffle modes, as follows:**

    *   **Off.** Tracks are played in the order they appear in the selected playlist or other play sequence.

    *   **Songs.** Tracks are played in a random order, starting with the first track selected.

    *   **Albums.** Tracks are played sequentially within a given album, and the next album is selected randomly from the available albums. Note that this option only plays those tracks that are in the current selection, and so if you are playing from a playlist that only includes three tracks from a given album, only those three tracks are played in the order they appear on the album, and then the next set of tracks is selected randomly. Naturally, this option only has an effect if your playlist contains tracks from more than one album.

| Settings | |
|---|---|
| About | |
| **Shuffle** | **Off** |
| Repeat | Off |
| Main Menu | |
| Music Menu | |
| Volume Limit | |
| Backlight | |
| Brightness | |
| Audiobooks | |

**Shuffle**

**Play Music Library in Sequence**

**8.5** iPod classic shuffle setting

4.  **Press the MENU button to return to the main menu.**

**Note**

If you have tracks that have been marked as Skip when shuffling in iTunes, these are excluded from any shuffle mode on the iPod classic, iPod nano (with video), or 5G iPod using firmware v1.2 or later, whether they are in the current playlist or not. Older iPod models only excluded these tracks when the main menu Shuffle Songs option was selected.

On the iPod classic and third- and fourth-generation iPod nano, shuffle mode can be enabled directly from the Now Playing screen. Simply press the center SELECT button three times to bring up the shuffle options, and then use the click wheel to select the appropriate shuffle mode. Note that this option is only available when listening to music tracks.

# Configuring shuffle settings on the iPhone and iPod touch

On the iPhone and iPod touch, the process for shuffling songs is slightly different. Each track listing includes a Shuffle option at the very top that can begin playing that entire set of tracks in shuffle mode, similar to figure 8.6.

Further, you can toggle Shuffle on and off while playing a given set of tracks:

1. **On the Now Playing screen, tap the album artwork image.** A track position indicator appears beneath the track title, as shown in figure 8.7.

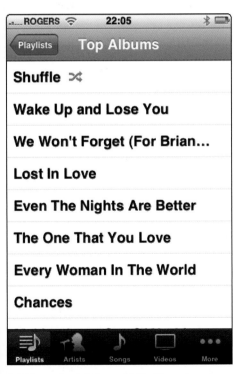

8.6 iPhone track listing with Shuffle option

8.7 iPhone Now Playing screen

2. **In the top-right corner of the screen, tap the shuffle icon.** The icon changes color to indicate the current shuffle mode status, with blue being ON and white being OFF.

3. **Tap the album artwork image again to return to the normal Now Playing screen.**

**Note** The iPod touch and iPhone do not presently support an album shuffle mode.

# Viewing Lyrics on the Go

Recent-model iPods have introduced the ability to view lyrics on your iPod, provided that these lyrics have been previously added to the tracks in iTunes. At this time, no purchased music from the iTunes Store includes lyrics, and so you're going to have to add these yourself. Chapter 3 discusses more about how to add lyrics to your tracks within iTunes.

Note that there is no specific option for lyric display on the iPod. In fact, the ability of the iPod to display lyrics at all remains hidden away unless you're actually playing a track that includes lyrics within the track.

If you're playing a track that includes lyrics on your fifth-generation iPod, iPod classic, or iPod nano, simply press the center SELECT button a few times to scroll through the different Now Playing screens until you see the lyrics appear.

If the track you are playing does not include lyrics, the iPod skips the lyrics screen entirely.

On the iPod touch or iPhone, displaying lyrics is even simpler: Just tap the album artwork from the Now Playing screen, and the lyrics overlay the album artwork.

Again, if the track you are playing does not include lyrics, no lyrics overlay is shown — only the track position and repeat and shuffle icons.

**Note** If you have recently added lyrics to your tracks and these are not appearing on your iPod, ensure that you have synchronized your changes from iTunes properly. Note that if you are using manual management for your iPod, you must recopy the tracks onto your iPod after adding lyrics, as you are not synchronizing changes from your main iTunes library in this case.

# Improving Your Podcast Experience

Listening to podcasts on the iPod can be a different experience from music playback, largely due to the episodic nature of these programs. Generally, most podcast listeners prefer to listen to new podcasts on a regular basis, and sometimes prefer to listen to several podcasts in sequence.

Although the iPod has supported podcasts since the fourth-generation models, there have been some changes and discrepancies to how podcasts are handled among different iPod models and firmware versions that you may find confusing, particularly if you've recently upgraded to a newer iPod.

The first thing that trips up most podcast enthusiasts is the change to Skip when Shuffling behavior in the recent iPod models. Podcasts downloaded by iTunes always have Skip when Shuffling enabled by default, and although you can change this for individual podcast episodes that you have already downloaded, you cannot change this default behavior for new episodes.

The problem comes into play when listening to podcasts with shuffle mode enabled on the iPod. In this case, the iPod plays a single podcast episode and then stops because all of the remaining podcast episodes are flagged to be skipped during shuffled playback. This has been the default behavior since the version 1.2 firmware update for the fifth-generation iPod, and continues onto the iPod classic and iPod nano.

In this case, if you want to listen to an entire series of podcast episodes, you must ensure that you disable shuffle on the iPod before you begin listening to the first podcast episode; otherwise, you can only play a single episode at a time. Even in this case, however, there are certain limitations:

- When playing podcasts from the Podcasts menu on the fourth-generation iPod nano, only the selected episode is played, after which the iPod stops, regardless of the shuffle settings.

- When playing podcasts from the Podcasts menu on the iPod classic and iPod nano, podcast episodes are listed in reverse-chronological order, with the newest episode at the top, which is the order they are played in.

**Note** Podcast behavior has been a bit of a moving target on the iPod and iPhone with each firmware update. For instance, prior to the iPhone and iPod touch v2.2 firmware, sequential podcast playback was not possible without using a Smart Playlist.

With these limitations in mind, a much better way to handle podcasts, if you regularly listen to several episodes in sequence, is to simply use playlists to organize your podcasts. You can either organize your podcasts into a standard playlist, or for more seamless podcast handling, create a Smart Playlist for each podcast that you would like to listen to in sequence:

1. **In iTunes, choose File ➪ New Smart Playlist from the iTunes menu.**

2. **Fill in the Smart Playlist dialog box, as shown in figure 8.8, specifying the title of the specific podcast that you would like to include in the Smart Playlist.**

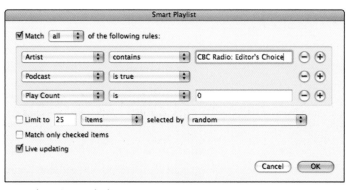

8.8 Podcast Smart Playlist

3. **Click OK.** The Smart Playlist dialog box closes, and the Smart Playlist appears in the iTunes Source list with the name highlighted for editing.

4. **Type a name for the Smart Playlist and press Return.**

5. **Select the Smart Playlist from the iTunes Source list.** Confirm that it includes the appropriate podcast episodes.

6. **Click the column heading for your preferred sort order (for example, Date Added).**

Once you have created this Smart Playlist and synced it to your iPod, you can listen to any unheard podcasts in the selected series from this playlist, instead of going to the Podcasts menu on the iPod. Further, as long as shuffle mode is turned off on your iPod, your podcast episodes are played sequentially in the order in which they were sorted in iTunes, and any podcasts you have listened to are removed from the Smart Playlist automatically.

**Genius**

You can also use a Smart Playlist to include episodes from several different podcasts. This can be useful if you listen to more than one podcast on a regular basis and want to group these episodes together in a single playlist.

# Adjusting Audiobook Playback Speed

One of the unique features of audiobooks on the iPod is that you can adjust their playback speed without affecting their overall sound quality. This feature is only available on tracks that have been properly imported as audiobooks, as described in Chapter 6.

To adjust audio playback speed on the iPod classic and iPod nano (with video), follow these steps:

1. **From your main iPod menu, select the Settings option.** The Settings menu is displayed.

2. **From the Settings menu, scroll to and select the Audiobooks option.** The iPod Audiobooks speed setting screen is displayed, as shown in figure 8.9.

3. **Use the click wheel to select your preferred audiobook playback speed, and press the center SELECT button.**

4. **Press the MENU button to return to the main menu.**

You can also adjust audiobook playback speed on the iPod touch and iPhone:

1. **From your home screen, tap the Settings icon.** The Settings menu is displayed.

2. **From the Settings menu, scroll to and tap the iPod option.** The iPod options menu is displayed, as shown in figure 8.10.

3. **Tap Audiobook Speed.** The audiobook speed options are displayed. Choices are Slower, Normal, and Faster.

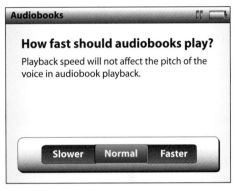

8.9 iPod Audiobooks speed setting screen

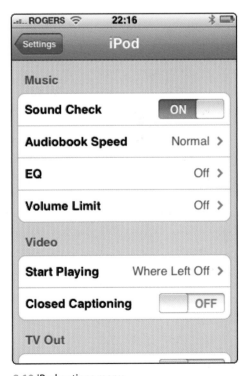

8.10 iPod options menu

4. **Tap the speed you would like your audiobooks to play at.**

5. **Press the HOME button to return to the home screen.**

# Listening to Music Videos

All of the iPod models that support video playback also support the storage and playback of music videos in addition to the other types of video content. However, music videos are normally treated as just another type of music content, and are organized alongside normal music tracks by the same artists.

Although you can play your music videos directly from the Videos menu on an iPod classic or iPod nano (with video), you can also access these same music videos from the Music section. When playing a music video from the Music menu, only the audio portion of the video is played back, with the normal Now Playing screen displayed as for any other audio track. This allows you to listen to your music videos mixed into your playlists alongside your normal tracks without having to actually display the video content on your iPod screen.

**Note**   Playing music videos in audio-only mode saves on the battery because the iPod screen is not used while these are being played. However, the iPod must still load in the entire video file, and with hard drive-based iPod models, this larger file results in more frequent hard disk access, which can still adversely affect battery life.

Prior to the new v2.0 firmware update, this worked the same way on the iPod touch and iPhone. As of v2.0, however, the iPod touch and iPhone now play music videos, regardless of where they are selected from. Music videos played from a normal playlist or track listing can be played in either portrait or landscape orientation, and can continue playing with the iPhone or iPod touch screen off.

# Using the On-The-Go Playlist

Normally, you build and manage your playlists in iTunes and then transfer them onto your iPod; however, the iPod also supports one special type of playlist known as the On-The-Go playlist. This allows you to queue up a list of tracks from your iPod into a temporary playlist. You can add and remove tracks from the On-The-Go playlist, and even re-order this playlist if you're using an iPod touch or iPhone.

When you sync your device with iTunes, the On-The-Go playlist is transferred back to iTunes, where you can rename it, reorganize it, or simply delete it.

On the traditional iPod models, such as the iPod classic, iPod nano (with video), and earlier, the On-The-Go playlist can be found at the bottom of your playlist menu. By default, the On-The-Go playlist is empty, and selecting it provides basic instructions on how to add tracks to this playlist, as shown in figure 8.11.

To add tracks to the On-The-Go playlist on an iPod classic or iPod nano, follow these steps:

1. **Locate the track that you want to add by browsing through the iPod Music window.**

2. **Press and hold the center SELECT button for about 1 second until the highlight bar flashes.**

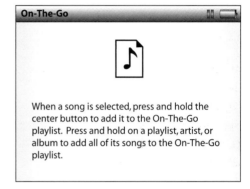

When a song is selected, press and hold the center button to add it to the On-The-Go playlist. Press and hold on a playlist, artist, or album to add all of its songs to the On-The-Go playlist.

**8.11** On-The-Go playlist on an iPod classic

**Note**  You can also add entire albums, artists, genres, or even other playlists; simply hold the center SELECT button on the appropriate menu entry rather than the individual track.

Removing items from the On-The-Go playlist is done in much the same way: Highlight the item that you want to remove and hold the center SELECT button on the iPod.

On the iPhone and iPod touch, the On-The-Go playlist behaves a bit differently. The On-The-Go playlist is listed near the top of your playlist menu, as shown in figure 8.12.

**Note**  On the 2008 iPod classic (120GB) and the fourth-generation iPod nano, holding down the center SELECT button presents an options menu instead of simply adding the current track to the On-The-Go playlist. With these models, simply select Add to On-The-Go from this pop-up menu when it appears.

Rather than adding items directly from the normal track browser menu, you go into the On-The-Go playlist to add tracks from there:

1. **From the top of the playlist menu, tap On-The-Go.** You are shown a list of all available songs, similar to figure 8.13.

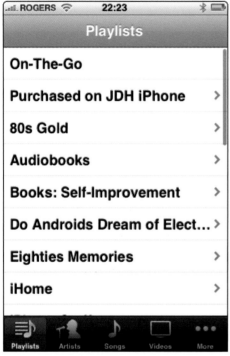

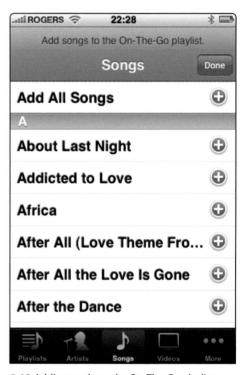

8.12 On-The-Go playlist on an iPhone    8.13 Adding tracks to the On-The-Go playlist

2. **Scroll to locate the song you want to add, and tap it to add it to your On-The-Go playlist.** You may also tap Add All Songs to add all of your songs to the On-The-Go playlist, or use the other menu buttons at the bottom of the screen to browse by other categories, such as playlist, artist, or album.

3. **Continue selecting songs to add to the On-The-Go playlist by browsing and tapping on those songs you want to add.**

4. **Tap Done.**

The iPhone and iPod touch also enable you to re-order tracks in an On-The-Go playlist directly on the device. To edit an On-The-Go playlist on the iPod touch or iPhone, follow these steps:

1. **From the top of the playlist menu, tap On-The-Go.** You are shown the current list of tracks in the On-The-Go playlist.

2. **Tap the Edit button.** The playlist switches to edit mode, similar to figure 8.14.

3. **You can make a few different edits from here:**

   - To move a track up or down in the playlist, tap and hold the icon to the right of the track name, and drag your finger up or down.

   - To remove a track from the playlist, tap the red delete icon at the left side of the track name.

   - To remove all tracks from the On-The-Go playlist, tap Clear Playlist at the top of the screen.

   - To add more tracks, tap the Plus button at the top-left corner of the screen.

4. **Tap Done when you are finished editing.**

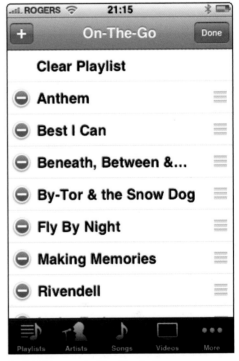

8.14 Editing an On-The-Go playlist

During the next sync, your On-The-Go playlist is transferred to your iTunes library as a new playlist, and the current On-The-Go playlist on the device is cleared. The new playlist created in iTunes may be renamed, edited, or deleted as with any other standard playlist.

# Creating and Using Genius Playlists

With the addition of the Genius feature in iTunes 8, the 2008 iPod classic and fourth-generation iPod nano also include direct support for creating and saving Genius playlists directly on your iPod. Support for this feature was also added to the iPhone and iPod touch through the v2.1 firmware update, and the Apple TV in the v2.2 firmware update.

The on-device Genius support allows your Genius playlists from iTunes to be recognized as Genius playlists and modified on the device. Further, Genius playlists may be created directly on your device and are automatically transferred back to iTunes during the next sync.

**Note**

Once you have enabled Genius in your iTunes library, you must sync your device with iTunes at least once before the Genius feature works on the device.

To create a Genius playlist on the 2008 iPod classic or fourth-generation iPod nano, follow these steps:

1. **Locate a song that you would like to use as the basis for your Genius list.** You can either find a song on the iPod track listing or use the currently playing track.

2. **Press and hold the center SELECT button for about 1 second until a menu appears, similar to figure 8.15.**

3. **From the menu, select Start Genius.** The current track is used to create a Genius playlist of 25 tracks, and the resulting list is displayed, similar to figure 8.16.

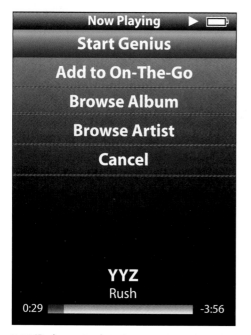

8.15 iPod nano track options menu

8.16 iPod nano Genius listing

184

**Note** Genius playlists created directly on your device are always limited to 25 tracks. You can, however, save them and sync them back to iTunes, where you can select a larger number of tracks.

From the Genius listing, you can simply begin playing back the content of your Genius playlist, refresh the content to select different tracks, or save the Genius listing as a separate playlist.

Selecting Save Playlist saves your Genius listing as a playlist named after the main track. This playlist is transferred back into iTunes the next time you synchronize your iPod.

**Genius** You can also refresh existing Genius playlists on your iPod, regardless of where they were created. Refreshed playlists are updated in iTunes when you sync your iPod.

Note that if you do not have sufficient tracks on your iPod to create a Genius listing, you instead receive an error message similar to figure 8.17, indicating that Genius is not available.

This message usually means that there are not enough tracks loaded onto your device to build a Genius listing. You may, however, still be able to create a Genius listing in iTunes, save it as a playlist, and then sync it with your device from iTunes. Additional tracks are copied from iTunes to your device as they would be for any other playlist.

On the iPhone and iPod touch, the concept behind creating a Genius playlist is the same, but the actual process differs slightly. To create a Genius playlist from the main playlist menu, follow these steps:

8.17 iPod nano screen stating that Genius is not available

1. **From the Playlists menu, select the Genius option, as shown in figure 8.18.**

2. **Browse for a song to use to create your Genius listing.** A Genius playlist is created and the selected song begins playing.

185

3. **To view your Genius listing, tap the left arrow button shown at the top-left corner of the Now Playing screen.** The Genius track listing appears, as shown in figure 8.19.

4. **Tap the Save button to save the Genius listing as a new playlist.**

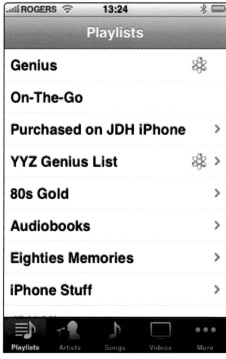

**8.18** Selecting the iPhone Genius option

**8.19** iPhone Genius track listing

You may also refresh your Genius listing with new tracks prior to saving it by tapping the Refresh button, or start over with a new Genius listing by tapping the New button.

**Genius**    You can also create a Genius listing directly from the Now Playing screen on your iPhone or iPod touch by tapping the screen and then tapping the Genius icon that appears at the center near the top of the screen.

As with the other iPod models, Genius playlists saved on your device are transferred back to iTunes during the next sync, and Genius playlists created from iTunes can be edited and refreshed on the device.

**Caution** While you can play your tracks directly from the main Genius listing, this queue is not saved back to iTunes when you sync your iPhone or iPod, and is actually cleared after you sync. Always ensure that you save your Genius listings as Genius playlists before syncing if you want to keep them.

# Connecting Your iPod to a TV

With the obvious exception of the iPod shuffle, all of the current iPod models now have the ability to display video on the iPod, but if you're tired of squinting at your iPod screen, you'll be happy to know that you can also view your iPod's video content on a normal television screen with the appropriate cables.

However, the question of which cables are appropriate for your iPod can be a bit complicated. Apple first brought video capabilities to the iPod with the fifth-generation iPod, released in 2005, and for two years this was the only video-capable iPod. This model supported video output through the iPod headphone jack with a simple minijack-to-RCA cable, such as the one shown in figure 8.20. Further, you could output video through the iPod Dock Connector with a variety of third-party cables and accessories, none of which required any more technology than the ability to take the video signal from the Dock Connector pins and push it out through a standard RCA video connection.

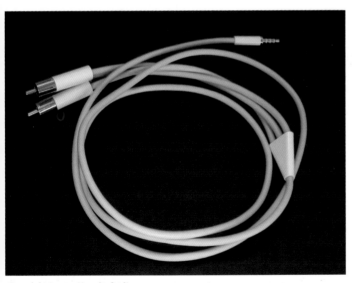

*Copyright Jeremy Horwitz for iLounge.com*

**8.20** iPod AV cable

**Genius**   If you have a fifth-generation iPod, you can use just about any camcorder minijack-to-RCA video cable with your iPod. Simply reverse the yellow and red leads when connecting it to your TV.

Unfortunately, when Apple released the 2007 iPod models — the iPod classic, iPod nano (with video), and iPod touch — it removed the ability to output video through the headphone port, rendering the first category of iPod video cables obsolete. More importantly, however, it also chose to restrict video output through the Dock Connector port to those accessories that were approved by Apple through the use of an authentication chip. It was no longer enough to build a video cable that took the video from the Dock Connector — rather, the accessory had to include an authentication chip supplied by Apple to unlock the video output capabilities. Without the presence of this chip, the iPod would simply refuse to output video through the accessory.

This had the unfortunate impact of rendering all video accessories manufactured for the fifth-generation iPod completely incompatible with the iPod classic. Users upgrading from the 5G iPod to the iPod classic (or iPod nano, iPod touch, or iPhone) had to buy new video accessory cables certified for these devices, and for the first six months, the only cables available were Apple's own Composite AV or Component AV cables, shown in figure 8.21, which were a bit on the expensive side compared to the fifth-generation AV cables.

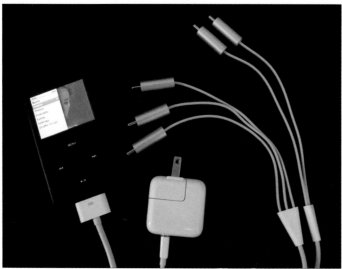

*Copyright Jeremy Horwitz for iLounge.com*

**8.21** Apple Composite AV cable

The bottom line is that when purchasing a video cable or other video-related accessory for your iPod, ensure that you check the packaging carefully to confirm that the cable or accessory is, in fact, compatible with your particular model of iPod (ie, the iPod classic, iPod nano (with video), and/or iPod touch). With the fifth-generation iPod on the market for over two years, many video accessories were manufactured for that model and simply listed as iPod-compatible. If in doubt, always do some online research before spending money on a cable. Sites like iLounge.com provide reviews of a wide range of iPod accessories, including AV cables.

**Caution** Beware of cables from unknown manufacturers that claim compatibility with the iPhone or newer iPod models. Building a video cable for the newer iPods requires a licensed authentication chip from Apple, and so only Apple Made-for-iPod-certified partners can manufacture these cables. Further, the licensing costs involved mean that these cables generally cost at least $30.

Once you have the appropriate cable and it's connected to your iPod and your TV, the next step is to enable TV output on the iPod. On the iPod classic and iPod nano (with video), follow these steps:

1. **From the iPod main menu, select Videos.** The Videos menu appears.

2. **From the Videos menu, select Settings.** The Settings menu appears.

3. **Select TV Out, as shown in figure 8.22, and press the center SELECT button.** The TV Out setting toggles between the following three options:

   - **Off.** Video is displayed on the iPod screen.

   - **Ask.** Whenever you start a video, the iPod asks whether you would like to use the screen or TV output.

   - **On.** Video is displayed using the TV output connection.

4. **Press MENU twice to return to the main menu.**

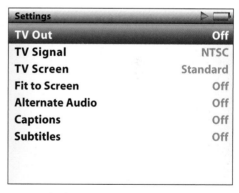

8.22 iPod video Settings menu

If no compatible video cable is detected, the iPod classic and iPod nano display a message asking you to connect a video accessory, similar to figure 8.23. If you see this message, check to ensure that your video cable is connected directly to your iPod and that you are in fact using a compatible video cable.

On the iPod touch and iPhone, the process is somewhat simpler: Just ensure that the video cable is connected before starting video playback, and you are prompted as to whether or not you want to use the TV output, similar to figure 8.24. Note that some AV cables trigger the video output on the iPhone or iPod touch automatically, without prompting.

If this prompt does not appear and your video still plays directly on your device's screen, then ensure that your video cable is connected directly to your iPod touch or iPhone rather than through a dock or extension cable, and that you do, in fact, have an iPod touch- or iPhone-compatible video cable.

**TV Out Enabled**
Please Connect Video Accessory

**8.23** Connect Video Accessory warning

**8.24** Display on TV prompt on an iPhone

**Genius**

A variety of video output accessories are available for the iPod, ranging from portable video displays to wearable video glasses. Despite the name, all video accessories connect to the iPod using the TV Out functionality. The same cautions apply with regards to video accessory compatibility, however — always ensure that the device you're thinking of purchasing is compatible with your particular iPod model.

# Adjusting Your iPod Video Settings for Optimal Display

When displaying video content on your iPod, you may find that the display is less than ideal, depending on the source content. Further, you may also need to adjust your settings for TV output, depending on what type of television you are connecting your iPod to.

These discrepancies exist primarily because some TV shows and movies use a different aspect ratio from the iPod screen. To put it simply, most movies today are released in a widescreen format, while the iPod still uses the traditional 4:3 aspect ratio from standard televisions. See Chapter 9 for more information on aspect ratios.

Although the iPod screen fits traditional TV content with no problems, when watching widescreen movies on the iPod screen, the content does not fit perfectly on the screen. Instead, your movies are either displayed in a letterbox format with black bars at the top and bottom, or they are displayed to fill the entire screen with the left and right edges cropped.

You can choose which playback mode you prefer by going into your iPod video settings:

1. **From the iPod main menu, select Videos.** The Videos menu appears.

2. **From the Videos menu, select Settings.** The Settings menu appears, similar to figure 8.25.

3. **Select Fit to Screen and press the center SELECT button.** The Fit to Screen option toggles between ON and OFF each time you press the SELECT button. OFF presents your widescreen content in a letterbox format, while ON zooms in on the screen, cropping the sides to fit the image to the screen.

4. **Press MENU twice to return to the main menu.**

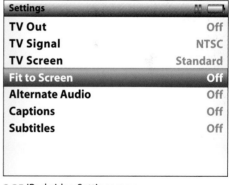

8.25 iPod video Settings menu

When displaying your iPod content on a TV, you must also specify whether you are using a standard 4:3 TV set or a widescreen 16:9 TV set so that your iPod knows how to present the TV output in the proper aspect ratio:

1. **From the iPod main menu, select Videos.** The Videos menu appears.

2. **From the Videos menu, select Settings.** The Settings menu appears, similar to figure 8.26.

3. **Select TV Screen and press the center SELECT button.** The TV Screen option toggles between Standard and Widescreen.

4. **Press MENU twice to return to the main menu.**

On the iPod touch and the iPhone, the aspect ratio issue on-screen is handled a bit differently. First, the iPod touch and iPhone each use an aspect ratio midway between standard TV and widescreen, meaning that they can handle both aspect ratios reasonably well, with either minimal letterboxing or minimal cropping. Secondly, instead of a Fit to Screen setting, the iPod touch and iPhone zoom in and out simply by double-tapping the screen while a video is playing.

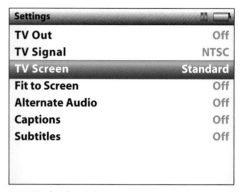

8.26 iPod video Settings menu

For TV output from the iPod touch and iPhone, you must still select your appropriate TV type, however:

1. **From your home screen, tap the Settings icon.** The Settings menu is displayed.

2. **From the Settings menu, scroll to and tap the iPod option.**

3. **Scroll down to the TV Out section, as shown in figure 8.27.**

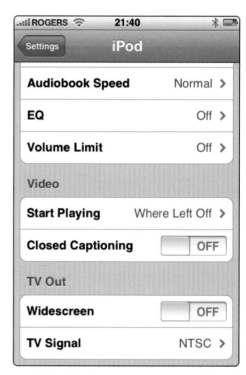

8.27 iPhone iPod options menu

4. Tap the button beside Widescreen to toggle the setting on or off, depending on the TV that you are connecting your device to.

5. Press the HOME button to return to the home screen.

**Note**

If your videos look distorted when playing them back on your TV, chances are that the TV Screen setting is incorrect. Try changing this setting to see if this resolves the problem. If not, then there may be an encoding problem with the video file, particularly if this is a video that was encoded from a source other than the iTunes Store. See Chapter 9 for more information on encoding your own videos.

# How Do I Get My Own Movies onto My iPod?

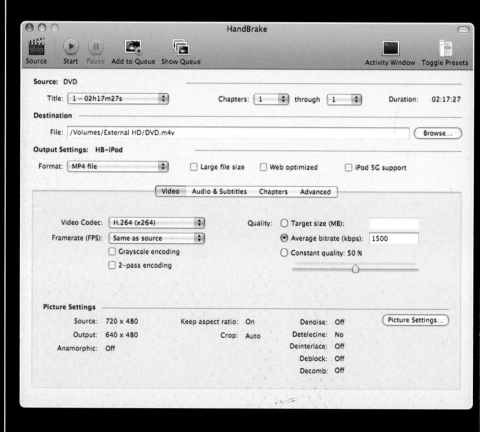

The iTunes Store is a great source of video content for your iPod, but it is not the only option available. Further, you might not even live in a country where video content is available on the iTunes Store. Fortunately, you can also encode your own movies and other videos into an iPod-ready format through the use of a variety of third-party tools.

# About Converting Video for the iPod

Unlike the world of digital audio formats, where the MP3 format is the reigning standard, the world of digital video formats can be much more confusing. At this point, there is no single standard video format, and therefore you are going to find a wide variety of different formats on the Internet, and a wide variety of conversion tools to support these different formats. Further, even videos that you record yourself are unlikely to be in an iPod-ready format and will therefore also require conversion for viewing on your iPod.

The most important point to keep in mind when converting video for the iPod is that the iPod actually supports a very limited set of video formats and display resolutions, so you must convert your videos into an iPod-ready format. To add to the confusion, iTunes supports a much wider range of video formats than the iPod, so being able to watch a video in iTunes is not an indication that it can be played on your iPod.

## Video formats supported by the iPod

The iPod supports video formats based on the MPEG-4 standard, subject to certain limitations, which are discussed shortly. Specifically, the iPod supports the MPEG-4 standard, and the H.264 standard, which is an evolution of the MPEG-4 standard optimized for portable devices with smaller file sizes at the same quality level.

The original fifth-generation iPod introduced video playback into the iPod family at a very limited 320 × 240 resolution. Because this resolution is still the size of the iPod classic screen today, this may not have seemed like a serious problem, until you consider that the iPod supported TV output capabilities, and even the most basic television can display a 640 × 480 image. The result was that the videos played back from the original fifth-generation iPod on a television generally looked somewhat blurry.

Fortunately, Apple chose to increase this maximum resolution to 640 × 480 in subsequent firmware updates. Today, all iPod models, including the iPod touch and iPhone, support this 640 × 480 resolution for their video content, a resolution suitable for display on any standard television set.

In addition to these maximum resolutions, the iPod is also limited to certain maximum bit-rates for video content. The published specifications indicate a maximum bit-rate of 1500 kbps for H.264 files and 2500 kbps for MPEG-4 files, although in my experience you can get away with pushing these slightly higher, depending on your source video.

Keep in mind that iTunes supports any video format that can be played by QuickTime. As a result, just because your video can be imported into iTunes does not mean that it can play on your iPod.

## Recommended video conversion settings

For most video content, the recommended conversion format is H.264 in a 640 × 480 resolution at 1500 kbps (or 1.5 Mbps). The H.264 format provides equivalent quality at a lower bit-rate, and therefore a smaller file size and more efficient battery life.

In principle, video bit-rates work in much the same way as audio bit-rates do. Put simply, a lower bit-rate produces a smaller file size while sacrificing quality, because there is less data available to store the actual video content. With video files, however, there is a direct correlation between the resolution of a video and its bit-rate. Because higher-resolution videos contain more data (more pixels on the screen), a higher bit-rate is needed to produce an acceptable quality. The iPod's standard limit of 1500 kbps at 640 × 480 is typical of the generally acceptable bit-rates for the H.264 codec, and generally produces standard TV-quality video, depending largely on the source material.

**Note** When choosing your bit-rate, keep in mind that the way digital video compression works, the optimal bit-rate is based on the amount of motion in the video. Compressed digital video formats work by encoding the differences and motion between frames, so a video of a newscaster talking is going to require less data to effectively reproduce than an action movie.

When converting video content, it is also important to keep in mind the intended playback methods to be used. If you are converting video solely for playback on your iPod screen, for example, and never intend to play this video back on a TV screen, you can get away with much smaller files by encoding at 320 × 240 (the size of the iPod's screen), and therefore also use a lower bit-rate of approximately 750 kbps to produce an acceptable-quality video file. Keep in mind, however, that the encoding process for your own videos takes a while, so it's always a good idea to plan for the future rather than having to go back and reconvert your videos into a higher-quality format.

**Note** The Apple TV permits much higher resolutions and bit-rates for your videos: up to 1280 × 720 (720p HD) resolution at bit-rates of up to 4000 kbps (4 Mbps). However, videos encoded in these higher resolutions cannot be played on your iPod or iPhone.

## Aspect Ratio

One other concern when dealing with video conversion is the aspect ratio. The aspect ratio of a video refers to the ratio between the width of the image and the height of the image, and can also be thought of as how square or rectangular the image is. There are three common aspect ratios in use today:

- **4:3 (or 1.33:1)** is used for some older movies and most standard-definition TV content. Standard TV screens use this aspect ratio, and this is also the aspect ratio used by the fifth-generation iPod, iPod classic, and iPod nano (with video).

- **16:9 (or 1.78:1)** is the standard widescreen format used by some movies and all high-definition TV content. Widescreen and HDTV screens use this aspect ratio and this is the native aspect ratio of the Apple TV.

- **2.35:1**, also known as Cinemascope, is an extremely widescreen presentation used by many theatrical movies. There are very few home-based devices available that use this aspect ratio — it is normally only seen in movie theaters.

Knowing which aspect ratio your source material uses is often useful for ensuring the best-quality conversion. The aspect ratio of a video can be computed simply by dividing the width of the video by the height. For example, for a 640 × 480 video, you would divide 640 by 480, yielding an amount of 1.33, making the aspect ratio of a 640 × 480 video 1.33:1.

# Converting DVDs

In the same way that many iPod and iTunes users begin with an established library of music on CDs, you may also have a collection of existing DVDs that you want to be able to play on your iPod. Unfortunately, while iTunes makes importing CDs extremely easy, DVD conversion is a more complicated process, both due to the video formats involved and the legal issues around the conversion of copy-protected DVDs. Put simply, Apple cannot legally include DVD-importing technology within iTunes, at least not for copy-protected content.

However, in many other countries the copyright laws do not prohibit you from converting content you already own into another format, regardless of whether or not it is copy protected. If you live in one of these countries, there are a number of ways that you can do this with third-party software.

**Caution** The legality of copying commercial DVDs varies in different countries. For example, in the United States, the Digital Millennium Copyright Act effectively makes it illegal to copy a commercial DVD's content for any reason due to digital copy protection. Always be sure to check the laws in your particular jurisdiction.

# Using Handbrake for one-step DVD conversion

The most popular software application for converting your DVDs into an iPod-ready format is Handbrake (www.handbrake.fr). This is a free, open-source application that can handle the entire process for you, including extracting the content from the DVD and converting it into an iPod-ready format.

The Handbrake application provides a wide range of options for advanced users, while also being perfect for users who want a simple way to convert their DVDs into an iPod-ready format. Handbrake provides a standard iPod preset that creates H.264 video files in a 640 × 480 resolution at 1500 kbps, and preserves the original aspect ratio of the source video.

To convert a DVD using Handbrake, follow these steps:

1. **Insert the DVD into your computer's DVD drive.**

2. **Start Handbrake.** On initial startup, Handbrake prompts you to select a video source with a standard file open dialog box, as shown in figure 9.1. If this does not appear, click the Source button in the top-left corner to open the file selection dialog box.

9.1 The Handbrake file open dialog box

**Note** Handbrake is available for both Mac OS X and Windows, although the Windows version does not include the ability to decrypt copy-protected DVDs due to the lack of Windows versions of the necessary open-source libraries. Windows users can still use Handbrake to copy unprotected DVDs, and may want to look for a tool called DVD43, which can present a copy-protected DVD to Handbrake as if it were unprotected. However, you should always consult the laws in your particular jurisdiction before using a tool like this.

3. **Choose your DVD from the file open dialog box and click Open.** Handbrake scans the DVD content and displays the main Handbrake window, similar to figure 9.2.

4. **From the Title drop-down menu, choose the title for the main video feature.** Most DVDs have multiple titles for additional content, previews, special features, and so forth. The length of each title is shown beside the title number. For a DVD movie, the main title is usually the longest one.

5. **Click the Browse button under Destination to choose a destination file and folder for the converted DVD file.**

9.2 The Handbrake main window

**6. From the presets list on the right, choose HB-iPod to load the Handbrake iPod preset.**
Click the Toggle Presets button in the top-right corner if the presets list does not appear.

**7. Click Start to begin conversion.**

Handbrake begins converting the selected title from the DVD into an H.264 file. This process can take anywhere from 2 to 10 hours for an average movie. When the process is complete, the resulting MP4 file can be imported directly into your iTunes library.

**Genius**

If you want to convert multiple titles from the same DVD in one session, click the Add to Queue button instead of the Start button. Handbrake adds the currently selected title to the queue, and you can then select another title from the same DVD. When you are finished adding to the queue, click the Start button to begin conversion.

## Anamorphic Encoding

Standard DVDs store their video files in a 720 × 480 resolution, which works out to a 1.5:1 aspect ratio. It may occur to you that this doesn't match either of the standard TV or widescreen aspect ratios. This is because DVDs actually use a process known as anamorphic encoding to either stretch or compress the video image, depending on the required aspect ratio.

What is happening in this case is that the video is actually stored on the DVD in a 1.5:1 aspect ratio, and the DVD player or playback application is advised to either stretch the video to 854 × 480 for widescreen (16:9) presentation, or compress it to 640 × 480 for standard TV (4:3) presentation, depending on the content. DVD players also add letter-boxing (black bars above and below the image) or pillarboxing (black bars to the sides of the image) as necessary to present the full-screen image, regardless of the aspect ratio of your TV set. This is done by setting a Pixel Aspect Ratio (PAR) flag, which renders the pixels as rectangular instead of square.

This comes into play for your own video conversion as the iPod also supports the PAR flag, which means you can use anamorphic encoding for your own iPod videos with an application that supports it, such as Handbrake. This is especially useful with widescreen content, because a 16:9 movie without anamorphic encoding can only be a maximum of 640 × 352 resolution, whereas anamorphic encoding can take a 640 × 480 video and stretch it to 854 × 480, pushing the vertical resolution to the full 480 lines used by standard television sets and producing much better on-TV output quality.

# Importing digital copies from DVD

In January 2008, several movie studios began including iPod-compatible digital copies with some of their DVD releases. This provides a simple and legal means to import these DVDs directly into iTunes while still preserving the copy protection of the original DVD.

Digital copies are normally included on a second disc, separate from the standard DVD that you would play back in your DVD player. This second disc is encoded in a format that is specifically designed to be imported into iTunes when inserted into your computer. Digital copies also normally come with an insert containing an unlock code that you must enter during import.

Keep in mind that you must have an iTunes Store account to use a digital copy, as the digital copy remains copy protected and tied to your iTunes Store account in the same way as any item purchased from the iTunes Store.

To import a digital copy into your iTunes library, follow these steps:

1.  **Check to ensure that you are using iTunes 7.6 or later.** Previous versions of iTunes do not support digital copy technology.

2.  **Insert the digital copy disc into your computer.** iTunes should detect the digital copy disc and display it in the iTunes Source list in the same way that an audio CD would appear.

3.  **Select the entry for the digital copy disc from your iTunes Source list.** An information and import screen should appear, similar to figure 9.3.

4.  **Type the code that came with your DVD, and click the Redeem button.**

iTunes begins importing the digital copy into your iTunes movie library. This process occurs in the same manner as when a movie is downloaded from the iTunes Store, and, in fact, the import even appears in the normal download queue. In this case, however, the download is actually occurring from the DVD to your iTunes library, rather than over the Internet.

**Note**    Even though Digital Copies come from your DVD, you must still be connected to the Internet when importing them in order to authorize them with the iTunes Store.

Once imported, the digital copy is stored as a copy-protected movie in your iTunes library in the same way as any other movie purchased from the iTunes Store, with the same usage restrictions applied to it. The code contained within the DVD packaging is essentially an activation code that ties the digital copy to your iTunes Store account as a zero-dollar purchase. In fact, you even receive an e-mail receipt from the iTunes Store. You may use the same code from the DVD packaging to re-import the digital copy as often as you like using the same iTunes Store account, but you cannot use this code with any other iTunes Store account.

**9.3** An iTunes digital copy import screen

**Caution** Not all digital copies provided with DVD releases are iTunes compatible. Always be sure to check the fine print on a DVD package before purchasing it for the digital copy feature.

# Converting unprotected DVD VOB files

If you are working with noncopy-protected DVDs, or you've already extracted the DVDs into an unprotected format using another DVD extraction tool, you have a few more options for conversion.

The video files on DVDs use a VOB extension, but in reality these are just MPEG-2 format files, and you can therefore view or convert them with any number of tools that can read the MPEG-2 format. The only problem is that if you're reading the VOB files directly from the DVD, there is rarely a one-to-one match between VOB files and DVD content, so it may be difficult to find or stitch together the exact files you're looking for.

Handbrake can still read an unprotected DVD, of course, but another tool that is worth looking at for this purpose, particularly if your conversion needs are more complex, is MPEG Streamclip, available for free from www.squared5.com. This is a tool designed for the express purpose of working with various flavors of MPEG video content, and it provides editing capabilities in addition to the ability to convert these files into an iPod-ready format.

# Converting Video Files

In addition to converting your own DVDs, you may find various video files from other sources on the Internet that you want to copy onto your iPod. There are a considerable number of tools available today to convert just about any unprotected video format into the H.264 format used by the iPod.

**Note**

Video files that you download from the Internet come in a wide variety of formats and resolutions. One important thing to keep in mind is to adjust your output settings to match the source file. Nothing is gained by converting a 160 × 120 video clip to 640 × 480, except wasted space.

## Converting video files with QuickTime and iTunes

The first and simplest tool, if not the fastest, is iTunes. Although the iPod's supported formats are quite limited, iTunes can import and play any video supported by QuickTime.

If you can import your video and play it in iTunes, then you can convert it directly within iTunes, without the need for any other third-party software:

1. **Import your original video into iTunes.** Your video appears in the Movies section by default.

2. **Select Movies in the Source list, and locate and select the video that you just imported.**

3. **From the iTunes Advanced menu, choose Create iPod or iPhone Version to create a version that can be played on your iPod, iPhone, or Apple TV, or Create Apple TV Version to create a version using the higher-quality Apple TV settings.** iTunes begins converting the video, with its progress displayed in the status panel at the top of the iTunes window, as shown in figure 9.4.

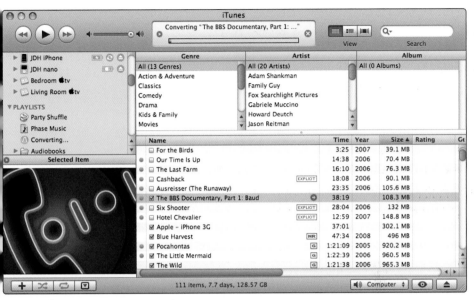

**9.4** The video conversion status panel

4. **When conversion is completed, a second copy of the movie appears in your iTunes library, ready to be synced to your iPod, iPhone, or Apple TV.**

**Note**
iPod or iPhone videos can also be played on the Apple TV, so the Create Apple TV Version option is only useful when you are converting higher-quality source material such as HD TV programming that can take advantage of the higher resolutions and bit-rates offered by the Apple TV and are not concerned about iPod or iPhone compatibility.

This method of conversion has the advantage of being built into iTunes so that no additional software is required; however, it does not support all formats and provides absolutely no conversion options. Further, QuickTime conversion to H.264 is presently the slowest of all of the tools that are available.

**Caution**
iTunes and QuickTime Pro can also convert MPEG-2 video files with the QuickTime MPEG-2 plug-in available from Apple. However, QuickTime does not support multiplexed MPEG video files. This usually results in the video being properly encoded, but having no actual audio track, and is a frequent source of confusion for many new users to iPod video conversion.

# Converting video files with third-party tools

If you are looking for either faster video conversion or support for more formats than QuickTime provides, there are a number of additional software tools that can assist you with this.

As of version 0.93, Handbrake now supports converting almost any standalone video file format into the H.264 format in much the same way as it does for DVDs discussed earlier in this chapter. Converting video files with Handbrake is handled in the same manner as converting DVDs — simply choose a file from the Source browser rather than a DVD.

To convert a video file using Handbrake, follow these steps:

1. **Start Handbrake.** On initial startup, Handbrake prompts you to select a video source with a standard file open dialog box. If this does not appear, click the Source button in the top-left corner to open the file selection dialog box.

2. **Choose your source file from the file open dialog box and click Open.**

3. **Click the Browse button under Destination to choose a destination file and folder for the converted file.**

4. **From the presets list on the right, choose HB-iPod to load the Handbrake iPod preset.** Click the Toggle Presets button in the top-right corner if the presets list does not appear.

5. **Click Start to begin conversion.**

**Note**

Another tool that was extremely popular among Mac users was iSquint from Techspansion. Unfotunately, in November 2008 Techspansion indicated that it would be ceasing further development of iSquint. That having been said, iSquint is a free and useful tool that can still be found on various software download sites if you're interested in checking it out.

Although Handbrake is available in both Mac and Windows versions, there are numerous other tools available for Windows users. The landscape of these video conversion applications for Windows users is much more varied and can be a bit confusing, although for basic video conversion, most of these tools perform similarly. One of the first iPod video conversion tools that still remains a popular choice today is Videora, a free conversion application that can be downloaded from www.videora.com.

# Converting Home Movies

Another type of content that you may be interested in converting for display on your iPod is your own home movies. Depending on how and when these were recorded, they may be in a range of different formats, but they are otherwise converted in much the same way as any other digital video file.

## Types of digital home video formats

Digital video cameras normally record in one of four possible formats:

- **DV.** Short for digital video, this is the standard format used by the first digital camcorders, and uses a minimally compressed video stream recorded onto a digital videotape. DV is normally transferred from the camcorder to your computer through a FireWire connection, although some cameras also provide USB transfer capabilities.

- **MPEG-2.** Similar to the format used by the DVD standard, some newer hard drive- and DVD-R-based camcorders have adopted the MPEG-2 format. Most camcorders that use the MPEG-2 format save recorded videos into a file system on either an internal hard drive or a recordable DVD. These files are then transferred either through USB or directly from the DVD onto the computer.

- **MPEG-4.** Some newer camcorders and most digital cameras and cell phones that provide video-recording capabilities record directly in different variations of the MPEG-4 format. Despite this format being directly supported by the iPod, not all cameras necessarily use a resolution or bit-rate that is iPod-compatible, and so these files may still require conversion. Recorded videos are usually stored on internal flash memory and transferred to your computer through a USB connection.

- **AVCHD.** This is a high-definition video format based on the H.264 codec to provide a high level of compression. As this is a high-definition format, however, videos are likely to be in a much higher resolution than is supported by the iPod, and therefore still require conversion into an iPod-ready format.

## Converting standard digital video

Standard digital video (DV) is usually transferred from your camcorder to your computer through a FireWire connection using an application such as iMovie or Windows Movie Maker. Because these videos must first be preprocessed by an actual video-authoring application, the usual method of converting these files into an iPod-ready format is to export them directly from these applications.

In fact, most recent versions of iMovie provide a direct iPod export option that uses the underlying QuickTime engine to generate an optimized iPod-compatible file that is transferred directly into your iTunes library.

Windows users may find this a bit more challenging, however, as the included Windows Movie Maker application does not provide any direct support for MPEG-4 or H.264 video output. In fact, almost all of its output formats are based on the Windows Media Video (WMV) codec. This makes it necessary to use another tool such as Videora to convert the resulting file into an iPod-compatible format.

**Genius**

When exporting videos from Windows Movie Maker for iPod conversion, use the DV-AVI output setting for the best results. DV-AVI provides the lowest amount of video compression, and is therefore less likely to suffer from additional quality loss that normally results from converting between lossy video formats.

## Converting MPEG-2 or MPEG-4 home video

If you are using a camcorder or digital camera that already encodes your videos into MPEG-2 or MPEG-4 formats, these are normally saved as files on your device and transferred to your computer through USB. These video files can be converted into an iPod-ready format using the same tools as for any other digital video file discussed earlier in this chapter.

## Converting VHS recordings

If you have old home movies on VHS videotapes, you can also convert these for viewing on your iPod, but the process is a bit more complicated and requires additional hardware.

The first and most important requirement for accomplishing this is a video capture card that you can use to connect your VCR to your computer, because you're essentially going to be recording your videotapes manually into your computer. Most capture cards available on the market today also include software to handle the recording aspects and save your recordings to a digital video file.

If your particular capture card and software support MPEG-4 or H.264 in the appropriate bit-rates and resolutions for the iPod, then this can make the conversion process much simpler. If not, you must save your captured videos into an intermediate format, and then use one of the tools discussed earlier in this chapter to perform the actual conversion for the iPod.

For Mac users, one very useful application for performing video capture and iPod conversion is the EyeTV software from Elgato. This software is normally included with video capture and TV tuner devices from Elgato, as well as several other manufacturers.

In addition to acting as a TV tuner/recorder, EyeTV provides a VHS Assistant feature (shown in figure 9.5), which guides you step by step through the process of connecting your VCR and capturing your VHS tapes, and then converting them into an iPod-ready format.

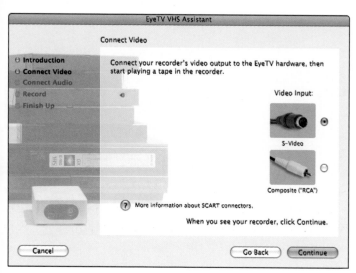

9.5 The Elgato EyeTV VHS Assistant window

# How Do I Get Content from My iPod Back to My Computer?

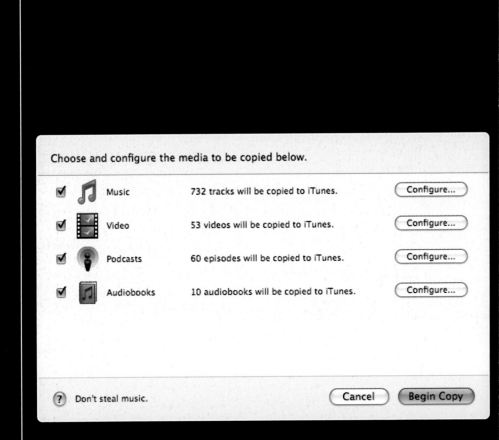

Choose and configure the media to be copied below.

| | | | | |
|---|---|---|---|---|
| ☑ | ♫ | Music | 732 tracks will be copied to iTunes. | Configure... |
| ☑ | 🎞 | Video | 53 videos will be copied to iTunes. | Configure... |
| ☑ | 👤 | Podcasts | 60 episodes will be copied to iTunes. | Configure... |
| ☑ | 📖 | Audiobooks | 10 audiobooks will be copied to iTunes. | Configure... |

(?) Don't steal music.

Cancel    Begin Copy

No matter how well you manage your content in your iTunes library, sooner or later you're going to come across the situation where you need to copy some or all of the content from your iPod back onto your computer. Unfortunately, iTunes has traditionally been a one-way conduit for your content — it flows from your computer out to your iPod, but seldom in the other direction. However, as with most things in the world of technology, where there is a will, there is a way, and many enterprising software developers have stepped in to fill the void.

# Transferring Purchased Content

For years, iTunes provided no means for getting back any content that was stored on your iPod. Content was synced from your computer to iTunes, but other than ratings and play counts, nothing was ever transferred back in the other direction.

iTunes 7 changed this slightly, however, by introducing the ability to transfer any content you have purchased from the iTunes Store back onto any of your authorized computers. This seemed like a reasonable enough compromise from the point of view of Apple, because although your iTunes purchases were potentially vulnerable to loss, presumably any music or other content that you had not purchased from the iTunes Store would be available on physical media in your CD collection.

The process for transferring purchases is intended for mass transfers of your purchased content to another library or recovery of purchased content in the event that you have lost your main iTunes library. This feature is an all-or-nothing deal in that there is no way to selectively transfer specific content from your iPod back to your computer; every purchased item on your iPod that the con-nected computer is authorized to play and that does not already exist in your iTunes library is copied back from your iPod.

To transfer purchases from your iPod back to your iTunes library, follow these steps:

1. **Ensure that the computer is author-ized for the iTunes Store account that corresponds to the content that you are transferring.** More information on authorizing your computer can be found in Chapter 2.

2. **Connect your iPod to your computer.**

3. **Right-click your iPod in the iTunes Devices list.** A context menu appears, similar to figure 10.1.

4. **From the context menu, choose Transfer Purchases.** iTunes scans through your iPod to locate any pur-chased content that the current com-puter is authorized to play and that does not already exist in the current library. These items are transferred back to your iTunes library.

10.1 An iPod context menu

The Transfer Purchases feature includes all types of purchased items that are found on your iPod, including not only music and video content, but also iPod or iPhone games and applications.

**Note** If you have content on your iPod that was purchased with different iTunes Store accounts, simply ensure that all of your accounts are authorized on your computer before using the Transfer Purchases feature. iTunes copies purchased content that is authorized by any account in the current iTunes library.

The Transfer Purchases feature works whether you are using automatic synchronization or managing your iPod content manually, and it can be used with any iTunes library that is authorized for your iTunes Store account. In fact, if you are using automatic synchronization and connect your iPod to a different iTunes library, you are given the option to transfer purchases in the standard warning dialog box that indicates that your iPod is linked to another iTunes library, as shown in figure 10.2.

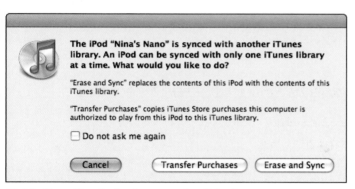

10.2 An iTunes Transfer Purchases warning dialog box

Note that a similar dialog box, shown in figure 10.3, also appears when you connect your iPod to your primary library if iTunes detects purchased content on the iPod that does not also exist in iTunes.

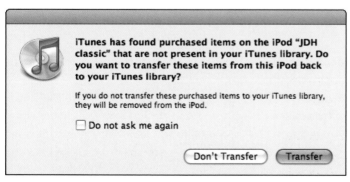

10.3 An iTunes Transfer Purchases warning dialog box

213

In this case, if you had recently deleted purchased items from your iTunes library intentionally, you would probably want to select the Don't Transfer option to remove these purchased items from your iPod as well.

**Caution**  If you have deleted nonpurchased items from your iTunes library that are still on your iPod, these are not transferred back by iTunes, and they are lost if you allow your iPod to automatically sync with your computer. With a different iTunes library, you are warned that your iPod is linked to a different library, but if you're syncing to the same library, iTunes removes any content from your iPod that is no longer in your iTunes library.

# Transferring Content Manually

The iTunes built-in capability for transferring your purchased content is a useful feature for moving iTunes purchases between libraries, but it is not a practical solution for recovering your entire library. This is because very few users have iTunes libraries that consist exclusively of purchased content.

Fortunately, if you're using a Click Wheel iPod model such as the iPod classic or iPod nano, there is actually a fairly straightforward way to copy all of the content from your iPod back to your computer en masse. The secret is that a traditional iPod model simply appears to your computer as an external USB mass storage device in the same way as any other external USB hard drive or memory key does. In fact, this is how iTunes communicates with your iPod, by simply copying your media files to it in the same way that Windows Explorer or the Mac Finder does, and updating the iPod's database directly. As a result of this, you can quite easily retrieve your music and video content from your iPod by copying it back in the other direction. All of your content is sitting on your iPod as files on a hard drive — you just have to know where to look for it.

**Note**  The iPhone and iPod touch use a completely different synchronization method and do not appear as external hard drives. As a result, manually copying your content off is not possible on these devices. If you're using one of these devices skip ahead to the next section and use a third-party application instead.

However, there are some difficulties in actually getting at your media content on your iPod. If you're trying to recover your content into a new iTunes library, the first problem is that iTunes is going to try and sync your iPod to the new, blank library, which could result in it erasing all of the content on your iPod. Many users are afraid to connect their iPod to a new computer for fear that they will lose the content on it by iTunes synchronizing it with a blank library. However, this is only a concern in the rare case that you have specifically deleted items from within your existing iTunes library database so that they're not even listed anymore. Even if you have lost the actual media files from your computer, iTunes does not remove anything from your iPod as long as it remains listed in your iTunes library.

However, if you're looking to recover all of the content from your iPod, chances are that you're starting over with a brand-new library database, either because you have formatted your computer and reinstalled your OS, or because you're using a new computer entirely. When you're using a new library, iTunes recognizes that your iPod has been automatically synchronized with a different library, notifies you of this, and asks you what you want to do, as shown in figure 10.4.

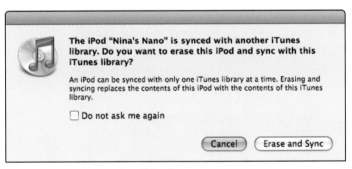

10.4 An iTunes sync warning dialog box

Simply click the Cancel button in this dialog box to prevent iTunes from performing an automatic sync. Your iPod remains connected and visible in iTunes, so you can adjust any other settings, but no synchronization occurs.

**Genius**

If you're recovering your iPod to a brand-new computer, or you have restored your computer from scratch, then the simplest method is to connect the iPod and copy the content off before you install iTunes. In this case, the iPod simply shows up as an external drive and you don't need to worry about avoiding interference from iTunes in the process.

In addition to iTunes trying to sync your iPod to a new library, the second problem is that iTunes does not normally leave your iPod connected long enough for you to see it appear as an external drive unless you have your iPod set to either manage the content on it manually or you have enabled disk use in iTunes. Basically, you have to tell iTunes that you want to access your iPod as an external hard drive; otherwise, it simply assumes that it no longer needs to remain connected after syncing.

1. **With your iPod connected to your computer, select it from the iTunes Devices list at the left side of your iTunes window.** A Summary screen appears, similar to figure 10.5.

10.5 The iPod Summary screen

2. **From the Summary screen, click the check box beside Enable disk use.**

3. **Click Apply to save this setting.** You may see a dialog box advising you that you now need to manually eject your iPod after use. If this dialog box appears, simply click OK to acknowledge it. Your iPod now appears as an external drive in Windows Explorer or the Mac Finder.

**Genius**

There's nothing particularly magical about the Enable disk use option in iTunes. Your iPod always appears to your computer as an external hard drive, regardless of whether this option is set. Enabling this option merely tells iTunes not to automatically eject your iPod when it's finished syncing.

Once you are able to access your iPod as an external drive through Windows Explorer or the Mac Finder, you then need to actually locate your media content on your iPod. The next problem is that the folder containing your content is actually hidden from normal view, and so you need to configure Windows Explorer or the Mac Finder to display hidden folders.

If you're using Windows, this setting can be found under your Folder options:

1. **From a Windows Explorer window, select Tools ⇨ Folder Options.** The Folder Options dialog box appears.

2. **Select the View tab.** The view options display, similar to figure 10.6.

3. **Click the radio button beside Show hidden files and folders.**

4. **Click OK.**

In Mac OS X, showing hidden files and folders is slightly more complicated, as you need to adjust a setting in the Mac OS X Terminal application.

1. **Open the Mac OS X Terminal application.** This can be found in your Applications/Utilities folder.

2. **At the Terminal prompt, type** defaults write com.apple.finder AppleShowAllFiles TRUE **and press Enter.**

3. **At the Terminal prompt, type** killall Finder **and press Enter.**

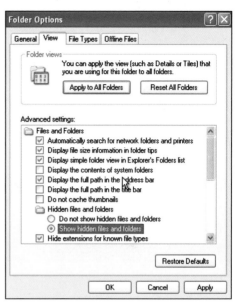

10.6 The View tab of the Windows Explorer Folder Options dialog box

The Mac OS X Finder application restarts, and you can then see all hidden files. To later turn off the display of hidden files, simply follow the same steps again, replacing TRUE with FALSE in step 2.

Once you have enabled the display of hidden files and folders, open Windows Explorer or the Mac Finder, and select your iPod from the list of drives. You should see a folder named iPod_Control at the very top level. This folder contains your iPod's internal database files, as well as all of your actual media content. Specifically, your media content can be found under the Music subfolder, laid out in a series of subfolders, similar to figure 10.7.

Despite the name, this folder contains all of your media content with the exception of your photos. Recovering photos from your iPod is covered at the end of this chapter.

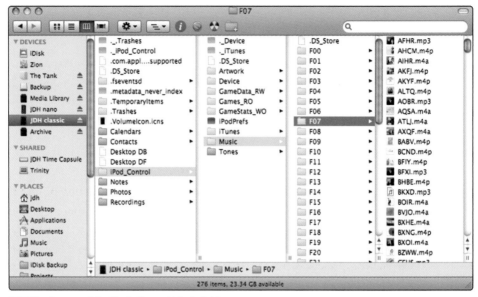

**10.7** The layout of the iPod_Control Music folder

You may notice that the files stored in this folder are not named in any useful manner. This is because iTunes renames them when transferring them onto your iPod to ensure that the filenames conform to the iPod's file system. Further, the files are not organized in any way that is meaningful to a person; they're merely spread out across a series of meaningless sub-folders. The good news, however, is that the actual tag information within these files is all completely intact, and in the end, iTunes only cares about the tags inside your files, and not the names of the files.

So, once you can actually see the files, recovering the content is really as simple as copying it all back onto your computer and then importing it into iTunes as you normally would for any other set of files.

**Note**

Traditional iPod models use a disk format specific to your host computer's operating system. Although Mac OS X can read Windows-formatted iPods, the reverse is not true. This means that if you are trying to recover a Mac-formatted iPod on a Windows PC you must install an additional software application such as MacDrive by MediaFour (www.mediafour.com) to allow your Windows PC to read your Mac-formatted iPod.

# Third-Party Programs for Transferring Music and Video Content

The manual method described earlier in this chapter is the most straightforward and inexpensive method for recovering content from your iPod. If you're in a situation where you've lost your entire iTunes library and simply want to get your content back without any concern for any of your additional library information such as playlists, ratings, and play counts, then the manual method works well and has the advantage of being free.

However, this method is not without its limitations. The first is that the layout of the files on the iPod makes it difficult to restore content selectively. If you need to pull off a single track or a set of tracks, the manual approach is not practical. Secondly, when copying your media content back to your computer manually, only the data that is stored within the actual media files is recovered. This includes most of the important information like track name, artist, album, and genre, but information such as ratings and play counts are only stored in the iTunes and iPod database and not in the actual files. The same thing applies to your playlists.

Fortunately, there are a number of third-party software applications available that know how to read the iPod database and not only selectively recover a listing of tracks, but in many cases recover your additional library data as well, such as ratings, play counts, and playlists. Many of these applications also work with the iPhone and iPod touch, for which the manual recovery method is not even possible due to the lack of direct disk access.

**Note** These applications are intended to assist you in recovering your own content from your iPod, a feature that Apple has omitted from the iTunes application in order to discourage piracy. The existence of these third-party tools should not be an encouragement to pillage content from other people's iPods.

The downside is that most of these applications are not free; you can expect to pay around $20 to $30 for a good iPod recovery application. The few free applications that are available are generally quite limited in how much data they can recover, and do not necessarily work with all iPod models.

**Caution** When looking for iPod recovery applications, always be sure that the application supports the iPod model you're looking to recover your content from and the version of iTunes you're looking to recover your content to. None of these applications are officially supported by Apple, and they usually need to be updated when a new iPod model or iTunes version comes along.

One of my preferred solutions for handling iPod recovery is a program called Music Rescue, by KennetNet Software (www.kennetnet.co.uk). This application is available for both the Mac and Windows platforms and supports all current iPod models including the iPhone and iPod touch. The application costs about $20; however, a trial version is available that is fully functional except for a registration reminder screen that comes up intermittently while copying data from your iPod.

Music Rescue offers a number of excellent advanced features over other software applications, including the ability to do a complete one-button recovery of your entire iPod back to your computer, or set up sophisticated rules to copy only selected content back. All additional metadata, such as ratings, play counts, last-played dates, skip counts, last-skipped dates, and playlists, are copied back during this process as well.

To perform a full recovery from your iPod using Music Rescue, follow these steps:

1. **Download and install the Music Rescue application.**

2. **Connect your iPod to your computer.** If you are using a traditional iPod model, ensure that the Enable disk use option has been checked, as described earlier in this chapter. If you are using an iPhone or iPod touch, you must have iTunes 7.4 or later already installed on the computer.

3. **Open Music Rescue.** Any iPod or iPhone devices attached to your computer are shown, similar to figure 10.8.

10.8 The Music Rescue iPod selection screen

4. **Select your iPod and click the QuickRecover button.** A QuickRecover welcome screen appears.

5. **Click Continue.** A Recovery Setup screen appears, similar to figure 10.9.

6. **Click the check boxes beside the types of content you would like to recover, and click the Continue button.** A setup screen appears for the first type of content you have selected, similar to figure 10.10.

10.9 The Music Rescue Recovery Setup screen

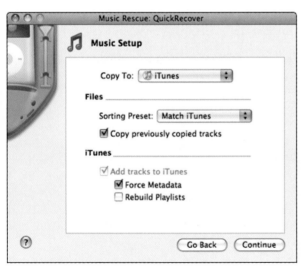

10.10 The Music Rescue Music Setup screen

7. **If you would like to recover your content to a location other than your iTunes library, select a different location from the Copy To drop-down menu.**

8. **If you do not want your recovered tracks automatically added to iTunes, click the check box beside Add tracks to iTunes to deselect it.**

9. **If you would like Music Rescue to also rebuild all of your playlists, click the check box beside Rebuild Playlists.**

221

10. **Click Continue to proceed to the next screen.** Similar setup screens appear for any other types of content that you selected in step 6.

11. **Repeat steps 7 to 10 for each subsequent screen.** When you have completed all of the setup screens, a Summary screen appears, similar to figure 10.11.

12. **Click Continue to begin copying content back to your computer.** A progress screen similar to figure 10.12 appears.

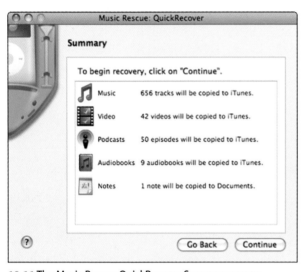

10.11 The Music Rescue QuickRecover Summary screen

10.12 The Music Rescue QuickRecover Copying progress screen

13. **Once the copying has completed, click Continue to close the Music Rescue: QuickRecover window.**

In addition to performing a full recovery of content from your iPod back to your computer, Music Rescue can also selectively recover individual tracks from your iPod.

1. **Download and install the Music Rescue application.**

2. **Connect your iPod to your computer.** If you are using a traditional iPod model, ensure that the Enable disk use option has been checked, as described earlier in this chapter. If you are using an iPhone or iPod touch, you must have iTunes 7.4 or later already installed on the computer.

3. **Open Music Rescue.** Any iPod or iPhone devices attached to your computer display.

4. **Select your iPod or iPhone and click the Open button.** The main Music Rescue window appears with a list of content on your iPod, similar to figure 10.13.

10.13 The Music Rescue main screen

5. **From the main Music Rescue screen, you can browse through your iPod content in much the same way as you would in your iTunes library, including your categories and playlists.** Note that Music Rescue also scans your iTunes library for matching items — a green dot to the far right of each item indicates that the item already exists in your iTunes library.

6. **To search for a specific item, type it into the Search box in the top-right corner of the Music Rescue window.**

7. **The check marks beside each item indicate which items are queued for copying to your computer.** If you want to select only a few items, choose Queue ➪ Unqueue All to clear all check marks on the current screen and then specifically check those items that you want copied.

8. **Once you have selected which items you want to copy back to your computer, click the Begin Copy button in the bottom-right corner.** A media selection screen appears, similar to figure 10.14.

9. **From this screen, click the check boxes beside each item type to select which types you want to copy to your computer.**

10. **To configure the copy settings for a specific item type, click the Configure button beside that item type.** A configuration screen appears, similar to figure 10.15.

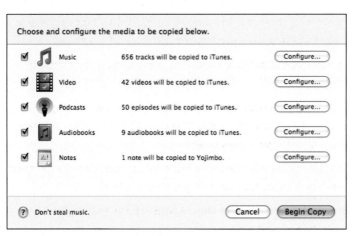

10.14 The Music Rescue media selection screen

10.15 The Music Rescue copy configuration screen

11. **From the configuration screen, choose from the following options to determine how and where your content is copied:**

   • **Copy To.** From this drop-down menu, select either iTunes to copy your tracks directly into your iTunes Music folder and import them into iTunes, or an alternate folder where you would like your content copied to.

   • **Sorting Preset.** Choose Match iTunes to copy your tracks into an album and artist folder structure in the same way that iTunes would store them, or choose an alternate file and folder layout if you would like your recovered tracks to be organized differently.

   • **Copy Previously Copied Tracks.** Choose whether Music Rescue copies over tracks that already exist in the target location.

   • **Add Tracks to iTunes.** Check this check box to have Music Rescue automatically add your tracks to iTunes after they have been copied. Note that this is mandatory if you are copying your tracks directly into your iTunes Music folder.

   • **Force Metadata.** This option determines whether Music Rescue overwrites the metadata in iTunes for any tracks that it copies that are already present in iTunes.

   • **Rebuild Playlists.** Enable this option to have Music Rescue rebuild your playlists in iTunes using the information on your iPod.

12. **Click Done when you have finished adjusting these options.**

13. **Click Begin Copy to begin copying the selected items back to your computer.**

Music Rescue also offers a number of more advanced features, such as the ability to recover your Smart Playlists and the ability to build complex rules to quickly select items for recovery, based on search criteria and whether an item is already present in iTunes.

Music Rescue is licensed either by computer or by iPod. A computer license allows you to use the software with multiple iPods on a single computer, while an iPod license allows you to use the software on a single iPod across multiple computers. Music Rescue can actually be stored on your Click Wheel iPod and carried around with you for multiple computer use. Note that a single iPod license can be used for both the Windows and Mac versions of the software.

There are a number of other applications that are also available to perform iPod recovery, with a couple of noteworthy ones being CopyTrans (www.copytrans.net), a $20 Windows-only application that can perform either full or selective iPod recovery, and iPod Access (www.findley designs.com), another $20 application available in both Mac and Windows versions. These two applications work quite well and generally perform the same tasks as Music Rescue, although I personally prefer Music Rescue for its cleaner user interface, quick recovery mode, and advanced selection features.

**Note** Searching the Internet for iPod recovery software is going to turn up dozens of options; however, a lot of iPod recovery software does not work as advertised. As with anything else you find on the Internet, it is always wise to do some research before deciding on an application. iPod review sites like iLounge (www.ilounge.com) are generally a good place to get information on reputable applications.

# Copying Photos

While the methods described previously in this chapter work great for recovering your audio and video content, photos are a special case when it comes to the iPod. This is because your photos are stored on your iPod differently from other types of media content.

The first and most important thing to keep in mind with photos on your iPod is that iTunes resizes your photos when they are transferred to your iPod, with the largest photo size stored by iTunes being approximately 720 × 480, depending upon your iPod model. For the traditional iPod models, such as the iPod classic and iPod nano, iTunes offers an option to store original full-resolution copies of your photos, which is discussed in Chapter 7; however, this option is not available for the iPod touch or the iPhone.

If you have stored full-resolution versions of your photos, you can very easily access these by opening up your iPod in disk mode through Windows Explorer or the Mac Finder, and simply browsing into the Photos/Full Resolution folder. Original copies of your photos are stored within this folder, organized into sub-folders by year, month, and date, and can be copied off in the same way as any other file.

Unfortunately, if you did not opt to store the full-resolution copies of your photos, the best you can recover is a considerably lower-resolution version. For most traditional iPod models with photo support, this is approximately 720 × 480 — the version used for on-TV display. For the iPhone and iPod touch, this is a 640 × 480 version. To put things in perspective, these equate to approximately 0.3 megapixels. Note that if you have a first- or second-generation iPod nano, which do not have TV output support, you can only recover a 176 × 132 version of your photos.

However, if you find yourself in a situation where you have lost your entire photo collection from your computer but still have it stored on your iPod, a 0.3-megapixel version of a precious memory can be far better than nothing. The photos themselves are stored as uncompressed 16-bit bitmaps in a thumbnail database format on your iPod that is not easily recoverable without third-party tools. Fortunately, however, like other forms of iPod recovery, third-party developers have provided tools to facilitate this.

Two recommended software applications that can perform iPod photo recovery are iPod Access Photo (www.findleydesigns.com), a $13 application available for both Mac and Windows, and CopyTrans Photo (www.copytrans.net), a $20 Windows-only application. Either of these tools can read your iPod, including the iPod touch and iPhone, and recover your photos for you in the maximum resolutions possible. Note that CopyTrans Photo has recently been updated to also provide photo-management support, offering an alternative to iTunes for putting photos onto your iPod.

# Copying Games and Applications

You may have noticed that none of the utilities described thus far provide any method for transferring games and applications from your iPod or iPhone. However, because all games and applications are purchased from the iTunes Store, no separate tools are necessary to transfer these from your iPod back into iTunes. The Transfer Purchases feature in iTunes, covered at the beginning of this chapter, also transfers back any games from your Click Wheel iPod or applications stored on your iPhone or iPod touch, provided your host iTunes computer is authorized for the iTunes Store account that was originally used to purchase them.

# How Do I Manage Content on an iPhone or iPod Touch?

he iPhone and iPod touch represent a significant new direction from
Apple's traditional iPod models, providing not only the traditional media-
related features of the iPod, but also providing personal digital assistant-type
functionality and the ability to run third-party applications. These devices are
more mobile computer than iPod, and as a result there are some significant
differences in how they interface with iTunes.

# Synchronizing Content with an iPhone or iPod Touch

For the most part, synchronizing your media content with an iPhone or an iPod touch works much the same as synchronizing it with a traditional iPod model. Your iPhone or iPod touch appears in the Devices list in iTunes in the same way as your iPod does, and most of the synchronization settings are exactly the same.

There are a few differences worth noting, however:

- **Disk mode.** The iPhone and iPod touch do not support any form of disk mode, and so the Enable disk use option does not appear on the Summary tab in iTunes, nor do these devices appear in Windows Explorer or the Mac Finder. iTunes uses a different synchronization protocol for the iPhone and iPod touch that does not require direct file-system access.

- **Album artwork.** With traditional iPod models, an option appears on the Music tab allowing you to choose whether you would like to have your album artwork displayed on your iPod. With the iPhone and iPod touch, album artwork is always transferred to the device and cannot be disabled.

- **Full-resolution photos.** Traditional iPod models with photo support provide an option to transfer full-resolution copies of your photos onto the device, which can later be retrieved in disk mode. Because the iPhone and iPod touch do not have a disk mode, there is no point in storing full-resolution photos, and this option is therefore not available for these devices.

- **Videos.** For the iPhone, movie and TV show synchronization settings are combined into a single Videos tab.

- **Movie sync.** Traditional iPod models allow you to sync all movies, or sync movies based on playlists. The iPhone and iPod touch only allow the selection of individual movies for synchronization.

- **Info tab.** The iPhone and iPod touch have an additional tab for synchronizing other information to the device, such as your contacts, calendars, e-mail accounts, and bookmarks. This replaces the Contacts tab for traditional iPods. Synchronizing contacts is discussed in the next section.

- **Applications tab.** The iPhone and iPod touch have an Applications tab instead of a Games tab to control the synchronization of applications onto your device.

- **Ringtones tab.** The iPhone also includes an additional tab for synchronizing ringtones to your device.

- **iPhone manual mode.** Although you can enable manual mode on the iPhone, unlike the iPod touch and traditional iPod models, you can only add content from a single iTunes library. The iPod touch does not have this limitation and works like a traditional iPod in manual mode.

In addition to the above differences, iTunes also performs a backup operation on the iPhone and iPod touch whenever they are connected to your computer. This allows you to restore the settings for your device should you need to wipe it or replace it with a new one. Information on your backups can be found on the Devices tab in your iTunes preferences.

# Synchronizing contacts

Although traditional iPod models allow you to synchronize your contacts to your device, this has always been a one-way trip — information was simply copied from your desktop address book application for viewing on your iPod.

However, the iPhone and iPod touch include a full contacts application where you can view your contacts, and also make changes to them or even add new ones. As a result, iTunes has to handle two-way synchronization of your contacts between your device and your desktop application.

As with the traditional iPod models, you can synchronize your contacts with the Mac OS X Address Book or with Microsoft Outlook or Windows Address Book. In addition, iTunes provides full two-way synchronization of contacts from your Yahoo! or Google address books for the iPhone or iPod touch.

To configure contact synchronization for your iPhone or iPod touch, follow these steps:

1. **Connect your iPhone or iPod touch to your computer.**

2. **Select your device in the iTunes Devices list.**

3. **In the main window, choose the Info tab.** The Info sync settings appear, as shown in figure 11.1.

4. **Under Contacts, click the check box beside Sync Address Book contacts.**

5. **Click the radio button to choose either All contacts or Selected groups.** The Selected groups option is only available if you have groups in your Address Book application.

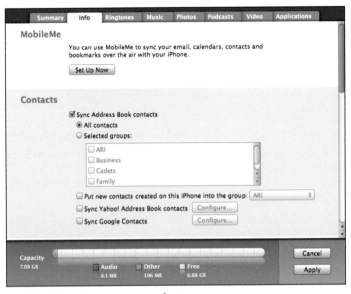

11.1 The iPhone Contacts sync preferences

6. **If you have chosen Selected groups, click the check box beside each group that you would like to sync with your device.**

7. **Optionally, if you would like to have all contacts created on your device placed in a specific Address Book group, click the check box beside Put new contacts created on this iPhone into the group, and choose a group from the drop-down menu.**

8. **Optionally, if you would also like to synchronize with your Yahoo! Address Book, click the check box beside Sync Yahoo! Address Book contacts, and type your Yahoo! username and password.**

9. **Optionally, if you would also like to synchronize with your Google contacts, click the check box beside Sync Google Contacts, and type your Gmail username and password.**

10. **Click Apply to save your settings and sync your contact information with your iPhone or iPod touch.**

For Windows users, the above process differs slightly in that you can only synchronize to a single contacts application. Outlook, Windows Address Book, Google Contacts, and Yahoo! Address Book are all supported for this, but you must select which one you want to use. Further, the Contact Groups feature is only available if you are synchronizing with an application that supports groups.

# Synchronizing calendars

Like Contacts, Calendars could also be synchronized to older iPod models in a view-only mode; however, the iPhone and iPod touch provide a two-way synchronization of your calendar information, with iCal in Mac OS X, or Microsoft Outlook 2003 or later in Windows.

To configure calendar synchronization for your iPhone or iPod touch, follow these steps:

1. **Connect your iPhone or iPod touch to your computer.**

2. **Select your device in the iTunes Devices list.**

3. **In the main window, choose the Info tab.** The Info sync settings appear, similar to figure 11.2.

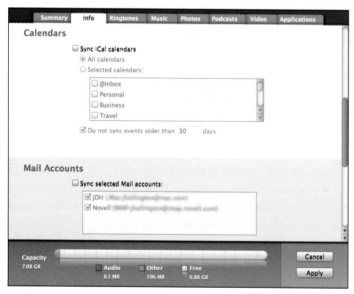

11.2 The iPhone calendar sync preferences

4. **Under Calendars, click the check box beside Sync iCal calendars.** In Windows, this option is Sync calendars with Outlook.

5. **Click the radio button to choose either All calendars or Selected calendars.** The Selected calendars option is only available if you have more than one calendar in your calendar application.

6. **If you have chosen Selected calendars, click the check box beside each calendar that you would like to sync with your device.**

7. **If you would like to limit the amount of calendar data that is synchronized with your device, click the check box beside Do not sync events older than, and type a number of days' worth of calendar information that you would like to sync with your device.**

8. **Click Apply to save your settings and sync your calendar information with your iPhone or iPod touch.**

If you have selected multiple calendars for synchronization, each calendar appears in your Calendar application on the iPhone or iPod touch, and you can select which calendar you would like new items to be created in by default from your device settings.

**Note**

If you're a MobileMe user, you can sync your Calendar directly with your MobileMe account over the air rather than going through iTunes. In this case, the Calendar sync settings in iTunes are disabled with a note that you are using MobileMe instead.

**Genius**

If you're a Google Calendar user, you can synchronize your Google calendar to your iPhone indirectly by first synchronizing it with iCal or Microsoft Outlook. If you're a Mac user, check out either BusySync (www.busymac.com) or Spanning Sync (www.spanningsync.com). For Microsoft Outlook users, Google provides its own Google Calendar Sync application.

# Synchronizing applications

The iPhone and iPod touch support a wide variety of third-party applications. These are managed and synced by iTunes in much the same way as games are for the traditional iPod models:

1. **Connect your iPhone or iPod touch to your computer.**

2. **Select your device from the iTunes Devices list on the left side of the iTunes window.**

3. **Click the Applications tab.** The screen switches to your Applications sync settings, similar to figure 11.3.

4. **Click the check box beside Sync applications if it is not already checked.**

5. **Click the radio button next to either All applications or Selected applications to choose which applications you would like to synchronize to your device.**

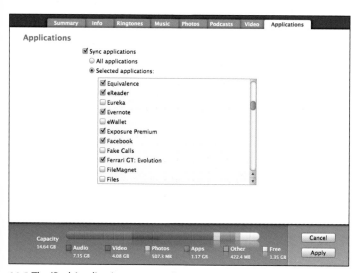

**11.3** The iPod Applications sync settings

6. **If you have chosen Selected applications, click the check box beside the applications that you would like to synchronize to your device.** Note that unchecking previously selected applications tells iTunes to remove these from your device on the next sync.

7. **Click the Apply button in the bottom-right corner of the iTunes window.** iTunes saves the settings for your device and begins synchronizing the selected content.

Applications must always be automatically synchronized to your iPhone or iPod touch. There is no manual-management option available.

# Synchronizing bookmarks

Because the iPhone and iPod touch include a mobile version of the Safari browser, iTunes also provides the ability to synchronize your Internet bookmarks from your computer to your device, and vice versa. In Mac OS X, bookmarks are synced from your Safari browser. Windows users can choose to sync bookmarks with either Internet Explorer or Safari for Windows. Firefox is not supported at this time.

To configure bookmark synchronization, follow these steps:

1. **Connect your iPhone or iPod touch to your computer.**

2. **Select your device in the iTunes Devices list.**

3. **In the main window, choose the Info tab.**

4. **Scroll down on the Info tab to see the Web Browser section, as shown in figure 11.4.**

11.4 The iPhone bookmark sync preferences

5. **Click the check box beside Sync Safari bookmarks (Mac) or Sync bookmarks with (Windows).** If you're using Windows, choose a browser to sync your bookmarks with the drop-down menu.

6. **Click Apply to save your settings and sync your bookmark information with your iPhone or iPod touch.**

**Note**

If you're a MobileMe user, you can sync your bookmarks directly with your MobileMe account over the air rather than going through iTunes. In this case, the Bookmark sync settings in iTunes are disabled with a note that you are using MobileMe instead.

# Purchasing Applications from the iTunes App Store

In July 2008, Apple launched another section on the iTunes Store to sell third-party applications for the iPhone and the iPod touch. Unlike other iTunes Store content, which was generally managed and sold directly by Apple, the iTunes App Store is actually a showcase of applications available from third-party developers. In this case, Apple is providing the storefront while the developers submit the applications to Apple for inclusion, and generally manage their own application pages and descriptions. The iTunes Store is discussed in greater detail in Chapter 2.

You can access the iTunes App Store by clicking the App Store link on the main iTunes Store home page; this takes you to the App Store home screen, similar to figure 11.5.

**11.5** The iTunes App Store home page

You can browse through or search the iTunes App Store in the same manner as any other section of the iTunes Store. Applications are grouped into general categories such as Games, Productivity, and Social Networking. Prices for applications are set by the individual application developers, and may vary widely, from completely free to $20 or more. Most applications on the App Store can be purchased for $10 or less.

Unfortunately, the App Store does not offer a demo or trial feature, therefore often the only indication you get as to the quality of an application is found in the application screen shots and reviews from other users. While originally any user could review any application, in September 2008, Apple changed this to only allow reviews by users who had purchased the application being reviewed. Some App Store vendors do offer both free and paid versions of their applications, with the free version generally intended as a trial or a limited-feature version.

**Note**   Unlike most other types of content on the iTunes Store, you can redownload an application that you have already purchased without having to pay for it again. To do this, simply attempt to buy the application as you normally would, and iTunes notifies you that you have already purchased it and offers to let you download it again for free.

Applications purchased from the iTunes App Store appear in the Applications category in your iTunes library. From this view, you can delete an application in the same way as any other item in iTunes, or choose File ⇨ Get Info to check the version number and other particulars about an application, as shown in figure 11.6.

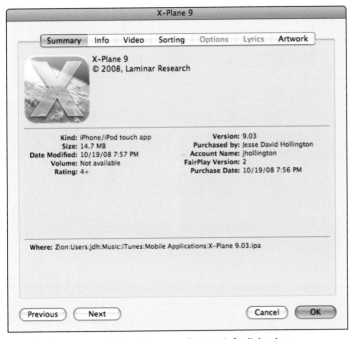

11.6 The Summary tab of an iTunes application info dialog box

Applications on the iTunes App Store are updated by their developers from time to time, and these updates are generally provided free of charge. iTunes periodically checks for App Store updates and notifies you of them, but you can also check for updates and download them manually:

1. **Select Applications from the iTunes Source list.**

2. **From the bottom-right corner of the Applications screen, choose Check for Updates.**
   iTunes checks the iTunes Store for updates to any of the applications presently in your
   library. If updates are found, iTunes displays the dialog box shown in figure 11.7.

11.7 The iTunes application update notification dialog box

3. **Click View Updates to see the list of available updates.** You are taken to an iTunes Store
   updates page similar to figure 11.8. From this screen, you can click the Get Update button to
   download individual updates, click the application to view the application's Store page, or
   click the Download All Free Updates button in the top-right corner to download all of the
   free updates shown.

11.8 The iTunes Application Updates page

**Note** iTunes checks your purchase history to determine if you are eligible for an update or not, regardless of whether the application is in your iTunes library. To receive a free update, you must be logged in with the same iTunes Store account that was used to initially purchase the application.

# Purchasing Music on the iPhone and iPod touch

Because the iPhone and iPod touch both support wireless connections, you can also purchase some content from the iTunes Store directly from your device. The iTunes Store app is an application that comes preinstalled on your iPhone or iPod touch that allows you to purchase music from the iTunes Store over a Wi-Fi connection. Although originally the iTunes Store application on the

iPhone and iPod touch was only available over Wi-Fi connections, as of January 2009 users can now browse the iTunes Store and purchase music over a cellular data connection as well. Note that you must be running at least the version 2.2 firmware on your device to access the iTunes Store over the cellular network.

To purchase music on your iPhone or iPod touch, follow these steps:

1. **Open the iTunes application on your device.** You should see the iTunes Store app home page, similar to figure 11.9. From this screen, you can either browse the iTunes Store app from the main screen categories, or tap the buttons located at the bottom to see top-ten listings or search for content directly.

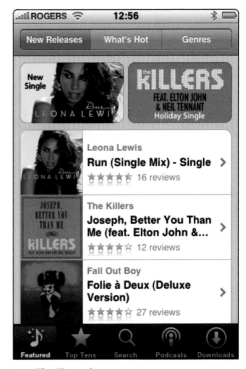

11.9 The iTunes Store app screen

2. **Tap a track name to listen to a 30-second preview of the track.**

3. **To purchase a track or an entire album, tap the price.** The price changes to a Buy Now button.

4. **Tap Buy Now to purchase the item.**

5. **If you are not signed in to the iTunes Store already on your device, you are prompted for your iTunes Store username and password, as shown in figure 11.10.** Otherwise, you are simply asked to confirm your password.

6. **Type your iTunes Store account information and tap OK to complete your purchase.**

You can monitor your downloads from the Downloads section in the iTunes Store application. Note that downloads continue even if you close the application. Purchased items are placed in a Purchased playlist on your device and are synced back to iTunes automatically the next time you connect your device to your computer. Purchases made on your device are placed in their own special Purchased playlist ending with the name of the device, similar to figure 11.11.

11.10 The iTunes Store app sign-in screen

11.11 iTunes Purchased playlists

**Note**

The iTunes Store app uses your iTunes account information from your computer, so whichever account you were signed into when you last synced your device is the one that it uses. You are only prompted for your account information if you were not signed in to any account on your computer when you last synced your device. You can confirm which account you are currently signed into by scrolling down to the bottom of any store page.

The iTunes Store app can only download music content, not videos or digital booklets. If you purchase an album from the iTunes Store that includes this type of content, the additional content is placed in your iTunes Store queue for download by your computer the next time you connect to the iTunes Store. The unsupported items and an explanation of this are shown at the bottom of the track listing for that album, as shown in figure 11.12.

# Downloading Podcasts on the iPhone and iPod touch

With the version 2.2 iPhone and iPod touch firmware update released in November 2008, the iTunes Store app gained the ability to stream or download podcast episodes directly over the air to your device. This works for both

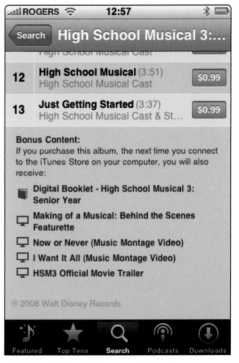

11.12 An iTunes Store app additional content listing

video and audio podcasts, and you can download podcasts either over Wi-Fi or a cellular data connection; however podcast episodes downloaded over the cellular network are limited to 10 MB in size.

It is also important to note that this feature only allows you to download individual podcast episodes manually — you cannot subscribe to a podcast directly from your device and new podcast episodes for podcasts you have subscribed to in iTunes are not downloaded automatically over the air.

To download podcasts on your iPhone or iPod touch, follow these steps:

1.  **Open the iTunes application on your device.** You should see the iTunes Store app home page. From this screen, you can either browse the iTunes Store app from the main screen categories, or tap the buttons located at the bottom to see top-ten listings or search for content directly.

2. **Tap the Podcasts button to browse through a list of podcasts.** Alternatively, you can use the Search button to search for a specific podcast or episode by title. Tapping on a podcast title presents a list of individual podcast episodes.

3. **To listen to or watch a podcast over the air, simply tap anywhere on the episode title.** To download a podcast to your device for later viewing or listening, tap the Free button, which appears to the right of the episode title. The Free button changes to read Download, as shown in figure 11.13.

4. **Tap Download to begin downloading the episode.** Note that you do not need to be signed into the iTunes Store to download podcast episodes to your device.

11.13 Downloading a Podcast Episode

As with music purchases, you can monitor your downloads from the Downloads section in the iTunes Store application. Note that downloads continue even if you close the application. New podcast episodes are placed directly within the Podcasts section in the iPod application, and are synced back to iTunes automatically the next time you connect your device to your computer. Note that unlike music, new podcast episodes are not added to the Purchased playlist on your device or in iTunes. Podcast episodes synced back to iTunes from your device appear within the iTunes Podcasts section with a Subscribe button next to them as shown in figure 11.14 so that you can easily subscribe to the entire podcast through iTunes should you so desire.

**Note**

If you have one or more episodes for a podcast already stored on your device, you can access the iTunes Store listing for that podcast directly from the iPod application. Simply go to the listing of podcast episodes you already have, and tap on the Get More Episodes link shown at the bottom of the list.

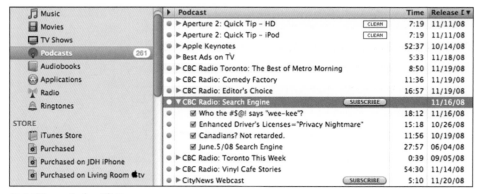

11.14 iTunes Podcast listing

# Purchasing Applications on the iPhone and iPod touch

You can also purchase iPhone and iPod touch applications directly from your device using the iTunes App Store application. The App Store runs just fine over a cellular 3G/EDGE connection or a Wi-Fi connection. However, only applications smaller than 10MB can be downloaded over a 3G/EDGE connection. If you purchase an application larger than this, it is queued up for download when you're next on a Wi-Fi connection or at your computer.

To purchase applications on your device from the iTunes App Store, follow these steps:

1. **Open the App Store application on your device.** You should see the iTunes App Store home page.

2. **Either browse the App Store from the main screen, or tap the button located at the bottom of the screen to browse by categories, as shown in figure 11.15.** You can also see listings for the top 25 free and top 25 paid applications or search for content directly.

11.15 The iTunes App Store home page

3. **Tap an application to display a description and screenshot of the application.** You can also scroll down to read customer reviews on that particular application, or tap the Tell a Friend button to send an e-mail with a link to the application.

4. **To purchase an application, tap the price.** The price changes to a Buy Now button.

5. **Tap Buy Now to purchase the item.** If you are not signed in to the iTunes Store already on your device, you are prompted for your iTunes Store username and password, as shown in figure 11.16. Otherwise, you are simply asked to confirm your password.

6. **Type your iTunes Store account information and tap OK to complete your purchase.**

11.16 The iTunes App Store sign-in screen

The application is downloaded directly to the first available slot on your home screen. The application icon appears faded with a progress indicator while the application is downloading, and it lights up normally once the application download and installation are complete. Applications downloaded directly to your device are automatically synced back to your iTunes library the next time you connect your device to your computer.

**Note**

The iTunes App Store uses your iTunes account information from your computer, so whichever account you were signed into when you last synced your device is the one that it uses. You are only prompted for your account information if you were not signed in to any account on your computer when you last synced your device. You can confirm which account you are currently signed into by scrolling down to the bottom of any store page.

The App Store can also be used to download updates for existing applications on your device. The iPhone and iPod touch automatically check for application updates in the background from time to time and display a number badge over the App Store icon indicating how many updates are pending. To download pending updates, simply open the App Store, select the Updates button, and download the applications as if you were purchasing them. You can also tap the Update All button in the top corner of the updates screen to download all updates.

**Note**

From the updates screen in the iTunes App Store, you can also tap on the title of any application to see a summary of changes in the update.

# Deleting Applications from the iPhone or iPod touch

If you decide that you no longer want an application on your device, you can easily delete it directly without having to wait to connect to iTunes:

1. **Move to the screen containing the application you would like to remove.**

2. **Tap and hold your finger on the application for about 2 seconds.** All of the application icons start jiggling.

3. **Tap the X beside the application icon that you want to delete.** A confirmation dialog box appears, similar to figure 11.17.

4. **Tap Delete to confirm that you actually want to delete the application.**

11.17 The iPhone application deletion confirmation dialog box

5.  **If you are using iPhone firmware version 2.2 or later, a dialog box similar to figure 11.18 appears prompting you to rate the application you are deleting.**

6.  **Tap the stars to assign a rating and then the Rate button, or type No Thanks to skip rating the application.** The application disappears from your device, along with all of its data, and is deselected for synchronization from iTunes the next time you connect to your computer.

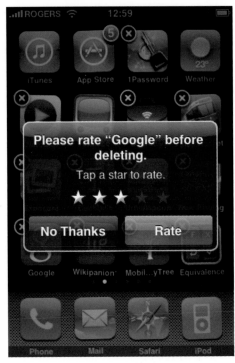

Note that the application is not actually removed from your iTunes library, only from the device. Of course, if you have just purchased the application and haven't synced it back to iTunes yet, then it does not appear in your iTunes library either.

**11.18** Rate an application before deleting it.

Note, however, that deleting applications from your iTunes library directly does remove them from any iPhone or iPod touch devices synced with that library.

# Purchasing Ringtones for the iPhone

In September 2007, Apple introduced the capability to create and purchase ringtones for your iPhone from the iTunes Store. This feature allows you to select a clip of up to 30 seconds from a track that you have already purchased from the iTunes Store and download that segment as a ringtone for an additional $0.99. If you have not already purchased a copy of the track that you want to use as a ringtone, you must first purchase the track as you normally would, and then pay an additional $0.99 to select a portion of it as a ringtone.

**Note**

Despite the worldwide availability of the iPhone 3G, ringtones remain available only on the U.S. iTunes Store.

Note that only certain tracks are eligible to be used as ringtones. These tracks can be identified within the iTunes Store by the small bell icon that appears in the track listing, as shown in figure 11.19.

**11.19** iTunes Store Ringtone-eligible tracks

You can also use the iTunes Store Power Search feature to limit your search to include only tracks that can be turned into ringtones by clicking the appropriate box as shown in figure 11.20.

**11.20** iTunes Store Power Search for ringtones

The ringtone column can also be enabled in your own library view to identify those tracks you already own that are eligible for use as ringtones. Converting these tracks still costs you an additional $0.99 to purchase them as a ringtone. Essentially, this means that to purchase a ringtone from the iTunes Store for a track you do not already own, the total cost is $1.98: $0.99 for the complete track, and an additional $0.99 to use a portion of it as a ringtone.

To convert an eligible track in your iTunes library into a ringtone, follow these steps:

1. **Select the track that you would like to convert into a ringtone.**

2. **From the iTunes menu, choose Store ⇨ Create Ringtone.** The ringtone creation tool appears at the bottom of your iTunes window containing a visual display of the track with an initial 15-second segment highlighted, as shown in figure 11.21.

**11.21** iTunes Ringtone Creation screen

3. **Click the Preview button to listen to the selected segment.**

4. **To choose a different segment of the track, drag the blue selection overlay across the track.**

5. **To change the length of the selected segment, drag the left or right side of the blue selection overlay.** You can select as little as 3 seconds or as much as 30 seconds of the track.

6. **To adjust whether the segment fades in at the beginning of fades out at the end, click the appropriate boxes at the top left and right corners of the blue selection overlay.**

7. **The selected segment repeats automatically when used as a ringtone.** To adjust the delay between loops, choose the desired gap from the Looping drop-down menu.

8. **Once you are satisfied with your ringtone, click the Buy button to purchase and download the selected segment to your Ringtones section.**

Newly added ringtones are automatically queued for synchronization to your iPhone. You can see a list of all of the ringtones in your iTunes library by selecting Ringtones from the iTunes source menu, and you can control which ringtones are synchronized to your iPhone from the Ringtones tab on your iPhone's synchronization settings.

**Note** Each ringtone you create costs $0.99, even if it comes from a song that you have already purchased a ringtone from. In other words, if you wanted to create another ringtone from a different section of the same song, you need to purchase it as a new ringtone.

# Creating Your Own Ringtones

Purchasing ringtones from the iTunes Store is a limited and relatively expensive option; each ringtone costs you $0.99 on top of the price of the song, the selections of songs that can be turned into ringtones is sparse, and ringtones are only available on the U.S. iTunes Store. When Apple first announced this feature, the iTunes Store was the only legitimate source of ringtones, and Apple took very proactive measures with a series of iTunes updates to disable any ringtone-creation capability offered by third-party developers. Approximately three months after this initial announcement Apple opened up the ability to create your own ringtones, and even added this capability to GarageBand '08 through a software update.

**Note** Only unprotected tracks can be converted into ringtones. This includes any music you've imported yourself as well as iTunes Plus music from the iTunes Store. Normal iTunes Store purchases cannot be turned into ringtones directly, although you can always burn a protected track to a CD and then reimport it as an unprotected track, which can then be converted into a ringtone.

Although there are a number of third-party tools to assist with creating ringtones, the reality is that as long as you're using iTunes 7.5 or later, creating your own ringtones is relatively straightforward and you can do it yourself with no third-party tools required.

1. **Locate a song that you would like to convert into a ringtone.**

2. **Listen to the song to decide on which segment you would like to use as a ringtone.** Ringtones can be no more than 40 seconds in length.

3. **Make a note of the start and stop times for your chosen segment.**

4. **With your chosen track highlighted, choose File ⇨ Get Info from the iTunes menu.**

5. **From the iTunes File Info dialog box, choose the Options tab. The track options appear.**

6. **Click the boxes beside Start Time and Stop Time and enter the times you noted in step 3.** This should look like figure 11.22.

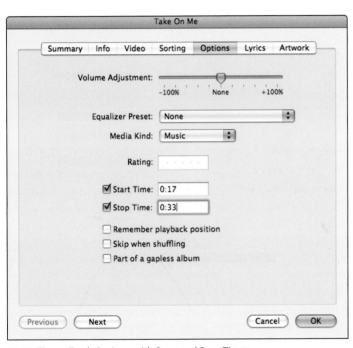

**11.22** iTunes Track Options with Start and Stop Times

7. **Click OK.**

8. **Double-click on the track to play back the selected segment and confirm that it sounds how you want.**

9. **From the iTunes menu, choose Advanced ⇨ Create AAC Version.** An AAC version of the track is created using the designed start and stop times. If the Create AAC Version option is not available you need to go to your iTunes Preferences and change your default import format to AAC. Only AAC files can be used as ringtones. More information on changing your default import format can be found in Chapter 1.

10. **Drag the new track from the iTunes window to your desktop.** The track appears on your desktop with an M4A extension.

11. **Rename the file on your desktop to give it an M4R extension.**

12. **Drag the file from your desktop back into the iTunes window.** iTunes sees the M4R extension and imports the file as a ringtone instead of a normal audio track.

13. **Select the Ringtones section from the iTunes source listing to confirm that your new track appears.**

14. **Once you have imported your ringtone, go back and delete the converted track from your iTunes library, and ensure that you uncheck the Start and Stop time boxes in your track settings.**

**Note**   If your ringtone does not appear in iTunes after you drag it into the iTunes window, ensure that the file is actually less than 40 seconds in length. iTunes does not display any error messages if a ringtone cannot be imported, it simply fails quietly.

New ringtones are automatically transferred to any iPhones that you are synchronizing with the current library. You can select which ringtones you want on your iPhone via the Ringtones tab in your iPhone's sync preferences.

This approach is the most straightforward way to turn a selected segment of a track into a ringtone without requiring any additional software. However, this method does not give you control over things like fading in or out, loop delays, or other effects you may want to add. If you want to create more sophisticated ringtones, you can of course use any AAC-compatible audio editor to create a ringtone segment of your own design and then save it as an AAC-format audio file with an M4R extension to import into iTunes. If you're a Mac user with iLife '08, a great tool for this is GarageBand '08, which can not only import your unprotected AAC files directly, but also provides a Send Ringtone to iTunes menu option under the Share menu to export your finished work directly into your iTunes Ringtones section.

Other iTunes-specific ringtone creation tools are available if you're looking for a more simplified method of creating ringtones, however unlike the method described above, most of these dedicated ringtone-creation applications are not free.

# How Do I Manage Content on an Apple TV?

*Copyright Jeremy Horwitz for iLounge.com*

# Synchronizing Content with an Apple TV

With the v2.0 firmware release in February 2008, the Apple TV can now function almost completely by itself without requiring an iTunes library on the back end. However, most Apple TV users are likely also iTunes users, and synchronization with your iTunes library continues to be an important feature of the Apple TV.

Although the Apple TV appears alongside your iPod devices in your iTunes Devices list, iTunes takes a considerably different approach to synchronizing content with the Apple TV. Firstly, synchronization occurs entirely over your home network, using either a Wi-Fi or Ethernet connection. Although the Apple TV has a USB port, this is only used for diagnostic purposes. Whenever your Apple TV is powered on and on the same network as your computer, it simply shows up in your iTunes Devices list.

Secondly, unlike the iPod, the Apple TV offers no manual-management mode, and, in fact, the Summary screen for an Apple TV looks considerably different, as shown in figure 12.1.

12.1 The iTunes Apple TV Summary screen

Instead, the Apple TV offers two synchronization modes:

● **Automatic Sync.** In this mode, iTunes chooses which content to synchronize to your Apple TV. Basically, iTunes copies as much content as it can fit on your Apple TV, giving priority to video content and newer items. In this mode, you have no direct control over the content that is synchronized to your Apple TV, with the exception of rented movies and photos. However, content that has not actually been synchronized to your Apple TV is still available when iTunes is running on the same network.

● **Custom Sync.** In this mode, you control the items that are synchronized to your Apple TV in much the same way as you would for an iPod or iPhone. Settings tabs become available to manually adjust synchronization settings for movies, TV shows, music, and podcasts, in addition to the Photos tab. You can also decide whether only content actually stored on the Apple TV is shown by clicking the check box beside Show only the synced items on my Apple TV. When this setting is enabled, only content actually synced to and stored on the Apple TV is available, regardless of whether or not iTunes is running on your home network.

When using Custom Sync mode, synchronization of content to the Apple TV is handled in much the same way as it is for an iPod or iPhone by adjusting the settings on the appropriate tabs. Content is synced in the order in which the tabs are displayed, which means that if you are syncing a lot of movie or TV show content, you may find that no podcasts are actually transferred to your Apple TV.

**Note**   You can give priority to the synchronization of photos to ensure that you have your pictures on your Apple TV, regardless of how much other content is stored on it. Simply check the Sync photos before other media check box on the Photos tab.

# Accessing Content from Multiple iTunes Libraries

Although the Apple TV can only synchronize content from a single iTunes library, you can easily set it up to allow you to access content from alternate iTunes libraries by streaming the content from iTunes to the Apple TV. This can be useful if you have more than one computer in your house and each family member has an iTunes library on his or her own computer.

1. **On the computer containing the iTunes library you would like to share with the Apple TV, open your iTunes preferences and select the Apple TV tab.**

2. **Ensure that the Look for Apple TVs check box is checked, as shown in figure 12.2.**

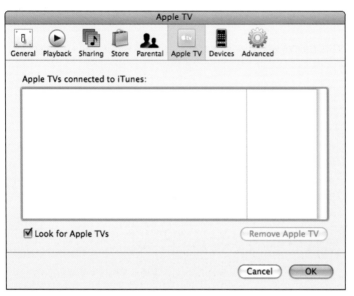

12.2 The Apple TV tab of the iTunes Preferences with the Look for Apple TVs option selected

3. **From the Apple TV main menu, choose Settings ⇨ Computers.** The Apple TV computer setup screen appears, similar to figure 12.3.

12.3 The Apple TV computer setup screen

4. **Choose Add Shared iTunes Library.** The Connect to iTunes screen appears, as shown in figure 12.4.

5. **Go to the computer containing the library that you would like to connect to your Apple TV, and start iTunes if it is not already running.** Your Apple TV appears in the iTunes Devices list on the left side. If it does not appear, check your iTunes preferences again in steps 1 and 2.

6. **Select the Apple TV from the iTunes Devices list.** The Apple TV setup screen appears, as shown in figure 12.5.

**Connect to iTunes**

To stream iTunes content to your Apple TV, open iTunes and select Apple TV from the Devices list. You will need to enter this passcode:

7  7  8  7  1

Apple TV requires iTunes 7.6 or later

12.4 The Apple TV Connect to iTunes screen

12.5 The Apple TV iTunes setup screen

7. **Type the five-digit code shown on the Apple TV from step 4 into the spaces provided in iTunes, and press Enter.**

Once you have completed these steps, your shared library is listed on the Apple TV's computer setup screen, and an additional Shared menu appears in each category, which you can use to access content from your secondary libraries. For example, below My Movies, you see another option for Shared Movies, and likewise for Shared TV Shows, Shared Music, and so forth.

In the secondary iTunes library, the Apple TV can be accessed through your Devices list; however, only a basic set of Apple TV configuration screens are available. Because you are only streaming content rather than synchronizing it, the Apple TV simply accesses all of the content from your shared iTunes library and there is no need to select individual items. The exception to this is photos — because you may not want to make your entire photo collection available to your Apple TV, iTunes allows you to select which photo albums are available from the Apple TV. This is handled in the same manner as synchronizing photos to the Apple TV or to an iPod or iPhone, except that photos are not actually transferred onto your Apple TV — they are simply available for viewing.

**Note** iTunes must be running on the shared computers for their shared libraries to appear on your Apple TV. The Apple TV does not show the Shared menus unless there are shared libraries available and running on your network.

# Purchasing Content on the Apple TV

With the Apple TV v2.0 update released in February 2008, you can now purchase content directly on your Apple TV, subject to availability in your particular country's iTunes Store. The Apple TV supports direct browsing and purchasing of movies, TV shows, music, and music videos directly from your couch.

In fact, most of the menus on the Apple TV are clearly designed to direct you toward browsing through the iTunes Store. For example, on the Movies sub-menu, shown in figure 12.6, only the last option — My Movies — is to access your own content. The first four menu items allow you to browse for and search content from the iTunes Store directly on your Apple TV.

12.6 The Apple TV movies menu

# Configuring your Apple TV for the iTunes Store

Before you can purchase content on your Apple TV, you must first be logged in to your iTunes Store account for your country of residence.

**Note**

Unlike the iPhone and iPod touch, your iTunes Store account settings do not synchronize from your iTunes library.

1. **From the Apple TV main menu, choose Settings ⇨ General ⇨ iTunes Store.** The iTunes Store Configuration menu appears, as shown in figure 12.7.

2. **Choose Location.** A list of countries appears.

12.7 The Apple TV iTunes Store configuration menu

3. **Scroll to and choose the country for your iTunes Store account.** A check mark appears next to the selected country, as shown in figure 12.8.

4. **Press the Menu button on your remote to return to the iTunes Store configuration menu.**

5. **Select Sign in.** A screen appears for you to enter your Apple ID for the iTunes Store, as shown in figure 12.9.

6. **Using the remote control to select letters, enter your Apple ID.** Click Done when finished to proceed to the password entry screen.

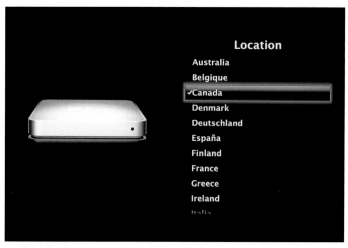

12.8 The Apple TV iTunes Store country listing

12.9 The Apple TV iTunes sign-in screen

7. **Enter your password using the remote control to select letters.** Click Done when finished.

8. **The next screen asks you whether you want the Apple TV to remember your password.** Selecting No requires you to enter your password each time you make a purchase from your Apple TV.

9. **Press and hold the menu button to return to the main Apple TV menu.**

**Genius**  If you have an iPhone or iPod touch, you can save yourself some time entering text on the Apple TV by downloading the Remote application from the iTunes App Store. Among other things, this application allows you to use your iPhone or iPod touch keyboard to enter information into Apple TV text entry fields. I discuss this application later in this chapter.

Once you have configured your Apple TV for your iTunes Store account and country, the menus on the Apple TV reflect content that is available in your particular country's store. For example, if TV content is not available on your iTunes Store, then the TV Shows menu does not show any browsing or purchasing options for TV Show content.

**Note**  You can select different countries in the Apple TV iTunes Store configuration menu and browse the content from those stores, but you cannot purchase that content unless you have an account for that country. In fact, if you try to purchase from a different country's store, the Apple TV simply gives you an error message and requires you to return to the configuration menu to set your store to the correct country manually.

## Previewing and purchasing content

Once you have configured your iTunes Store account on your Apple TV, purchasing content on the Apple TV is relatively straightforward — simply browse or search for content using the displayed menus. Selecting an individual song or video provides options for previewing or purchasing the song or video, as shown in figure 12.10.

For music, TV shows, and music videos, the preview is generally the same 30-second extracted clip that is available through iTunes on your computer. Movies, on the other hand, generally provide theatrical trailers instead of extracted previews.

Show Details
44 minutes
Original air date 8/1/08
Widescreen
★★★★☆
(29 Reviews)

Preview     $1.99
            Buy

**12.10** An iTunes Store item's general purchase options on an Apple TV

Purchasing an item on your Apple TV immediately downloads it from the iTunes Store directly to your Apple TV. As an added bonus, you can actually begin watching content while it is still downloading; the Apple TV notifies you when enough of a movie or TV show has been downloaded to begin watching.

Items purchased directly on the Apple TV are automatically transferred back to your primary iTunes library the next time you sync with your Apple TV, and placed in a purchased playlist with the name of your Apple TV.

# Adding movies to your wish list

In addition to purchasing movies directly on your Apple TV, you can also keep a wish list of movies that you might want to purchase or rent at a later time. You can add content to your wish list directly from any iTunes Store movie item screen.

1. **Browse to and select a movie that you would like to add to your wish list.** The movie information screen appears.

2. **Choose More, as shown in figure 12.11.** A more detailed information screen appears, including a summary of the movie, and cast and crew information.

3. **Select Add to Wish List.** The item is added to your wish list and the menu item toggles to read Remove from Wish List.

**12.11** The option buttons, including the More button

4. **Press the menu button on your remote to return to the main movie information screen.**

**Genius**

From the detailed information screen, you can also select the name of a cast or crew member to see a list of other works available on the iTunes Store for that person.

Once your wish list contains at least one item, a Wish List menu option appears on your Apple TV main Movies menu, where you can review the contents of your wish list.

**Note**

Your wish list is only stored locally on the specific Apple TV that you create it on. It does not sync back to your iTunes Store account, iTunes library, or any other Apple TVs in your house.

# Keeping track of your favorite TV shows

Like the wish list for movies, iTunes also allows you to keep track of your favorite TV shows by adding them to a Favorites list. This list works on the basis of complete shows, rather than individual seasons or episodes, and can be a very useful way to quickly check for new episodes for shows that you're following, particularly when no Season Pass option is available.

To add a TV show to your Favorites list, follow these steps:

1. **Browse to and select a TV show title that you would like to add to your Favorites.** The TV show's episode listing screen appears.

2. **Select Add to Favorites, as shown in figure 12.12.** The item is added to your Favorites and the menu item toggles to read Remove from Favorites.

3. **Press the menu button on your remote to return to the TV Show listing screen.**

Your Favorites can be accessed from the Favorites menu, which appears on the Apple TV's main TV Shows menu.

**Corner Gas, Season 3**

Add to Favorites
Buy Season                              $29.99
Other seasons in this series      >

1 Dress for Success
2 Key to the Future
3 Dog River Vice
4 Will and Brent
5 The Littlest Yarbo
6 Mail Fraud
7 Fun Run

**12.12** Select Add to Favorites to add an item.

**Note** Your Favorites list is only stored locally on the specific Apple TV that you create it on. It does not sync back to your iTunes Store account, iTunes library, or any other Apple TVs in your house.

# Downloading Podcasts on the Apple TV

The Apple TV not only includes the ability to purchase content such as movies, TV shows, and music, but you can also search for, play, and download free podcast episodes directly from your Apple TV. In addition to these podcasts being completely free, there are a number of stunning high-definition podcasts available through iTunes that really show off the HD capabilities of the Apple TV.

Browsing for and finding a podcast on the Apple TV works in much the same way as it does for other types of content, with podcasts grouped by genre or provider and a search option available for locating specific podcasts. Selecting a podcast episode shows an information screen similar to figure 12.13, where you can choose to either play the podcast episode back by streaming it directly from the source or download it to your Apple TV for later listening or viewing.

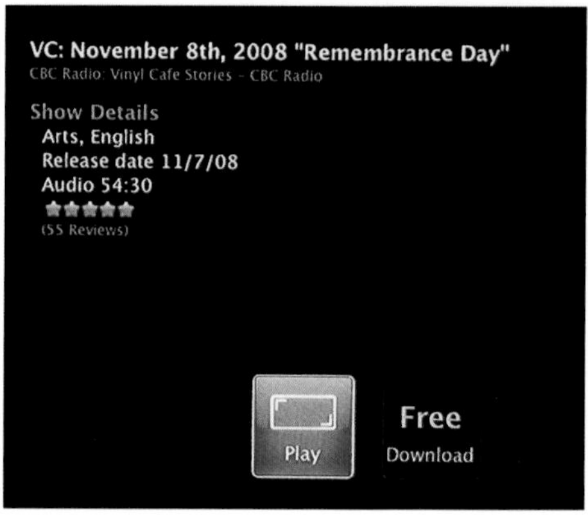

Note that you cannot subscribe to a podcast directly from the Apple TV — you can only listen to or download individual episodes.

**VC: November 8th, 2008 "Remembrance Day"**
CBC Radio: Vinyl Cafe Stories - CBC Radio

Show Details
Arts, English
Release date 11/7/08
Audio 54:30
★★★★★
(55 Reviews)

Free
Play   Download

**12.13** An Apple TV podcast episode information screen

However, podcasts can be added to a Podcast Favorites list, which works in the same manner as the TV Shows Favorites list described earlier in this chapter.

Further, podcast episodes downloaded to your Apple TV sync back to your primary iTunes library automatically during the next sync operation. These individual episodes appear in your Podcasts section in iTunes, and a Subscribe link appears next to them, allowing you to subscribe to the podcast from iTunes, after which any new episodes are automatically downloaded to your computer and synced back out to your Apple TV.

# Renting Movies with Your Apple TV

One of the big announcements from Apple in 2008 was its entry into the movie-rental business, greatly expanding the role of the Apple TV in the living room. In addition to purchasing movies to keep in your library, iTunes began offering the ability to rent movies for a limited time, similar to the video-on-demand services available from many cable and satellite providers.

Apple TV movie rentals also come with an additional benefit: high-definition (HD) movies. While iTunes had traditionally only offered standard-definition (SD) movies for purchase, this new announcement introduced the availability of certain titles to be rented in HD resolution for a slight premium over the SD equivalent. Further, many of the HD movies available for rental on the iTunes Store also include a Dolby Digital 5.1 soundtrack, taking advantage of the Apple TV's digital audio output capabilities.

**Note** HD movies are available only for rental and not for purchase, and are available only from the Apple TV and not through iTunes on your computer. This is in contrast to HD TV shows, which can be purchased in HD quality from either Apple TV or iTunes.

Renting a movie on the Apple TV is handled in the same way as purchasing a movie — you simply choose the movie, and if it is available for rent, the appropriate rental options are shown on the movie information screen, as shown in figure 12.14.

12.14 The options for rental of an Apple TV iTunes Store movie

Note that not all movies are available for both purchase and rental, and it is not uncommon for movies to be made available for purchase several weeks prior to their rental availability. In the event that a movie is scheduled to be available for rent on a specific date in the future, this is also shown on the Apple TV's movie information screen, as shown in figure 12.15.

12.15 The Apple TV iTunes Store movie information screen indicating that the movie is not yet available for rent

You can access your movie rentals from the Apple TV's Rented Movies menu option at the top of your Apple TV's main Movies menu. This menu option only appears when your Apple TV contains at least one rented movie.

**Note** The Apple TV has a maximum 720p resolution, and so even HD content on the Apple TV is not of the same quality as a Blu-Ray disc, which is 1080p. This should not be a significant limitation for most users, however.

Rented movies remain on your Apple TV for 30 days, after which they are automatically deleted, whether your have watched them or not. Once you begin watching a rented movie, it is set to expire 24 hours after you begin watching it if you purchased it from the U.S. iTunes Store, or 48 hours later if you purchased it from the Canadian or U.K. iTunes stores. Note that if you are in the process of watching a movie when it expires, the Apple TV allows you to continue watching it — it is deleted as soon as you exit the movie or finish watching it.

**Note** Unlike movies rented through iTunes on your computer, movies rented on the Apple TV cannot be transferred back to your iTunes library or to another Apple TV. Because there is no difference in quality between an SD movie rented on the Apple TV and the same movie rented through iTunes on your computer, for maximum flexibility you may want to consider renting an SD movie through iTunes and transferring it up to your Apple TV unless you are certain you are only going to watch it on your Apple TV.

# Using On-The-Go and Genius Features on the Apple TV

The Apple TV provides support for On-The-Go and Genius playlists in much the same way as described in Chapter 8 for the iPod. The On-The-Go playlist appears at the bottom of the main Playlists listing under the Apple TV's My Music menu. To add tracks to the On-The-Go playlist, follow these steps:

1. **Locate a track that you would like to add to the On-The-Go playlist.** You can also use a grouping of tracks, such as an album, artist, genre, or even another playlist.

2. **Press and hold the Play/Pause button on the Apple remote.** A pop-up menu appears.

3. **Select Add To On-The-Go, as shown in figure 12.16.** The track is added to the On-The-Go playlist.

Note that you can also add tracks to the On-The-Go playlist from the Now Playing screen in the same manner — simply press and hold the Play/Pause button while a track is playing.

On-The-Go playlists can be saved and named directly on the Apple TV. Simply select the Save as Playlist option from the top of the On-The-Go playlist.

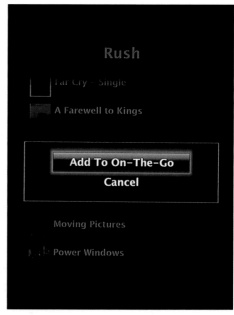

12.16 The Apple TV On-The-Go playlist option

**Note** Unlike the iPod and iPhone, the On-The-Go queue from the Apple TV is not synchronized back to your iTunes library, nor is it cleared by syncing with iTunes. If you want to transfer your On-The-Go playlist of selections to your iTunes library, you must first save it as a playlist manually on the Apple TV.

Building a Genius playlist from a track is handled in a similar manner:

1. **Locate a track you would like to base a Genius playlist on.** You must select an individual track, although you can also use a track that is currently playing.

2. **Press and hold the Play/Pause button on the Apple remote.** A pop-up menu appears.

3. **Select Start Genius, as shown in figure 12.17.**

12.17 The Apple TV Start Genius option

A new Genius list is created in your top-level playlists folder, and the selected track immediately begins playing back from the Genius list.

You can save the current Genius list by selecting the Save as Playlist option from the top of the Genius list. Saved Genius playlists are transferred back to your iTunes library during the next synchronization.

## Setting up a Video Party Mix

The Apple TV v2.2 firmware update released in October 2008 also added another feature that many users had been awaiting since the Apple TV's initial release.

With this update, you can now set up a playlist of music videos on your Apple TV and play them either sequentially or shuffled in the same way as a normal playlist. In addition to playing the videos without stopping, the Apple TV also provides a small overlay in the bottom-left corner of your TV screen at the beginning of each new video track showing the album artwork, artist, and album name. This allows you to create an MTV-style video party mix.

Video playlists are created in the same way as any other playlist, and you can either create them from iTunes or use an On-The-Go playlist. You can even mix video and audio together in the same playlist — the Apple TV switches seamlessly back and forth between video playback for your videos and the normal Now Playing screen for audio tracks.

269

**Note** Genius lists are not automatically saved, nor are they synced back to iTunes unless they have been saved as a playlist.

**Note** On-The-Go and Genius support was added in the Apple TV v2.2 firmware update in October 2008. If you cannot access these features, then ensure that you are running the latest Apple TV firmware.

# Displaying Slide Shows on Your Apple TV

As with the iPod and iPhone, you can also sync your photos from your computer onto your Apple TV through iTunes. The sync process works in the same way as it does for an iPod or an iPhone (see Chapter 7 for more information).

The Apple TV is much better suited for displaying your photo slide shows, providing the ability to play back transitions between slides, accompany your slide shows with music, and provide a Ken Burns effect (where your slides slowly move across the screen during playback). These settings can be set on the Apple TV and apply to any normal photo albums that you use to play slide shows from.

As an added bonus, if you're a Mac iPhoto user, you can set up customized slide shows in iPhoto and play these back with the same settings on your Apple TV. Slide shows from iPhoto synchronize to your Apple TV through iTunes in the same way that normal iPhoto albums do, but when you play them back, the effects, transitions, and music set in iPhoto are used on the Apple TV.

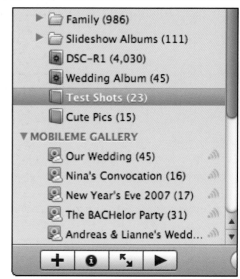

1. **Open iPhoto on your computer.**

2. **Select the photos that you would like to include in your slide show.**

3. **Click the Add button.** This button is located at the bottom-left corner of your iPhoto window, as shown in figure 12.18. It looks like a plus sign. A Create New Item panel appears.

12.18 The iPhoto Add button

4. **Select Slideshow from the panel, as shown in figure 12.19.**

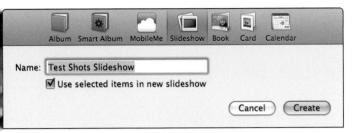

12.19 The Slideshow panel of the create new item panel

5. **Type a name for your slide show and click the Create button.**

6. **The new slide show appears in the Slideshows section of your iPhoto library, similar to figure 12.20.**

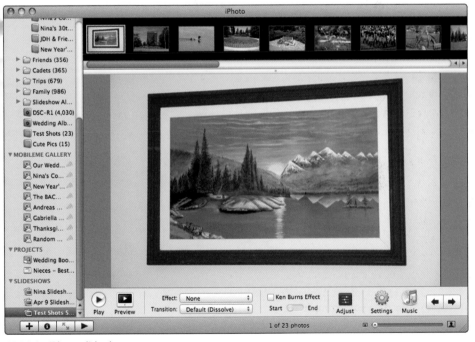

12.20 An iPhoto slide show

7. **Click the Settings button in the lower-right to adjust global slide show settings.** A dialog box similar to figure 12.21 appears to allow you to adjust features of your slideshow such as display interval and default transition effects.

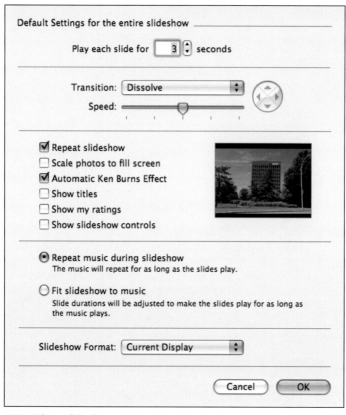

Default Settings for the entire slideshow

Play each slide for [ 3 ] seconds

Transition: [ Dissolve ]
Speed: ————————●————

☑ Repeat slideshow
☐ Scale photos to fill screen
☑ Automatic Ken Burns Effect
☐ Show titles
☐ Show my ratings
☐ Show slideshow controls

◉ Repeat music during slideshow
The music will repeat for as long as the slides play.

◯ Fit slideshow to music
Slide durations will be adjusted to make the slides play for as long as the music plays.

Slideshow Format: [ Current Display ]

( Cancel )    ( OK )

**12.21** iPhoto slide show settings

8. **Select 16:9 Widescreen from the Slideshow Format drop-down menu.** This ensures that your photos will be scaled properly for output on your widescreen TV.

9. **Click OK.**

10. **Click the Music button, located just to the right of the Settings button in the lower-right.** The music selection listing appears, as shown in figure 12.22.

11. **Select a track or playlist from iTunes to use as musical accompaniment for your slide show.**

12. **Click OK.**

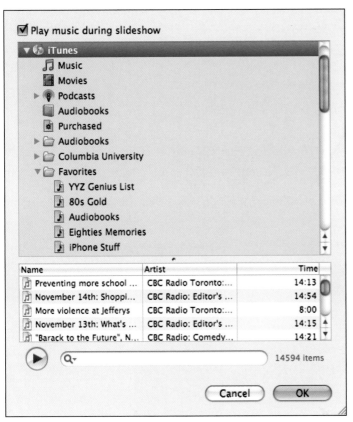

**12.22** An iPhoto slide show music selection

From this point, you can customize the slide show by using the option buttons at the bottom of the screen to add different transitions and effects on a per-slide basis — for example, every slide can use its own custom transition. Once you have customized your slide show to your preferences, simply select it in iTunes for transfer to your Apple TV as you would for any other photo album.

The photos and the slide show settings are copied to your Apple TV, and appear on the Apple TV's photos menu in the same way as any other photo album. However, unlike a normal photo album, selecting a slide show album immediately begins playback of the slide show, with the settings from iPhoto taking precedence over any global slide show settings on the Apple TV.

**Note** If you have selected musical accompaniment for your slide show, the music track or playlist must be available on your Apple TV during slide show playback, either streamed from your iTunes library or synced directly to the Apple TV. You must sync this playlist yourself — it does not come across with the slide show automatically.

# Using Your Apple TV with AirTunes

The Apple TV can also act as an AirTunes client for any of the iTunes libraries on your network. To configure the Apple TV to function as an AirTunes client, follow these steps:

1. **From the Apple TV main menu, choose Settings ⇨ AirTunes.** The AirTunes configuration screen appears.

2. **Ensure that AirTunes Speaker is set to on, as shown in figure 12.23.**

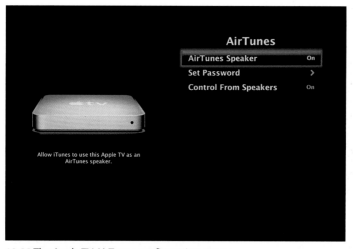

12.23 The Apple TV AirTunes configuration screen

3. **Optionally, select Set Password to require any connecting iTunes library to authenticate before being allowed to stream music through this Apple TV.**

4. **Press the Menu button to return to the previous menu.**

Once properly configured, your Apple TV appears by name in the AirTunes speaker list in the bottom-right corner of the iTunes window. AirTunes is discussed in Chapter 4.

With the Apple TV v2.3 firmware update, you can also now send your audio to other remote AirTunes-connected speakers. This works in much the same way as it does in iTunes. A list of any remote AirTunes speakers on your local network appears in the AirTunes configuration screen, similar to figure 12.24.

You can choose which speakers you want to play audio through by using the remote. A check mark appears beside the speaker names to indicate enabled speakers.

**Note** You can only stream audio content to remote speakers with AirTunes. When playing back video content, the audio track is always played only on your locally connected speakers regardless of the AirTunes settings.

12.24 List of remote AirTunes speakers on Apple TV

**Genius** You can quickly access the AirTunes menu while listening to an audio track by holding down the SELECT button on the Apple Remote and choosing Speakers from the pop-up menu that appears.

# Using Your iPhone or iPod Touch as an Apple TV Remote

If you have an iPhone or an iPod touch, it can also double as a remote control for your Apple TV when you install the free Apple Remote application from the iTunes App Store. This application allows you to browse and control the playback of your Apple TV content directly from your iPhone or iPod touch in a manner very similar to the built-in iPod application, but with even more advanced features such as the ability to search for content and create and edit playlists, all directly from your device.

Once you have installed the Remote application, you simply need to pair your Apple TV with your iPhone or iPod touch:

1. **Start the Remote application on your iPhone or iPod touch.** The Settings screen appears, similar to figure 12.25.

2. **Tap Add Library.** A four-digit numeric code appears, similar to figure 12.26.

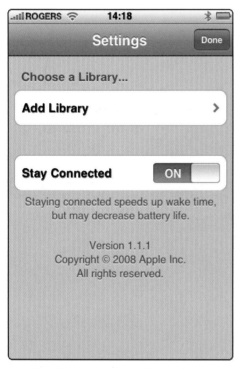

12.25 The iPhone Remote application Settings screen

12.26 The iPhone Remote application Add Library screen

3. **On your Apple TV, choose Settings ⇨ General ⇨ Remotes.** The Remote settings screen appears with your iPhone or iPod touch listed.

4. **Select your device, as shown in figure 12.27, and then press the Play/Pause button on your Apple remote.** A passcode entry screen appears.

5. **Using the arrow keys on your Apple remote, enter the passcode shown on your iPhone or iPod touch in step 2.**

12.27 Selecting your device

6. **Choose Done.** Your Apple TV shows your iPhone or iPod touch linked in the setting screen, and the Remote application on your device updates to show your Apple TV library content.

Once paired, you can browse through your Apple TV library in the same way as you would browse content stored directly on your device. Selecting content for playback immediately begins playing it on the Apple TV. The Remote application also supports searching, playlist creation, and the Genius feature.

One particularly useful feature of the Remote application is as a remote keyboard for entering information into the text-entry fields that appear on the Apple TV. Rather than fumbling with the normal Apple remote to try to scroll around to spell a word, simply start the Remote application on your iPhone or iPod touch. The current data-entry prompt appears on your device, with a keyboard that you can use to fill it in, as shown in figure 12.28.

This works on any data-entry field, so you can use it to enter passwords or fill in search fields.

12.28 The iPhone Remote data-entry screen

# Using a Third-Party Remote with the Apple TV

The Apple TV v2.3 firmware update introduced the ability for the Apple TV to learn commands from just about any infrared remote. While users of universal remote controls have likely already taken the opposite approach of teaching the Apple TV commands to your remote, this feature allows any remote to be used regardless of whether it is capable of learning commands or not — the Apple TV learns the commands directly from the remote.

Another advantage of this feature is that advanced playback controls can now be configured beyond the limitations of the Apple six-button remote. The learning process also allows you to have the Apple TV learn remote commands for specific functions such as play, pause, stop, rewind, fast-forward, previous track, next track, skip backward, and skip forward. Once programmed, the appropriate buttons can be used to trigger these functions directly from your remote.

To configure your Apple TV to use your own remote, follow these steps:

1. **Locate either a remote that you are no longer using, or a multifunction remote with a device that you are not using.** Many modern TV sets come with basic multifunction remotes to control several devices such as a cable box, VCR, or DVD player.

2. **Using your normal Apple Remote, from the Apple TV choose Settings ⇨ General ⇨ Remotes.** The remote control configuration screen shown in figure 12.29 appears.

12.29 Apple TV Remote Control configuration screen

3. **Choose Learn Remote.** You are prompted to choose an unused device setting on your other remote and then select Start using your Apple Remote to continue. The Learn Remote screen shown in figure 12.30 appears to guide you through the process.

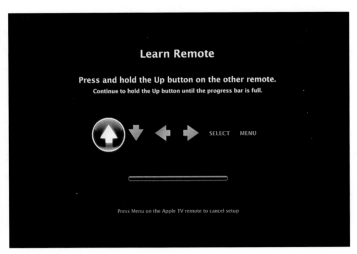

12.30 Apple TV Learn Remote screen

4. **Press and hold each button on your other remote as directed until the progress bar is full.** As you finish each button the Apple TV automatically proceeds to the next one. When you have programmed the final button, the Apple TV prompts you to name the remote control as shown in figure 12.31.

12.31 Apple TV Remote Control Name screen

5. **Using either your original Apple Remote or the new remote you have just pro-grammed, enter a name to identify the new remote and choose Done when finished.** The Apple TV displays a screen confirming that you are finished setting up your remote and asks if you want to set up playback buttons, as shown in figure 12.32.

**Setup Complete**

Your remote is ready to use with Apple TV. Choose Set Up Playback Buttons to set up additional buttons.

OK

**Set Up Playback Buttons**

12.32 Apple TV Remote Setup Complete

6. **Choose OK if you are finished configuring the remote to return to the main remote menu or choose Set Up Playback Buttons to configure additional buttons on your remote for use with your Apple TV.** If you choose to set up additional playback buttons, the screen in figure 12.33 is shown to allow you to set up your Apple TV to respond to additional buttons on your remote. Note that you do not need to program all of the listed buttons — you can use the left and right buttons on your remote to choose which buttons you want to program. Press the Select button on your remote when you are finished programming additional buttons.

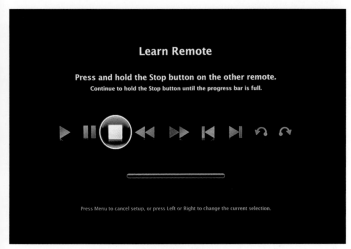

**12.33** Apple TV Learn Remote Buttons screen

When finished, you are returned to the Apple TV remote settings menu with your new remote configuration listed. You can select the remote from here to reconfigure, rename, or remove it, and you can even program your Apple TV to respond to additional third-party remotes.

**Note**

Programming a third-party remote does not disable the Apple Remote.

# How Do I Manage a Large iTunes Library?

Although you may only start out with a few dozen CDs and a few hundred music tracks in your iTunes library, with the wide variety of content supported by iTunes, it won't be long before you suddenly find yourself dealing with a much larger iTunes library. While iTunes handles most of your library management quite seamlessly, there are some advanced tips and tricks that are useful for getting the most out of iTunes when you're dealing with one or more larger iTunes libraries.

# Moving Your iTunes Library to an External Hard Drive

With higher bit-rate music formats becoming more common, as well as iTunes support for movies and TV shows, it's not going to be long before you find that your iTunes library has outgrown the capacity of the hard drive in your computer. At this point, you have two options: Buy a bigger hard drive and deal with the hassle of migrating your operating system over to it, or simply move the iTunes library to an external hard drive.

A common mistake made by many iTunes users is simply copying the entire iTunes Music folder to a new location and expecting iTunes to pick up this change. Unfortunately, this does not work, as iTunes is very specific about where its files are kept and how it manages them. As I discuss in Chapter 1, iTunes references files by their full path names, and so if you move a file to a new drive or partition, iTunes loses track of it, and the result is a broken link in your iTunes library.

**Note** Mac OS X users can get away with moving files between folders *on the same drive* because of the way that the underlying OS X operating system keeps track of file locations. However, this does not work when moving files to a different drive or partition.

If you have made this mistake and suddenly find that iTunes cannot find any of your tracks, the best solution is simply to move them back to their original location. Provided you have just copied the files over en masse and have not done any major reorganization of your file and folder layout, putting the files back in the locations where iTunes expects to find them should make everything match up again.

The good news is that iTunes provides a method by which you can move your files to a new location through iTunes, ensuring that all of your file locations are updated for the new location in the process.

**Note** The steps in this section make reference to using an external hard drive, but the same method can be used if you're simply looking to move your iTunes library to a second internal hard drive or a different partition on the same drive.

# Specifying a different iTunes Music folder location

By default, iTunes stores its library database and related information in a folder named *iTunes* under your *Music* (Mac) or *My Music* (Windows) folder. Your media content also lives here, in a sub-folder named *iTunes Music*. Don't let the name fool you, though: Your podcasts, audiobooks, TV shows, and movies are all stored here, too. In fact, the only types of content that are not located in this folder are your Click-Wheel iPod Games and your iPhone and iPod touch applications.

As I discuss in Chapter 1, this iTunes Music folder is where iTunes places content that you import from CD or download from the iTunes Store, including podcasts. Other files that you import directly into iTunes may also be stored in this folder or they may have been left in their original locations, depending on your preference settings.

You can change the location of your iTunes Music folder quite easily:

1.  **Open your iTunes preferences and click the Advanced tab, shown in figure 13.1.**

**13.1** The Advanced tab of the iTunes Preferences dialog box

2. **Click Change.** A file browser dialog box appears.

3. **In the file browser dialog box, specify a new folder location for your media content.**

4. **Click OK to apply the new settings.**

# Moving and consolidating your iTunes media

Changing your iTunes Music folder path tells iTunes where to place any new media that you import into your library; however, any existing files already in your library are left in their previous location. iTunes links to these files by their full path name so that it can still find them, but it begins treating them as unmanaged files like any other file outside of the iTunes Music folder.

However, iTunes has a feature designed to reorganize all of your files within your iTunes Music folder, copying in any tracks that are stored elsewhere in the process. While this feature is primarily designed to allow you to collect any tracks that you may have added to your library from their original locations, it works very well as a means for transferring your entire library to a new drive.

1. **In your iTunes preferences, set your iTunes Music folder location to the new drive that you want to store your media on.** More information on this can be found in Chapter 1.

2. **From the iTunes menu, choose File ⇨ Library ⇨ Consolidate Library.** Note that prior to iTunes 8, this option was found on the Advanced menu.

iTunes scans through your library, looking for files that are stored outside of the iTunes Music folder, and begins copying them in. In this case, because you have specified a completely new iTunes Music folder location, the result is to copy all of your media to this new location, updating your paths in the process.

Keep in mind that the Consolidate Library process *copies* your media files rather than moving them. This means that you still need to go back and manually clean them up from the original location to free up disk space once you've confirmed that everything is otherwise working properly.

**Note**  This method may not be desirable if you have chosen to not let iTunes organize your Music folder for you, as this option essentially reorganizes your entire library into the iTunes file-and-folder structure. Unfortunately, there is really no simple way to move a self-organized library to a new drive without reimporting all of your tracks again from the new location.

## External Hard Drives and Laptops

If you're a laptop user who travels often, there's no need to worry about lugging your iTunes media drive around with you unless you really need access to all of your media.

iTunes works just fine without the external drive connected, although, of course, you don't have access to any of your actual media files. Instead, iTunes shows them as broken links, and you may receive the occasional error about a file that cannot be found. Don't worry, as iTunes can pick these files up again as soon as the external hard drive returns.

More importantly, however, if you check your iTunes Music folder location while disconnected, you can see that iTunes has temporarily reverted back to the default location on your system drive. This means that you can use iTunes to download podcasts, purchase music, and even import CDs while you're on the road. These tracks are added to the local iTunes folder, where you can manage them normally and even sync them to your iPod or iPhone.

Further, you can even use automatic sync with your iPod while travelling. iTunes does not remove a file from your iPod as long as it remains listed in the iTunes library, even if the underlying file is not accessible.

When you return home and reconnect the external hard drive, the iTunes Music folder path should revert automatically back to the external path as soon as you restart iTunes, and then you can run another quick Consolidate Library operation to transfer any content that you've downloaded to the external drive.

# Moving the iTunes database to a new folder

The iTunes Music folder only specifies where your media content is stored. Your library database and other related support files remain in the default location under iTunes in your *Music* (Mac) or *My Music* (Windows) folder. These files generally take up very little space relative to your media collection, and so there is rarely any need to move them.

There are, however, cases where storing the iTunes library database in another location may be desirable, such as with an external hard drive that is used with multiple computers, or a shared network location.

Moving your iTunes database is a separate process from moving your iTunes Music folder, and does not change the path in which iTunes looks for your music. Because the iTunes media files are stored by default under the main iTunes folder, I strongly recommend that you move your iTunes Music folder first using the Consolidate Library function described earlier in this chapter before moving the main iTunes database.

Moving your iTunes database is relatively easy to accomplish, as long as you're using iTunes 7 or later:

1. **Shut down iTunes.**

2. **Using Windows Explorer or the Mac OS Finder, copy your iTunes folder to the new location where you want it to be stored.** Note that if your iTunes Music folder is still located under the iTunes folder, you may want to exclude this from the copy to save time, because it won't be used in the new location until you've copied it using the Consolidate Library function.

3. **Start iTunes while holding down the Opt key (Mac) or the Shift key (Windows).** Keep holding this key until iTunes prompts you with a dialog box similar to figure 13.2.

**Choose iTunes Library**

iTunes needs a library to continue. You may choose an existing iTunes library or create a new one.

Quit    Create Library...    Choose Library...

13.2 The Choose iTunes Library dialog box

4. **Click Choose Library.** A standard file browser dialog box appears.

5. **Browse to the location that you copied your iTunes folder to in step 2, and select the iTunes folder.**

6. **Click OK.**

iTunes starts up using the iTunes library folder in the new location, and continues to use this new location unless you change it again. Note that if you want to access this iTunes library database from other computers, you must repeat these steps on each additional computer.

**Caution**

If you choose to store your iTunes library on a network share for access by multiple computers, be very careful to not have iTunes running against the same library on more than one computer at a time. The iTunes database is not designed for simultaneous multiuser access, and corruption can occur in this situation.

# Moving Your iTunes Library to a New Computer

Migrating your entire iTunes library to a new computer is actually a fairly simple task, provided you plan to store your files in the same relative location on each computer. Ideally, if your iTunes Music folder is in its default location on your system drive, then copying your iTunes library to the new computer is really just a matter of copying over the entire iTunes folder from your original computer to the corresponding location on the new computer.

1. **Optional: Perform a Consolidate Library operation, as described earlier in this chapter.** This helps to ensure that all of your media files are contained within the iTunes folder.

2. **Shut down iTunes on both computers.**

3. **Locate your iTunes folder.** On a Mac, this is stored under your Music folder for the current user, while on Windows, it can be found under the My Music folder. See figure 13.3 for an example.

13.3 The iTunes folder location

4. **Copy the entire iTunes folder and all files and folders underneath it to the correspon-ding location on the new computer, directly under your Music or My Music folder.** You can copy these files using an external hard drive or USB memory key, by burning CDs or DVDs, or simply by copying them over a network connection between the two computers.

5. **If you receive an error message asking you whether you want to overwrite files in the destination folder, select Yes.** This can happen if you have already run iTunes on the new computer and created an empty iTunes database.

6. **Once the copying process is complete, start iTunes on the new computer.** It should pick up the copied library database and all of your content.

Note that your iTunes preferences are not copied from the original computer, and you should revisit your iTunes preferences screens to ensure that these are set the way you would like.

If you've stored your iTunes Music folder in another location, the process can be a bit trickier depending on how the new computer is laid out. If you store your iTunes Music folder on an external hard drive, you can still follow the previous steps to transfer your iTunes library database, and then simply make sure that the external hard drive is connected to the new computer.

If you're storing your iTunes library on a second hard drive inside your computer, then you either need to ensure that you copy the iTunes Music folder separately to the same location on the new computer (for example, D:\Music to D:\Music), or perform the Consolidate Library steps described earlier in this chapter to move the iTunes Music folder to a new location.

**Note**

Windows users may have problems with using an external hard drive on more than one computer, because drive letters may be assigned differently on different machines. You can reassign drive letters manually in Windows XP or Vista by visiting your Computer Management control panel and choosing Disk Management.

# Managing Your iTunes Media in Multiple Locations

As your iTunes library grows, one of the more frustrating limitations that you are likely to bump up against is the inability for iTunes to easily handle the storage of your media in more than a single location. Basically, you have one iTunes Music folder in which everything is stored, and although you can move your content en masse to a new location, as described earlier in this chapter, there's really no easy way to split it up. You can certainly choose to not copy files to the iTunes Music folder when adding them to your library, but this is not practical for those situations where your content is already in your iTunes library, and having some of your media stored outside of the iTunes Music folder can make things complicated when you want to relocate that content.

Fortunately, there are some tricks you can use in the underlying operating system to help you manage your content across multiple drives or partitions. These are not iTunes-specific features, but instead are ways to trick iTunes into storing or accessing your content elsewhere.

Both the Mac and Windows operating systems support a feature whereby you can link a sub-folder to a different file system location — even a completely different drive. In Mac OS X, these are referred to as symbolic links, while in Windows, they're called NTFS Junctions. Regardless of terminology, however, the function is the same: What looks like a normal sub-folder in your file system is actually linked to a completely different location.

This concept works with your iTunes library by allowing you to essentially chop off portions of your iTunes Music folder and relocate them elsewhere. For example, you could take the Movies sub-folder from your iTunes Music folder and copy it to a different drive or partition. You would then create a symbolic link or junction in place of the old Movies folder to point to this new location. As far as iTunes is concerned, the Movies folder is still there, but in reality, when it visits that location, it's actually referencing the files on the other drive.

The actual discussion of how to create symbolic links and NTFS Junctions is beyond the scope of this book, although numerous tutorials are available online.

# Creating Multiple iTunes Libraries on One Computer

It's not uncommon in many families to have multiple iPod users all sharing the same computer, sometimes with widely diverse musical tastes. Although you can easily share the same library and sync it with multiple iPods as discussed in Chapter 7, this may not work in many cases because the playlists, ratings, and other metadata are also shared across all iPods.

Fortunately, there are a few different ways you can manage multiple libraries on a single computer.

The first and simplest method is to just use separate user accounts. Your iTunes library is specific to your own user account, and if somebody else logs in on the computer, they get their own iTunes library. In this case, everybody has their own self-contained iTunes library database and iTunes Music folder automatically, with no further effort required to manage it.

On the other hand, if you're all sharing a single user account on the computer, this may not be a practical solution. In this scenario, iTunes allows you to create and choose different libraries manually. To create a new library for the current user account, follow these steps:

1. **Start iTunes while holding down the Opt key (Mac) or the Shift key (Windows).** Keep holding this key until iTunes prompts you with the Choose iTunes Library dialog box, shown in figure 13.4.

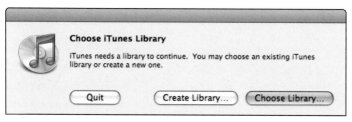

**Choose iTunes Library**

iTunes needs a library to continue. You may choose an existing iTunes library or create a new one.

( Quit )     ( Create Library... )     ( Choose Library... )

13.4 Creating a new iTunes Library

2. **Click Create Library.** A standard file browser dialog box appears.

3. **Browse to the folder where you want the new iTunes library to be stored.**

4. **Type a name for the new iTunes library folder.**

5. **Click OK.** iTunes creates a new, empty library at the specified location. To create additional iTunes libraries, simply repeat these steps.

When you restart iTunes, it uses the same library as it did last time unless you tell it to use a different one. To change between libraries, follow these steps:

1. **Start iTunes while holding down the Opt key (Mac) or the Shift key (Windows).** Keep holding this key until iTunes prompts you with the Choose iTunes Library dialog box.

2. **Click Choose Library.** A standard file browser dialog box appears.

3. **Browse to and select the folder where your alternate iTunes library is stored.**

4. **Click OK.**

**Caution**

iTunes preference settings are stored globally for your current user account, regardless of which library you are currently using. This can be especially important for settings such as the iTunes Music folder location. If you need to keep your iTunes preferences separate, then you must use different user accounts or an iTunes library-management tool such as AppleScript discussed in Chapter 15.

292

# Sharing your iTunes Library on a Network

iTunes provides built-in support for sharing and streaming your media content across multiple computers on the same network. This allows other users to connect to your iTunes library using their own copy of iTunes, and then to browse through and listen to your music. Note that remote users cannot actually copy or sync the music — your library is shared in listen-only mode.

**Note**
If you have protected iTunes content stored in your shared library, then the remote computers must be authorized for your iTunes Store account in order to listen to or view that content.

To enable sharing for your iTunes library, follow these steps:

1. **Open your iTunes preferences and select the General tab.**

2. **In the Library Name field at the top of the pane, type a name for your iTunes library.** This is the name that other users see in their list of shared libraries. In figure 13.5, you can see I named mine Main Library.

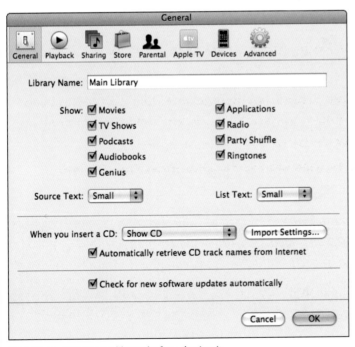

13.5 Name your iTunes library before sharing it.

3. **Select the Sharing tab.**

4. **Click the check box next to Share my library on my local network to enable it.**

5. **Choose whether you would like to share your entire iTunes library or only selected playlists, as shown in figure 13.6.**

**Genius**

There have been several tools available in the past, such as ourTunes, which allowed you to actually copy music from a shared iTunes library. While such tools are frequently handy for sharing music that you own across several computers in your household, they should of course not be used for stealing music from shared libraries that you do not own. Unfortunately, these tools work by reverse-engineering the shared library technology and are therefore frequently broken by iTunes updates. For instance, ourTunes does not presently work with iTunes 8.

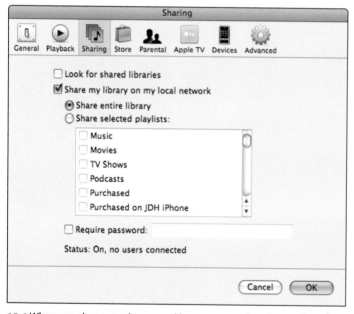

13.6 When you choose to share your library, you need to choose if you want to share all of the library or just parts of it.

6. **You can also click the check box beside Require password and type a password if you would like to restrict access to your iTunes library.** In this case, users attempting to connect to your iTunes library are required to enter this password before they can connect.

7. **Click OK.**

Once you have enabled library sharing, other users can see your shared library in their iTunes Source list immediately above their playlists, as shown in figure 13.7.

Accessing a shared library is handled in the same way as any other iTunes category, and the listing can be filtered and sorted in the same way. Clicking the triangle to the left of the shared library expands it to show a list of playlists from that library. Keep in mind that Cover Flow and Grid views are not available when accessing a shared library.

13.7 An iTunes shared library

**Note** If you are not seeing any shared libraries in your iTunes Source list, ensure that the Look for shared libraries option is enabled in your iTunes sharing preferences.

## Network Sharing and Synchronizing

iTunes library sharing works well enough for situations where you're really just concerned with letting other users listen to your music. However, many users also want a way to share a common set of music that they can sync to their iPod or take with them on a notebook computer.

If you have a home network server, you may simply be tempted to put your iTunes library on the server and point each of your computers at it. This solution is fraught with danger, however, because the iTunes library database is not designed for multiuser access, and so you must be very careful to not have more than one copy of iTunes running against it at a time. Another common method is to simply put the iTunes Music folder on a network drive and point each iTunes library at it. This creates less possibility of corruption, but you must again be very careful not to let one of your iTunes libraries reorganize your media files on you, or the other libraries will end up with broken links. Further, new music must be individually imported into each library, because the databases are separate.

Neither of the above methods is practical for creating a library that you can actually take with you. If you're a notebook user and you're away from the home network, you're pretty much cut off from your iTunes library.

Recently, however, some enterprising third-party software developers have stepped in to provide a much more elegant solution for sharing a common library of music by providing tools to synchronize iTunes libraries across multiple computers, rather than merely sharing a single library. In this case, each computer has its own standalone iTunes library, but a third-party application running on both ends reads the iTunes database and provides a number of different options for syncing either some or all of your iTunes libraries to keep them consistent.

If you have multiple computers and you want to share the same iTunes content between them, be sure to check out TuneRanger (www.acertant.com) or Syncopation (www.sonzea.com).

# What Can I Do When I Have Problems with My iPod?

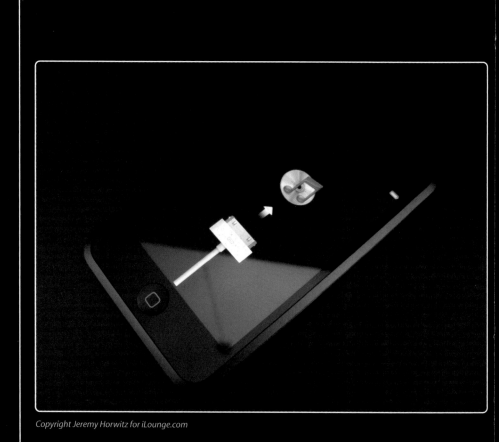

Although the iPod is a wonderful piece of technology, it's also a very sophisticated electronic device, and therefore it's not uncommon for problems to occur. A few simple troubleshooting steps can help you to determine whether you can solve your iPod's problems yourself or whether you should be taking it to your nearest Apple Store for professional help.

# Basic Troubleshooting

If you're having a problem with your iPod, you should start by following basic diagnostic procedures to see if this solves the problem you are having. Many common problems experienced by iPod users are caused by software conflicts on the iTunes computer, USB port or cable problems, or software or database corruption on the iPod.

## Reset

The first step is to simply reset your iPod. This is conceptually the same as rebooting your computer, and basically gives your iPod a clean start. This does not erase any of the content stored on your iPod, but simply restarts it from scratch.

You can reset a traditional click wheel iPod by holding down the CENTER and MENU buttons for about 6 to 10 seconds until you see the Apple Logo appear. On the iPod touch and iPhone, this is accomplished by holding down the HOME and SLEEP/WAKE buttons for about 8 seconds, again until the Apple logo appears.

While the click wheel iPods are fairly stable and rarely need to be reset, it's not uncommon for the iPhone or iPod touch to require a reboot every so often, particularly if you're using a lot of demanding third-party applications. Sluggish performance and inexplicable application crashes on the iPod touch and iPhone are frequently solved simply by restarting the device.

## Retry

The second R involves retrying the operation that you're having a problem with. For example, if you're having problems connecting or synchronizing your iPod, try using a different USB port or a different USB cable, if you have one available. Avoid using USB ports on keyboards or USB hubs — connect the iPod directly to a USB port on your computer.

Another good solution is to try a different computer if you have one available. A computer at a friend's house, or at school or work, can be useful in determining if the problem is with your iPod or with your computer.

## Restart

The third R is to restart your computer and try the operation again. Sometimes simply restarting your computer clears out its memory and resolves any problems you've been having.

If the issue remains after a simple restart, the next step is to try restarting your computer with fewer background applications running — try to start iTunes before you start anything else, and disable other applications that might be causing problems. You can identify and temporarily disable applications that start automatically in Windows by using the MSCONFIG tool. On the Mac, a list of applications that run automatically at start up for the current user account is found in your Account preferences.

You should also ensure that you are running the latest version of iTunes and the latest software updates for your operating system. You can check for updates for iTunes and Mac OS X by running Apple's Software Update on your Mac or PC, and you can check for updates and patches for Windows XP and Vista by running the Windows Updater tool.

Certain applications can commonly get in the way of synchronizing your iPod. Virus scanners and disk-management tools can cause problems because they see a traditional iPod as an external hard drive, and try to scan it or process it, which may interfere with the ability of iTunes to do so. Likewise, any USB drivers that you may have installed for other devices can easily interfere with your iPod's USB connection, particularly on Windows-based computers. Restarting Windows in Safe Mode is one method you can use to identify whether your problem is caused by third-party software and driver conflicts.

**Note**  Apple provides a Web-based walk-through diagnostic of each specific iPod model at www.apple.com/support/ipod/five_rs.

# Reinstall

The fourth R suggests reinstalling iTunes on your computer to clear up any driver-related problems or iTunes connection problems that you may be having. Note that you can uninstall and reinstall iTunes without losing any of your stored media content or your iTunes library — only the iTunes application files are affected when you uninstall. You should always download and install the very latest version of iTunes when doing this, rather than reinstalling your existing version. You can always obtain the latest version of iTunes for either Mac or Windows at the Apple iTunes download page at www.apple.com/itunes/download.

Once you've reinstalled the latest version of iTunes, you should also confirm that your iPod is running the latest iPod firmware. To check this, do the following:

301

1. **Connect your iPod to your computer.**

2. **Select your iPod from the iTunes Devices list.** The iPod Summary screen appears, similar to figure 14.1.

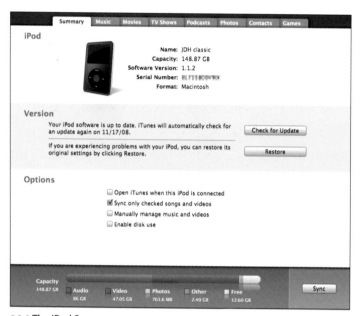

14.1 The iPod Summary screen

3. **Click Check for Update.** This tells iTunes to check with Apple to see if a newer firmware package is available for your iPod. If so, iTunes downloads and installs it onto your iPod.

## Restore

The fifth R is the final drastic step in the process — to actually restore your iPod. This effectively reformats your iPod, returning it to out-of-the-box factory settings and erasing all of the content that you have stored on it.

If you've been using automatic synchronization, all of your content is already stored in your iTunes library, and you can easily reload it onto your iPod after a restore. On the other hand, if you're using manual synchronization and do not have all of your iPod's content actually on your computer, then you should look at trying to back up the data from your iPod first — Chapter 10 has more information on how to do that.

**Note** Storing your media content solely on your iPod is generally a bad idea because your iPod is a portable device that can easily be lost or damaged. It's always a really good idea to keep a backup of your content somewhere else, even if it's not on your main computer.

To restore your iPod to its factory settings, follow these steps:

1. **Connect your iPod to your computer.**

2. **Select your iPod from the iTunes Devices list.** The iPod Summary screen appears.

3. **Click Restore.** iTunes checks for and downloads the latest firmware for your iPod, and then proceeds to format the drive and load the latest iPod firmware back on.

When this process is complete, your iPod is returned to its original configuration and you are taken through the iPod Setup Assistant as you would be for a new iPod.

**Note** In the case of the iPhone and iPod touch, iTunes offers to restore your device's preferences and settings from a previous backup. If you've been having problems, it may be worthwhile to skip restoring this backup to see if the same problem occurs in a clean configuration. You can always restore the backup later.

# Common iPod Problems and Solutions

With the way the iPod works and the wide variety of hardware and software configurations in use, there are a few problems that users most commonly run into regardless of configuration. You can solve some of these by going through the standard Five Rs troubleshooting process, but others have slightly different solutions.

## Your iPod is not detected by iTunes

The Five Rs often do you no good if your iPod isn't even being seen by your computer. Obviously, if your computer doesn't see your iPod, then updating or restoring it is not going to be an option.

If you're using a traditional iPod model, the first thing to check is whether your iPod appears in Windows Explorer or the Mac OS Finder when you connect it without iTunes running. If the iPod is showing up as an external drive, but iTunes is not picking it up, then this usually indicates a problem with your iTunes installation or drivers, rather than your computer's operating system or hardware. The fact that your computer sees your iPod as a hard disk indicates that the USB communication is working properly.

On the other hand, if the iPod is not showing up on your computer at all, then this could indicate a problem with your USB port or USB cable, or a driver conflict on your computer. Consider the following:

1. **Try a different USB port directly on the computer.** Do not use a USB hub or keyboard port, but plug the iPod directly into a USB port on your computer. If you're using a desktop PC, try one of the USB ports at the rear of the computer, as these are usually directly hard-wired to the computer's system board.

2. **Try a different iPod USB cable if you have one available.** If you do not have an extra USB cable or know anybody who does, you can visit an Apple Store or local Apple reseller to try one there.

3. **Try a different computer.** This is a very useful troubleshooting step to isolate whether the problem is with your iPod or your computer. If your iPod appears fine on the other computer — even as a removable hard disk — then you can focus on computer-related problems. If the iPod doesn't appear on any other computer that you try, then there's a good possibility that the iPod is the problem.

4. **Check for any new software or drivers that have been recently installed.** Something as seemingly innocuous as a printer or digital camera driver can create USB driver conflicts that can affect your computer's ability to see your iPod. Uninstalling or rolling back these drivers can often help resolve the problem.

5. **Unload any extra software or services.** Some background software applications can also conflict or interfere with your iPod being properly detected. Quit as many of these applications as possible and try connecting your iPod. Alternatively, if you're using Windows try restarting your computer in Safe Mode and connecting your iPod to see if it at least appears as a removable storage device.

You can also find some very good and specific troubleshooting information for each model of iPod in the Apple Knowledge Base at www.apple.com/support/.

# Your album artwork is not appearing properly on the iPod

Due to the way that iTunes and the iPod store album artwork on the iPod, it is not uncommon for this information to get out of sync such that either the wrong artwork appears on your iPod for certain tracks, or no artwork appears at all.

Restoring your iPod completely often fixes this problem, but taking that drastic step is rarely necessary. If you are using automatic synchronization and have a traditional iPod model, then you can easily reset the artwork on your iPod by following these steps:

1. **Connect your iPod to your computer.**

2. **Select your iPod from the iTunes Devices list.**

3. **Choose the Music tab from your iPod sync settings screen in iTunes.** The Music sync settings appear, similar to figure 14.2.

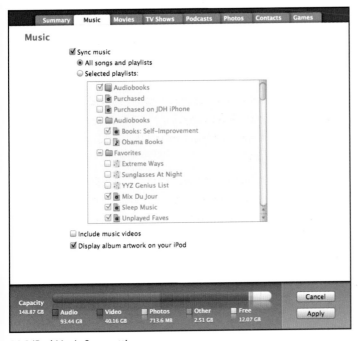

14.2 iPod Music Sync settings

4. **Click the check box next to Display album artwork on your iPod to deselect it.**

5. **Click Apply.** Your iPod begins synchronizing. During this sync, iTunes removes all album artwork from your iPod.

6. **Once the sync completes, click the check box next to Display album artwork on your iPod to re-enable it.**

7. **Click Apply.** Your iPod begins synchronizing again, with iTunes rebuilding the album artwork and retransferring it to your iPod.

Once the sync is complete, check the artwork on your iPod to see if it is now correct.

Unfortunately, the iPod touch and iPhone do not provide the option to turn off album artwork on these devices. If you are having artwork problems with an iPod touch or iPhone, the only way to reload the artwork is to actually remove the affected tracks themselves and reload them.

# Your songs skip on the iPod or do not play at all

Skipping is another problem frequently encountered by many users. Sometimes you can solve this problem simply by resetting the iPod, but if it persists, then the likely cause is corrupt or incompatible media files on the iPod.

If this problem is specific to a small number of tracks and these tracks play fine in iTunes, then you should try removing these tracks from the iPod and loading them back on. If you are using manual management, simply delete them directly from the iPod using iTunes, and then copy them back on using drag-and-drop. If you're using automatic synchronization, you can remove them by setting your iPod to only sync checked items:

1. **Connect your iPod to your computer.**

2. **Select your iPod from the iTunes Devices list.** The iPod Summary screen appears.

3. **Click the check box beside Sync only checked songs and videos to ensure that it is enabled, as shown in figure 14.3.**

4. **Click Apply.**

5. **Locate the affected songs in your iTunes library, and click the check box beside each song to deselect them.**

6. **Select your iPod from the iTunes Devices list.**

7. **Click the Sync button in the bottom-right corner of the iTunes window.** This removes all unchecked tracks from your iPod.

8. **Retransfer them onto your iPod by reselecting them in the iTunes library and syncing your iPod again.**

14.3 The iPod Summary screen with the Sync only checked songs and videos option selected

If you have retransferred the tracks onto your iPod and they still are not playing properly, then the other possibility is that there is an encoding problem with the tracks themselves. Depending on your iPod model and firmware version, you may have problems playing MP3 files with nonstandard bit-rates, or VBR files. Updating to the latest firmware often resolves these problems, but if not, then you may need to re-encode the affected files. The simplest way to determine if you have an encoding problem is to try converting the file to your preferred import format using iTunes. Follow these steps:

1. **Select an affected track.**

2. **From the iTunes menu, choose Advanced ⇨ Create AAC Version.** Note that if your default import format is something other than AAC, then this menu option lists that format instead (i.e., Create MP3 Version). Chapter 1 provides more detail on import formats and bit-rates. iTunes creates a new version of the selected track in the specified format and bit-rate.

3. **Transfer the new track to your iPod.**

**Caution** When converting tracks, iTunes creates a copy of each track and leaves the original in place, still taking up space in your library. To conserve space, you should ensure that you go back and delete either the original or the converted tracks when you are satisfied with the results.

Try playing the converted track. If it plays properly, then you may want to convert the remaining tracks that you're having problems with. Note, however, that converting these tracks using iTunes results in a quality loss; whether or not this loss is noticeable depends largely on the original file format, the bit-rate chosen, and the quality of your earphones. Ideally, if you have the original CDs available, you should simply rerip the tracks.

If a lot of tracks are skipping that did not previously skip, then there could be a problem with the iPod. Try restoring the iPod, and if this does not fix the problem, then the iPod likely needs to be serviced.

**Note**

In rare cases, protected iTunes tracks may end up on your iPod without the proper authorization being transferred. In this case, these tracks simply do not play on the iPod. Usually, retransferring additional tracks purchased from the same account solves this problem. However, this should rarely occur, as iTunes does not normally allow tracks to be transferred to the iPod unless they can be authorized.

# Advanced iPod Troubleshooting

If all of the standard troubleshooting steps have failed, there are still a few more solutions you can try to return your iPod back to normal operation.

## Downgrading your iPod firmware

If you're having an iPod problem that started after a recent iPod firmware upgrade, then it's possible that the problem lies in the new firmware. Fortunately, iTunes keeps older firmware versions that you've previously used on your computer, and you can downgrade your iPod to an earlier firmware version quite easily, although you need to perform a full restore on your iPod to do so:

1. **Connect your iPod to your computer.**

2. **Select your iPod from the iTunes Devices list.** The iPod Summary screen appears.

3. **While holding down the Opt key (Mac) or Shift key (Windows), click the Restore button in iTunes.** A file browser dialog box appears, prompting you to select a specific iPod software package.

4. **Browse to your iPod Software folder.** In Mac OS X, you can find it under your home folder in *Library/iTunes/iPod Software Updates*. In Windows XP, it is stored in *Application Data\Apple Computer\iTunes\iPod Software Updates* under your home folder, and in Windows Vista, in *AppData\Roaming\Apple Computer\iTunes\iPod Software Updates*.

5. **From the iPod Software Updates folder, select the package you would like to restore to your iPod.** Version numbers are normally listed at the end of each package name, as shown in figure 14.4.

6. **Click OK to begin restoring the older firmware onto your iPod.**

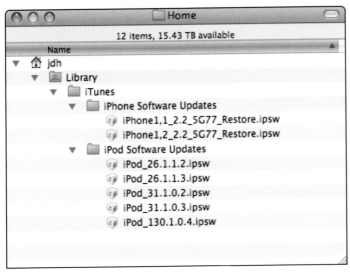

14.4 iPod Software packages

**Note** Older firmware packages are only available on your computer if you have previously updated or restored your iPod through iTunes. Although Apple does not supply older iPod firmware packages directly, links can be found on the Internet to download them.

# Starting your iPod in Disk Mode

Another very useful troubleshooting step for traditional iPod models is to force your iPod into Disk Mode. This mode bypasses any normal iPod function and forces your iPod to present itself to your computer as a removable hard disk. This can be very useful for situations where your computer cannot otherwise detect your iPod.

To force your iPod into Disk Mode, follow these steps:

1. **Hold down the CENTER and MENU buttons for about 6 to 10 seconds until the Apple logo appears.**

2. **When the Apple logo appears, release the MENU button immediately and hold down the PLAY/PAUSE button until the Disk Mode screen appears, similar to figure 14.5.**

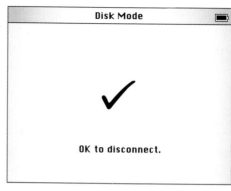

14.5 iPod Disk Mode screen

Once in Disk Mode, you can try connecting you iPod to your computer to see if it is properly detected. This can often allow you to restore your iPod in situations where it cannot otherwise be seen by your computer.

To return from Disk Mode, simply reset your iPod by holding down the CENTER and MENU buttons for about 6 to 10 seconds.

# Hard-restoring your click wheel iPod

In certain cases, particularly with older iPod models, you may find that iTunes still cannot see or restore your iPod, even after you've tried all the other troubleshooting steps, as well as forcing the iPod into Disk Mode.

In this case, as long as the iPod is visible to your computer as an external hard drive, you can often recover the iPod and get iTunes to recognize it by doing an operating-system-level format. Remember that the iPod is actually just an external hard drive as far as your computer is concerned, and you can therefore treat it like any other hard drive. If iTunes cannot see your iPod or cannot restore it, then there could be something wrong with the hard drive or flash memory on the device that can be fixed by doing a computer-level format.

In this case, simply shut down iTunes and format the iPod through Windows Explorer or Disk Utility (Mac) as you would for any other drive. This erases everything on the iPod, of course, including the iPod's own operating files; however, it also cleans up any file-system issues that may be preventing iTunes from doing its job. Once this process is complete, the iPod may not work at all (because the internal operating files have also been erased), but you may now have better luck getting iTunes to complete its restore process and returning the iPod back to normal operation.

These types of issues are less common with the newer iPod classic and iPod nano models, but many a third- and fourth-generation iPod have been saved by performing an operating-system-level format. It's definitely worth a try if you've tried everything else to get your iPod working and iTunes can't get the job done by itself.

# Hard-restoring your iPhone or iPod touch

The iPhone and iPod touch do not present themselves as an external hard drive, and therefore cannot be hard-restored using the same method as for click wheel iPods. Instead, these iPods support a hardware-based "DFU mode" that can be used to force the device into a restore mode where iTunes should be able to recognize it. To place your iPhone or iPod touch into "DFU mode" follow these steps:

1. **Connect your iPhone or iPod touch to your computer via the USB cable.** Don't worry if it doesn't show up in iTunes.

2. **Hold down both the Home and Sleep/Wake buttons on your device together until your device's screen goes blank.**

3. **Once the screen goes blank, release the Sleep/Wake button and continue holding the Home button until iTunes displays a message telling you that it has found your device in recovery mode, similar to figure 14.6.** Note that your device's screen should remain blank — if the Apple logo appears then return to step 2 and try again.

4. **Restore your device using iTunes as described earlier in this chapter.**

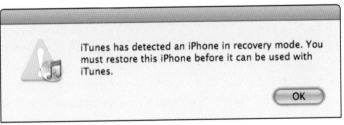

iTunes has detected an iPhone in recovery mode. You must restore this iPhone before it can be used with iTunes.

OK

14.6 iTunes has detected an iPhone in recovery mode.

**Note**

DFU mode bypasses the loading of the iPhone or iPod touch operating system entirely — it is a hardware-based restore mode. If iTunes still cannot detect your device in DFU mode even on multiple computers, then chances are that your device is damaged beyond repair.

311

# How Do I Use Scripts to Get More out of iTunes?

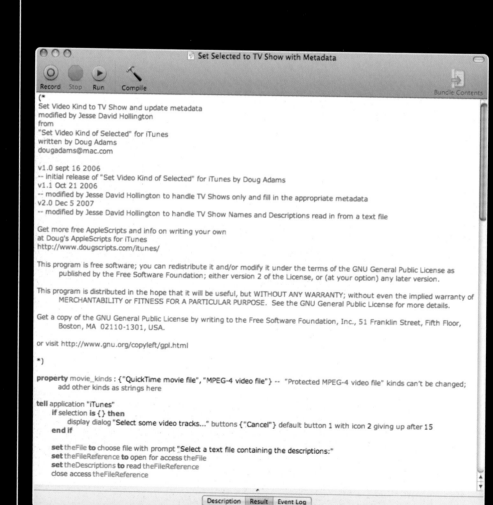

```
○ ○ ○                    Set Selected to TV Show with Metadata
○        ■        ▶        ✎
Record    Stop     Run       Compile                                          Bundle Contents
(*
Set Video Kind to TV Show and update metadata
modified by Jesse David Hollington
from
"Set Video Kind of Selected" for iTunes
written by Doug Adams
dougadams@mac.com

v1.0 sept 16 2006
-- initial release of "Set Video Kind of Selected" for iTunes by Doug Adams
v1.1 Oct 21 2006
-- modified by Jesse David Hollington to handle TV Shows only and fill in the appropriate metadata
v2.0 Dec 5 2007
-- modified by Jesse David Hollington to handle TV Show Names and Descriptions read in from a text file

Get more free AppleScripts and info on writing your own
at Doug's AppleScripts for iTunes
http://www.dougscripts.com/itunes/

This program is free software; you can redistribute it and/or modify it under the terms of the GNU General Public License as
    published by the Free Software Foundation; either version 2 of the License, or (at your option) any later version.

This program is distributed in the hope that it will be useful, but WITHOUT ANY WARRANTY; without even the implied warranty of
    MERCHANTABILITY or FITNESS FOR A PARTICULAR PURPOSE.  See the GNU General Public License for more details.

Get a copy of the GNU General Public License by writing to the Free Software Foundation, Inc., 51 Franklin Street, Fifth Floor,
    Boston, MA  02110-1301, USA.

or visit http://www.gnu.org/copyleft/gpl.html

*)

property movie_kinds : {"QuickTime movie file", "MPEG-4 video file"} -- "Protected MPEG-4 video file" kinds can't be changed;
    add other kinds as strings here

tell application "iTunes"
    if selection is {} then
        display dialog "Select some video tracks..." buttons {"Cancel"} default button 1 with icon 2 giving up after 15
    end if

    set theFile to choose file with prompt "Select a text file containing the descriptions:"
    set theFileReference to open for access theFile
    set theDescriptions to read theFileReference
    close access theFileReference

                    Description   Result   Event Log
```

One of the great features of iTunes is its extensibility through AppleScript and JavaScript on both the Mac and Windows platforms. This direct script integration allows for automated routines and access to features that aren't directly available through iTunes, greatly enhancing the power of iTunes as a media-management application.

# About Scripts and iTunes

For Mac users, Apple provides a convenient systemwide scripting system known as AppleScript, which allows many applications in Mac OS X to be controlled and enhanced through the use of scripts that can access features directly within an application. iTunes is no exception, with a comprehensive AppleScript dictionary that allows for sophisticated management of your iTunes library and control of iTunes.

Windows users are not entirely left out in the cold, however, as iTunes can also be extended through JavaScript on the Windows platform. The scripting capabilities are not quite as extensive, and the number of available scripts for Windows users is considerably smaller than for Mac users, but a number of useful scripts still exist to help Windows users manage their iTunes libraries as well.

If you have some experience with AppleScript or JavaScript, then you can also write your own scripts for iTunes quite easily. AppleScript, in particular, is a very user-friendly, natural language-scripting system, and can be quite useful for performing simple library-management tasks like mass-updating information in your tracks that isn't otherwise accessible through iTunes.

# Cool AppleScripts for Mac iTunes Users

The best source of AppleScripts for iTunes can be found on a site called Doug's AppleScripts for iTunes at www.dougscripts.com. As of this writing, over 400 scripts are available to handle a wide variety of different functions, extending the features in iTunes and allowing you to better manage your iTunes library. Many of the scripts are written by Doug Adams, although a number of user-contributed scripts can also be found on his site. With the exception of a few of the more sophisticated scripts, the majority of the AppleScripts available on this site are completely free.

**Note** For those users interested in writing their own AppleScripts or modifying existing ones, Doug Adams moderates an AppleScripts for iTunes forum on iLounge.com, where some great additional AppleScripting for iTunes information can be found.

## Find duplicate tracks in iTunes

Although iTunes has a built-in feature to show duplicate tracks, this is not particularly useful in a large iTunes library, because all it does is show you the tracks — you still have to go through and clean them up yourself. Dupin (dougscripts.com/itunes/itinfo/dupin.php) is a $15 shareware

AppleScript that automates the process of cleaning up duplicates for you. Follow these steps to use this AppleScript to clean up your duplicates:

1. **Download, install, and run Dupin.** The main Dupin window appears, similar to figure 15.1.

15.1 The main Dupin window

2. **From the Library section in the top-left corner, select the context or playlist in which you would like to search for duplicates.**

3. **From the Criteria list at the lower-right, choose the criteria that you would like to use to compare files and match duplicates.** Tracks are only considered duplicates if the properties of all selected criteria fields match between two or more tracks.

4. **Click Get Dupes to begin searching the selected context or playlist for duplicate tracks.** Dupin scans through your iTunes library in search of duplicate tracks, with the results shown in the main window, similar to figure 15.2.

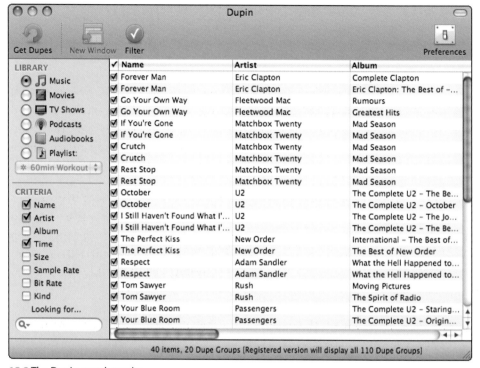

15.2 The Dupin search results

5. **Click the Filter button to determine which tracks to keep for each set of duplicates.** The Dupin Filter Controls dialog box appears, as shown in figure 15.3.

6. **Select the criteria that you would like to use for determining which duplicates to keep.**

7. **Click the Filter button.** Dupin scans through your list and indicates which items are going to be kept or deleted by displaying a check mark next to each keeper.

15.3 The Dupin Filter Controls dialog box

8. **When you are satisfied with the track selections, choose File ⇨ Purge from the Dupin menu to remove the unchecked tracks from your iTunes library.**

# Easily use multiple iTunes libraries

While iTunes allows you to switch libraries manually at startup by holding down the Opt key (Mac) or Shift key (Windows), if you regularly switch between iTunes libraries on the same computer and user account, this can quickly become tedious. Further, as I note in Chapter 13, switching to a different library with iTunes still maintains the preferences from your original library, making it more complicated to truly have multiple independent iTunes libraries.

Fortunately, iTunes Library Manager (dougscripts.com/itunes/itinfo/ituneslibrarymanager.php) is a $10 shareware script that addresses both of these problems. First, it prompts you at startup to select an iTunes library, so that you don't have to remember to hold down a key when starting iTunes. Second, it switches to library-specific preference settings, so that you can easily use different iTunes Music folder locations or other preferences unique to each library. To set up and manage multiple iTunes libraries with iTunes Library Manager, follow these steps:

1. **Download, install, and run iTunes Library Manager.** The main iTunes Library Manager window appears, similar to figure 15.4.

15.4 The iTunes Library Manager window

2. **Click the Save button to back up your current iTunes library before proceeding.**

3. **Type a name for your current iTunes library.** Once the backup is complete, your library should be listed in the main iTunes Library Manager window.

4. **To create a new iTunes library, click the New button.** iTunes Library Manager notifies you that it is going to back up the current iTunes library and then create a new, empty iTunes library.

5. **Click Proceed to continue.** An iTunes Library Manager dialog box asks whether you want to use your existing iTunes preference settings or create initialized preferences, as shown in figure 15.5.

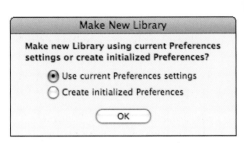

15.5 The iTunes Library Manager Make New Library dialog box

**Note** If you choose the Create initialized Preferences option, the new iTunes library acts just like a brand-new installation of iTunes, and the iTunes setup wizard appears.

6. **To switch among iTunes libraries in the future, simply load iTunes Library Manager, select the iTunes library that you would like to use, and click the Load button.** The current library is backed up, and the chosen library is swapped into its place.

# Convert lossless to AAC for your iPod

A common problem among fans of lossless music formats is how to store full Apple Lossless or AIFF files in your iTunes library while automatically syncing a more reasonably sized version to your iPod. iTunes can transcode higher bit-rate formats to 128 kbps AAC on the fly for iPod shuffle users, but this feature is unavailable in the sync settings for any other iPod model.

A free AppleScript comes to the rescue, however: Lossless to AAC Workflow (dougscripts.com/itunes/scripts/ss.php?sp=losslessaccworkflow) is designed to allow you to convert selected tracks to your preferred AAC format, and copy them onto an iPod that is set to manual management. To use this script, follow these steps:

1. **Download Lossless to AAC Workflow and install it into your Scripts folder, according to the provided instructions.**

2. **Ensure that your iPod is connected to your computer and set to manual mode.**

3. **In iTunes, select a lossless track that you would like to convert and transfer to your iPod.** You can also select multiple tracks.

4. **Run the Lossless to AAC Workflow
(iTunes ⇨ iPod) script.** iTunes converts
the selected lossless tracks to AAC files
and prompts you for what to do next, as
shown in figure 15.6, with a dialog box.

5. **Choose Add AACs to iPod or Create
New iPod Playlist.** Add AACs to iPod
copies the tracks directly to your iPod;
Create New iPod Playlist copies the
tracks to your iPod too, but in a new
playlist containing only the newly

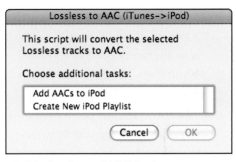

15.6 The Lossless to AAC dialog box

copied tracks. In either case, the converted tracks are removed from your iTunes library after
they are copied to your iPod.

The Lossless to AAC Workflow package also includes a second script that can be used to rip your
tracks directly from CD into a lossless file for your iTunes library, and an AAC file for your iPod, all at
the same time.

# Other cool AppleScripts

The library of AppleScripts at Doug's Scripts for iTunes contains dozens of other cool little scripts
that can perform a wide variety of useful functions, and best of all, they're free. Some additional
scripts worth taking a look at include:

- **Join Together.** This script allows you to automatically join multiple individual tracks into
  a single AAC file, optionally including chapter markers for each track. While its usefulness
  for music has been largely eliminated by iTunes and the iPod's Gapless Playback features,
  it may still be of interest to users of older iPod models, as it's a great way to create a
  gapless listening experience while still being able to skip to specific tracks. It is also
  extremely useful for dealing with multichapter audiobooks that come as a series of separate files. Join Together is available as both a full-featured free version, and a $7 pro ver-
  sion with some additional preflight and postop features.

- **Tracks Without Artwork to Playlist.** This free script collects any tracks in your iTunes
  library that do not contain album artwork, and groups them together in a single playlist,
  providing you with an easy way to search out tracks that need album artwork added.

- **No Lyrics to Playlist.** Similar to the Tracks Without Artwork to Playlist script, this script
  groups all tracks that do not have any lyrics into a single playlist.

- **Embed Artwork**. Artwork that you add to tracks yourself is stored within the AAC or MP3 file tags directly. However, this is not the case with artwork added automatically by iTunes. The free Embed Artwork AppleScript goes through your iTunes library and adds any automatically downloaded artwork into the tags of the MP3 or AAC files.

- **Assign Half-Star Rating.** It's a little-known feature, but iTunes actually supports half-star ratings. Although there is no way to assign these directly through iTunes, this free AppleScript allows you to do this. Note that half-star ratings can be shown in your iTunes library, but do not appear on iPod or iPhone devices — the rating is simply rounded down to the nearest full star.

- **Art to iChat.** This is a neat little free script that automatically updates your iChat Buddy icon with the artwork of the album that you are currently listening to in iTunes. Your original buddy icon is restored when you stop playback, or if you're listening to a track that does not contain any album artwork.

- **Super Remove Dead Tracks.** This free script searches your iTunes library for any tracks that cannot be found due to missing files, and removes these entries. Any playlists that are left empty as a result are also removed.

- **Gather up the One-Hits.** This free script collects all the "one-hit wonders" in your iTunes library and collects them in a single playlist.

# Cool JavaScripts for Windows iTunes Users

Although the selection of scripts available for Windows users is far more limited, a number of useful free scripts for common tasks can be found at http://ottodestruct.com/blog/2005/10/20/itunes-javascripts. Specifically, scripts are available to perform the following useful library-management tasks:

- **Create a playlist of the songs in your library with no artwork.**
- **Create a playlist of the songs in your library with no lyrics.**
- **Create a playlist of the "one-hit wonders" in your library.**
- **Import lyrics into iTunes.**
- **Reload and update your iTunes library database from the file tags.**
- **Create a list of dead tracks in your library.**
- **Remove dead tracks from your library.**

# Appendix A

## iPod and iTunes Resources

In addition to print publications like this book, there are a number of excellent online resources that iPod and iTunes users will find very useful when looking for more information on related products and accessories, or the latest technical information. This appendix lists a few of the more popular online sites where you can get technical assistance and find more iPod- and iTunes-related information.

## News and Technical Information

The popularity of the iTunes, iPod, and iPhone platforms has given rise to a large number of Web sites attempting to draw crowds by providing news and support information. Many of these are small sites with very little useful or original material, and it can sometimes be hard to sort out the good sources of information from all of the fly-by-night operations that are trying to capitalize on the iPod's popularity. This appendix contains some of the best sources of news, product reviews, and information for iTunes, the iPod, and the iPhone.

### Apple
www.apple.com

Naturally, as the manufacturer of the iPod and iTunes, Apple provides product information and specifications on the iPod and iPhone, a Knowledge Base of technical information, and a set of discussion forums. Its Knowledge Base is very good for established and known problems; however, Apple does not normally post information about unresolved problems, and so it can be difficult to confirm whether or not a problem you are having with your iPod or iTunes is actually a known issue that has simply not yet been fixed.

Note that although the Apple discussion forums are moderated to ensure that discussions remain appropriate, they are not staffed or specifically monitored by Apple support or engineering personnel, but are designed as user-to-user support forums. Posting support questions in the Apple discussion forums may be useful for getting support from other users, but they are not a conduit for reporting problems to Apple, or getting help directly from Apple. One notable area on the Apple Web site is its product feedback page at www.apple.com/feedback. This page allows users to submit feature requests and file bug reports for any Apple hardware or software products. Note that this is simply a method of reporting problems or suggesting features, and not a support page. Users posting on the feedback pages should not expect a response.

# iLounge

www.ilounge.com

Founded one week after the first iPod was announced back in 2001, iLounge (formerly known as iPodLounge.com) has become the de facto online resource for all things related to iPods, iPhones, and iTunes. In addition to providing iTunes- and iPod-related news and technical information, iLounge is an excellent resource for information on the seemingly endless supply of iPod- and iPhone-related accessories, with online reviews of thousands of iPod-related products such as cases, earphones, speakers, and applications. Each year before the holiday season, iLounge also publishes a free downloadable Buyer's Guide covering the latest and greatest iPod- and iPhone-related products and accessories. iLounge also provides the world's largest iTunes- and iPod-specific online discussion forums, with over 100,000 registered users.

# Doug's AppleScripts for iTunes

www.dougscripts.com

If you're a Mac user and you want to get more out of iTunes, you will most definitely want to take a look at Doug's AppleScripts for iTunes. The site features over 400 AppleScripts that add enhanced functionality to iTunes and iPod management. AppleScripts are discussed in Chapter 15.

# iPhone Atlas

www.iphoneatlas.com

iPhone Atlas, run by CNET, is a popular blog for iPhone-related news and information.

# iPodHacks

www.ipodhacks.com

If you're a more advanced user looking for ways to hack and modify your iPod or iPhone, iPodHacks provides specific information on hacking and modifying the iPod and iPhone at both a software and hardware level.

# Macworld

www.macworld.com

Although primarily focused on the Mac computing platform, Macworld occasionally covers iTunes-, iPhone-, and iPod-related news and software reviews.

# The Unofficial Apple Weblog

www.tuaw.com

Referred to by the initials TUAW, this is a Weblog focused on all things Apple, including the Mac, iPod, and iPhone platforms. It covers Mac-related iTunes and iPhone software announcements and other news.

# Content Providers

In addition to the iTunes Store, there are a number of other places where iPod-friendly content can be purchased or legally downloaded for free. Many of these sites offer pricing that is competitive with iTunes, with some offering music on a monthly subscription-based model, and even some free tracks.

# Music

Despite all of the new types of content that can now be played in iTunes and on your iPod, these devices are still used primarily for music playback. Online digital music is only increasing in popularity, and there are now dozens of sites offering legal iPod-ready music tracks for sale or even free download. iLounge also maintains an up-to-date listing of free music sites.

### iTunes

If you're looking for free music, keep in mind that iTunes frequently offers free tracks of the week and other similar promotions. iTunes offers a "free on iTunes" page that is sometimes linked from the main store page, or that you can search for. Further, there are some Internet sites, such as www.itsfreedownloads.com and freeitunesmusic.blogspot.com, which track weekly free iTunes downloads with links to them.

Free video content can also be found on the iTunes Store. Single episodes of TV shows are frequently made available for free as teasers, and iTunes has recently begun offering short movie featurettes for free download similar in concept to the extras found on many traditional DVDs.

### 3hive (http://3hive.com)

This site provides free MP3 tracks offered by record labels as samples to promote full album purchases.

## GarageBand (http://garageband.com)

This site provides free music from over 125,000 independent artists in an iPod-ready MP3 format.

## mfiles (http://mfiles.co.uk)

This site provides free downloads of classical music in MP3 format.

## Download.com (http://music.download.com)

CNET's Download.com service has a music-dedicated section that offers free MP3 tracks across a wide variety of different genres.

## Amazon.com (www.amazon.com)

As an alternative to the iTunes Store, Amazon.com provides DRM-free music for sale in the MP3 format. At this point, Amazon's digital music services are not available outside of the United States.

## eMusic (www.emusic.com)

This is a subscription-based service that allows you to download a fixed number of tracks each month for a monthly subscription fee. Tracks are in the MP3 format and unprotected by digital rights management. Unlike other subscription-based services such as Napster (which are not iPod-compatible), eMusic tracks are yours to keep even after you cancel your subscription. eMusic also offers an ad-supported variation on its service, where tracks can be downloaded for free by adding an advertising toolbar to your browser.

# Podcasts

Podcasts are a great source of free music from many independent artists. Simply search the iTunes Store for music-related podcasts, and you can find numerous podcasts being published by music reviewers, radio stations, and even some artists.

# Video

A search for iPod-ready video downloads on the Internet will turn up hundreds of links to questionable sites offering premium video content for free download, almost all of which is copyrighted content not licensed for distribution through these sites. At this time, the only legitimate source of television and movie content that is iPod-ready is for purchase from the iTunes Store itself. However, many free independent and educational videos can be found in the various video podcasts throughout the iTunes Store, and Google Video (video.google.com) also offers much of its content in an iPod-compatible format ready to be downloaded and synced directly to your iPod.

# Appendix B

## Third-Party Software

In addition to iTunes, there are a number of third-party tools and utilities discussed in this book for enhancing your iTunes experience. For your convenience, a listing of these tools is provided here for each topic.

## Adding Lyrics

Adding lyrics to your iTunes library is covered in Chapter 3. Here are suggested links for third-party software, with some basic information about each one:

### Sing That iTune! — for Macs

- www.apple.com/download
- Dashboard widget
- For Mac only
- Free

### Sing That iTune! — for PCs

- www.widgets.yahoo.com
- Dashboard widget
- For Windows (through Yahoo Widgets)
- Free

## iTunes Companion

- www.widgets.yahoo.com
- For Windows (through Yahoo Widgets)
- Free

## iTunes Lyrics Importer

- www.senthilkumar.googlepages.com/ituneslyricsimporter
- For Windows only
- Free

## GimmeSomeTune

- www.eternalstorms.at/gimmesometune
- For Mac only
- Free

# Tagging videos

Tagging videos is discussed in Chapter 3. Here are suggested links for third-party software, with some basic information about each one:

## AtomicParsley

- www.atomicparsley.sourceforge.net
- For Mac, Windows, and Linux
- Free

## Lostify

- www.lostify.com
- For Mac only
- Free

## Parsley is Atomically Delicious

- www.them.ws/pad/
- For Mac only
- Free

## Tagger

- tvtagger.wordpress.com
- For Windows only
- Free

# Adding album artwork

Adding album artwork is discussed in Chapter 3. Here are suggested links for third-party software, with some basic information about each one:

## CoverScout

- www.equinux.com
- For Mac only
- Priced around $40 (as of this writing)

## iArt

- www.ipodsoft.com
- For Windows only
- Priced around $10 (as of this writing)

# Internet Radio

Chapter 4 talked about the use of Internet Radio. There is only one piece of software that I specifically recommend in this category:

## iRADIOmast

- www.iradiomast.com
- For Mac or Windows
- Priced around $10 (as of this writing)

# Add-on visualizers

Add-on visualizers are covered in Chapter 4. Here are suggested links for third-party software, with some information about each one:

## JewelCase

- www.opticalalchemy.com
- For Mac only
- Priced around $10

## G-Force

- www.soundspectrum.com
- For Mac or Windows
- Prices range from free to around $20

## WhiteCap

- www.soundspectrum.com
- For Mac or Windows
- Prices range from free to around $20

## SoftSkies

- www.soundspectrum.com
- For Mac or Windows
- Prices range from free to around $20

# Converting audiobooks

Audiobooks are covered in Chapter 6. Here are a couple of suggested links for third-party software, with some information about each one:

## Audiobook Builder

- www.splasm.com
- For Mac only
- Priced around $10

## MarkAble

- www.ipodsoft.com
- For Windows only
- Priced around $18

# Accessing Mac-formatted iPods on Windows machines

This topic is discussed in both Chapters 7 and 10. Here is a link to a good piece of software to accomplish this task:

## MacDrive

- www.mediafour.com
- For Windows only
- Priced around $50

# Video conversion

Video conversion is covered in Chapter 9. Here are suggested links for third-party software, with some information about each one:

## HandBrake

- www.handbrake.fr
- For Mac or Windows
- Free

## MPEG Streamclip

- www.squared5.com
- For Mac or Windows
- Free

## EyeTV

- www.elgato.com
- For Mac only
- Priced around $80 as a standalone application (usually bundled with hardware tuners)

# Recovering iPod content

Recovering iPod content is discussed in Chapter 10. Here are suggested links for third-party software, with some basic information about each one:

## Music Rescue

- www.kennettnet.co.uk
- For Mac or Windows
- Priced around $15 USD

## CopyTrans

- www.copytrans.net
- For Windows only
- Priced around $20

## iPod Access

- www.findleydesigns.com
- For Mac or Windows
- Priced around $20

## iPod Access Photo

- www.findleydesigns.com
- For Mac or Windows
- Priced around $13

## CopyTrans Photo

- www.copytrans.net
- For Windows only
- Priced around $30

# Creating ringtones

Ringtones are discussed in Chapter 11. Here are suggested links for third-party software, with some basic information about each one:

## iToner

- www.ambrosiasw.com
- For Mac only
- Priced around $15

## MakeiPhoneRingtone

- www.rogueamoeba.com
- For Mac only
- Free

## iPhoneRingToneMaker

- www.efksoft.com
- For Mac or Windows
- Priced around $15

## iRingtunes

- www.ipodsoft.com
- For Mac or Windows
- Priced around $15

# Synchronizing iTunes libraries

Synchronizing iTunes libraries is covered in Chapter 13. Here are a couple of suggested links for third-party software, with some basic information about each one:

## TuneRanger

- www.acertant.com
- For Mac or Windows
- Priced around $30

## Syncopation

- www.sonzea.com
- For Mac only
- Priced around $25

# Index

# The Genius is in